Preface

In 1984, a plan to transfer the Still Photography Division from the National Film Board to the National Museums of Canada threatened to shelve the collection and terminate the programmes of the organization that for forty-five years had preserved and been the main support of contemporary Canadian photography. Among the many aspects of the programme then soon to be extinguished, publication was held by many to be the most important. The National Film Board had enjoyed popular success with its commemorative books while its catalogues, monographs and thematic books of images remained, faute de mieux, the basic sourcebooks for two decades of Canadian photography. It was curious indeed to mark the end of forty-five years of photographic activity by publishing the first comprehensive anthology of the NFB collection, *Contemporary Canadian Photography.* Fortunately, the end was also a beginning and in 1985, the photographic collection and activities of the NFB were perpetuated under the National Gallery of Canada by the creation of an affiliate museum, the Canadian Museum of Contemporary Photography.

Left out of this rather dry account is the process by which the photographic community made known its fierce attachment to the NFB programme and put forward recommendations for its continuance and improvement.

Chief among these was a permanent home for the collection but also as pressing was the request that the museum take a more active role in photographic publishing. Opportunities for critical writing were lacking in Canada. Research and documentation of the medium and its practitioners were limited to the occasional exhibition catalogue and to a few struggling magazines and journals. (Sadly, there are now even fewer that are dedicated to photography.) In such an environment, neither emerging nor seasoned writers could afford the luxury of research and reflection. To celebrate the 150th anniversary of the invention of photography, this is what CMCP thought to offer to some.

In 1987, Geoffrey James was approached to lead an editorial board that would select from solicited proposals between twelve and fifteen topics on which articles would be commissioned by CMCP for an anthology of new critical writing on photography. The members of the board were Richard Baillargeon, Cheryl Sourkes and myself. Our discussions centred on the interests of artists, critics, historians, curators, arts administrators and, above all, readers. And readers, in the end, is what we became ourselves: we read to choose the forty writers whose proposals would be solicited; we read their outlines; and chose thirteen; we read the thirteen essays; we read thirteen revised versions and the subsequent versions from the editors and translators; we read in advance of the reader; and now we cede that privilege to you.

The various contributors to this project were all equally generous in giving and receiving ideas. I mean, of course, the writers, the photographers, the board, the editorial team at Alphascript, the designer Robert Tombs and the project coordinator, Maureen McEvoy. Maureen and I would in turn thank our colleagues at CMCP who unstintingly give their support to one Herculean labour after another. To them especially, Happy Anniversary plus One.

Martha Langford
Director
Canadian Museum of
Contemporary Photography
Ottawa, 1990

Introduction

GEOFFREY JAMES

The habit of characterizing art by decades ordinarily has little to commend it. It is a form of nominalism that, in its crude use of the *Zeitgeist*, blurs distinctions and nuances, creates a false sense of order and eliminates the discrepant and the atypical, so often the most interesting work of any period. But with that said, it can be stated that in the last decade, when most of the work discussed in this book was made, there has been a profound and seismic change — a true shifting of the ground — in the way that photographs are both created and perceived.

Some idea of that change in attitudes — of the intellectual distance between now and a mere ten years ago — can be gleaned from a talk given to a colloquium on photography in Toronto in 1979 by the American art historian John Ward. Ward made a heroic attempt to construct a descriptive framework for photographic criticism, from the beginnings of the medium to what was then the present day. He set up two general classes of photographic criticism: categorical criticism, directed at photography as an entity or at a class of photographs, and specific criticism, which looks at individual images or groups of images. Under these large headings Ward outlined various approaches to the medium, ranging from a formalist reading of photographs to the application of Jungian archetypes. What was remarkable about the presentation was not what it contained but what it omitted: the entire body of European theoretical writing on semiology, psychoanalysis and textual analysis which has come to dominate current thinking on photography. His list of exemplary critics included Susan Sontag but not Walter Benjamin; Max Kozloff but not Roland Barthes. When a member of the audience asked about such an absence, the speaker replied with disarming frankness that "I didn't deal with it because I don't know much about it."[1]

My intention here is not to denigrate Ward's conscientious efforts but to stress how much the critical terrain has changed, how inadmissible such a position would be today. For, as this book of essays attests, the presence of these postwar European models (including Benjamin, whose influence was delayed) is pervasive. It can be seen in Georges Bogardi's use of a Barthesian model to reflect on the work of Donigan Cumming, in Robert Graham's reading of Jacques Lacan, in Peter Wollheim's reading of psychoanalytic literature and in Monika Gagnon's and Carol Phillips's varying uses of feminist theory. Such ideas have become the basis for what can be called the *post-modern sensibility*.

I use that term with reluctance, since to talk of the post-modern is to be immediately embroiled in an endless, overly familiar debate on the precise nature of the present, an exercise which tends more and more to resemble a nervous patient with little medical knowledge attempting to diagnose his own illness. (The trope of medicine, even of pathology, occurs frequently in writing on contemporary art.) Certainly the term *post-modern*, like the condition it describes, is unresolved and polyvalent, equally applicable to the decor of a hotel lobby as to what some perceive to be the deepest cultural rift in a century already characterized by profound cultural schisms. In its most literal sense *post-*, of course, means nothing more than coming after. But for the purposes of the current argument, let the prefix carry the implication less of a complete break than an inability entirely to shake off inherited preconceptions, as in post-impressionism or, say, post-Marxism.

But if the presence of modernism looms large, its tenets have been called in question, if not entirely recast. This is strikingly evident if one looks at the evolution of photographic practice and discourse over the past decade. Ten years ago the dominant manner of thinking about art photography was still to consider the medium's formal qualities, those apparently inherent characteristics that distinguish it from other forms of visual expression. A rough consensus surrounded the recently constructed history of photography. There was a notion of a tradition, once likened to a kind of vast gene pool from which future photographic possibilities could flow. In short, it was not difficult to believe in Photography with a capital *P* (or qualified as Fine Art), with the judgment seat located at the Museum of Modern Art in New York. The medium seemed to have won its advocates' long, slightly tedious search for respectability, even if it was not entirely at ease within the enterprise of high modernism. (As Michael Mitchell has pointed out, there are aspects of photography, especially its indissoluble link to the mimetic, that do not fit within the strictest modernist tenets; certainly Clement Greenberg never quite made his peace with the medium.)

It is perhaps a coincidence that the moment when fine-art photography became identified with the promotional apparatus of modernism was also the start of its declining authority. But without lapsing into the fashionably apocalyptic language of the moment, it is possible to talk of a crisis within photography, a faltering of confidence, a sense that perhaps certain possibilities have been used up. The gene pool is producing mutants and hybrids that bear little family resemblance to what has gone before — as can be seen in Denis Lessard's analysis of "altered" photography in Quebec. For many it becomes harder to maintain a belief in photography's transcendent power or to take pleasure in what has been termed "the inexhaustible plasticity of photographic description."[2]

This questioning of the nature of photography — sometimes resembling a full frontal assault — assumes several forms. There were the early structuralist attempts to show how photographs signify — which, while never very illuminating when applied beyond the world of advertising or journalism, had the virtue of underlining what has now become a commonplace: that all meaning is constructed. Keith Bell's investigation of Prairie photography demonstrates this quite literally as he shows how, for decades, powerful interests controlled and manipulated the image of an entire region. But doubts about photography's evidentiary weight run even deeper than this. As Donald Kuspit has written, in a remark that sums up much current art-world thinking about photography (but which would probably not be voiced in, say, a court of law), "The idea that it [photography] is the record of a direct observation seems quaint. Photography's truth claim seems of less interest than its power to position consciousness."[3] Kuspit's assertion is one that would seem to render beyond the critical pale those who believe in the documentary approach to photography. And indeed there is in Serge Jongué's account of the recent documentary movement in Quebec a sense of how intellectually disenfranchised that movement has become in relation to a wider art discourse.

A severer and more specific questioning of the foundations of modernist photography has been made by Abigail Solomon-Godeau, who claims that "art photography" has become hostage to a "modernist allegiance to the autonomy, self-referentiality, and transcendence of the work of art" and in doing so has "systematically engineered its own irrelevance and triviality." Solomon-Godeau characterizes current art photography as the "relentless overproduction of third- and fourth-generation variants of a vitiated academic formalism." Against this exhausted tradition she juxtaposed photographic practices that in a certain sense invent themselves for the project at hand. What differentiates the post-modern from the modern, she says, is how the two modes position themselves in relation to their institutional spaces — which she defines as "all the discursive formations — canons, art and photography histories, criticism, the marketplace — that together constitute the social and material space of art."

"Here the issue is not photography qua photography," she writes, "but its use toward a specific end."[4]

There is something familiar about Solomon-Godeau's call for an instrumental approach to the medium. It recalls Baudelaire's cry for photography "to return to its true duty, which is to be the servant of the sciences and arts — but the very humble servant, like printing or shorthand, which have neither created nor supplemented literature."[5] The same kind of demand was made by artists in the past who used photography to document ephemeral or otherwise inaccessible artworks — Lucy Lippard's "dematerialized" art objects — choosing the medium for its lack of preciousness, its very ordinariness. (Revealing in this regard is the remark made by the conceptual artist Lawrence Weiner about the late Gordon Matta-Clark, who made elaborate photographic collages to document his architectural interventions. "He liked photography a lot," said Weiner. "I think it was one of his weaknesses."[6]) Today the instrumental demand made upon photography, the new prescription of the critics, is to use the medium to lay bare the ideology of representation. Whether such an agenda can be sustained for three or four generations without lapsing into a vitiated academic formalism is a question that only time can answer. What is certain is that we are in a period of acute awareness of how photographs are implicated in larger spheres of meaning. Witness, for example, Carol Phillips's rereading of the work of Lynne Cohen, Clara Gutsche and Nina Raginsky in the light of feminist theory — work that only a few years ago would more likely have been interpreted within the formal codes of modernism. Gail Fisher-Taylor, in her treatment of work that is more explicitly feminist (especially that of Susan MacEachern), appears less interested in the application of feminist theory than in the development of a female critical voice that is non-authoritative, even vulnerable.

One of the paradoxes of post-structuralist thinking, particularly in its transposition to North America, is that despite its questioning of the idea of the author, it has itself become a system of authority. Ian Wallace, in his account of photoconceptualism in Vancouver, talks of that movement's unique links to the university. But the phenomenon is wider than that. Indeed, it could be argued that the greatest structural shift in the art world (which is increasingly the photography world) over the last decade has been the move into the university. Not only is the post-secondary education system the largest employer of advanced artists, but the very nature of the academic curriculum tends to favour the creation of work that is, before it is anything else, theoretically defensible. Dot Tuer's essay is an almost total renunciation of this mindset — in her quest for a photographic practice that will reveal the specific realities of Canada.

Raymonde April, the only artist in this book who writes of her own working methods, reveals the extent to which creation comes out of intuition and lived experience. Her essay, in our increasingly logocentric world, is a reminder that the gap that separates theory and practice can often be salutary.

1. Taken from the transcript of "Canadian Perspectives: A National Conference on Canadian Photography," March 1-4, 1979, mimeographed (Toronto: Ryerson Polytechnical Institute, 1979), p. 409. The question was posed by the author.
2. John Szarkowski, writing on the later work of Lee Friedlander in the essay "Understandings of Atget," in *The Work of Atget* (New York: Museum of Modern Art, 1985), vol. 4, *Modern Times*, p. 26.
3. Donald Kuspit, "Reification or Personalization: The Dilemma of Photography," *C* (Spring 1989), p. 60.
4. Abigail Solomon-Godeau, "Photography after Art Photography," in Brian Wallis, ed., *Art After Modernism: Rethinking Representation* (Boston: David R. Godine, Publishers, 1984), pp. 82, 85.

5. Charles Baudelaire, "The Salon of 1859," in *Art in Paris 1845-1862: Salons and Other Exhibitions*, trans. and ed. Jonathan Mayne (London: Phaidon Press, 1965), p. 154.

6. Quoted in Mary Jane Jacob, *Gordon Matta-Clark: A Retrospective* (Chicago: Museum of Contemporary Art, 1985), p. 141. Reinforcing Weiner's attitude toward photography is a remark by another conceptual artist, Joseph Kosuth: "I had criticisms of Gordon's work, which I discussed with him. I had problems with the photographs... I also understood the emotional, intellectual, and economic reasons for the photographs, and the whole issue is further complicated because the photographs are good." Ibid., p. 111.

1

Here's Me! *or*
The Subject in the Picture

R O B E R T   G R A H A M

Even at the age of four or so, coming down the stairs with his nurse-maid…
he would call out 'here's me!'

STAN GÉBLER DAVIES
James Joyce: A Portrait of the Artist

The young James Joyce has provided me with more than a title. His exuberant self-announcement in celebration of his being, and of his being seen, also contains an illuminating childish grammatical slip: misemploying the objective case. To shout joyfully, "Here I am — the object of your attention!" is to state precisely the ways in which the subject operates in the field of the Other. Or, as French psychoanalyst Jacques Lacan characterized the discourse of Jean Piaget's egocentric child, "a case of hail to the good listener!"[1]

For Lacan, the subject is a signifier within a topography of relational forces, not an entity, but a locus, the meeting point in a network of dynamic vectors. As the "I who counts"[2] or the "I" who says "I…," the subject/signifier is shifting and transient. Existing only in a present that quickly passes, the subject is constantly succeeded by a renewed subject in a new configuration of relations.

It is perhaps this very slipperiness of being which encourages psychocritical readings of the photograph to deal predominantly with the "scopophilic" urges of the photographer and the viewer, and to describe the photograph as an occasion for looking more than anything else. Paramount is the "I" who sees. Christian Metz, for example, has described the cinematic experience as a sequence of inscriptions in which the world imprints on the film, the projector projects on the screen, and the screenlight then illuminates the retina. The principal human activity in this model is that of the voyeuristic spectator, who identifies with and adopts the position of the camera lens. Transferred to the still photograph, Metz's description brackets the figure in the photo as "world" and neglects the dynamic process of exposure and self-exposure that occurs when a subject becomes a photo subject. While most people experience mass-media photo imagery as spectators, the experience of being a photo subject still merits examination. [3]

To be sure, we cannot re-illude ourselves into thinking that the figure in the picture is somehow co-present [4] when we examine the photograph. The moment of that subject is past.

Even when the person photographed is still living, that moment when she or he was has forever vanished. Strictly speaking, the person *who has been photographed* — not the total person, who is an effect of time — is dead. [5]

[2]

The camera does not provide, between figure and viewer, a subject-to-subject encounter of mutual observation or interaction. Nor can we renew naturalist readings of portraiture in which some interior identity is uttered and revealed through the picture. But the photograph remains and the subject in the picture knows that it will. The figure in the photo composes a "lasting impression." Thus the photograph serves as the record of a meeting between a subject and an unformed future. Our existence as viewers is foretold and anticipated within the picture. As sitters we attempt to predict a distribution of the image, and we position ourselves accordingly. Both the figure and the viewer imagine and construct each other as potential beings. The viewer exists as an imaginary entity; or more properly, the abstracted viewer is plural and heterogeneous and, in some ways, objectified. Precisely because we cannot control the fate of our pictures there is discomfort: we address ourselves for the camera in the present and for an unknown context in the future.

In *Camera Lucida*, Roland Barthes describes his delicious anxiety at being photographed:

But very often (too often, to my taste) I have been photographed and knew it. Now, once I feel myself observed by the lens, everything changes: I constitute myself in the process of "posing," I instantaneously make another body for myself, I transform myself in advance into an image. This transformation is an active one: I feel that the Photograph creates my body or mortifies it, according to its caprice... [6]

This passage helps us to mark out a common analysis of the photographic dynamic: in the hierarchy of photographic participants, the figure is the most passive, the one transformed and least in control, and, in short, all too often the victim of the encounter. Photographic thought has become irreversibly sensitive to this condition and seeks in its practice to compensate for, or to acknowledge in its analysis, the subversion of the subject at the moment of the photographic exposure. In logical extreme, Martha Rosler considered her unpeopled project, *the bowery in two inadequate descriptive systems*, "a work of refusal,"[7] in not doubly harming derelicts by also showing them.

The legend of Marilyn Monroe leaves the suspicion that whatever the painful flaw in her life, it was somehow related to her superb skill as a photographer's model. Feminist critiques of representations of the female body are well established on the basis that the objectification of the camera recapitulates and supports a position of male/viewer dominance.[8]

Let me invoke Barthes twice more, first as he describes his defensive preparation for the session:

> I lend myself to the social game, I pose, I know I am posing, I want you to know that I am posing, but (to square the circle) this additional message must in no way alter the precious essence of my individuality: what I am, apart from any effigy.[9]

As soon as there is mention of a game, we know we are dealing with rules, conventions and codes. Thus the pose is a playful performance, a self-imitation. But, more seriously, it must not contradict an identity, a self-image. To become a photo subject is to transform oneself, to reconstitute oneself as an image. In posing for a photograph, the sitter must "write" with the body. But what the body says is a deceit and a betrayal of the "self":

> …each time I am (or let myself be) photographed, I invariably suffer from a sensation of inauthenticity, sometimes of imposture (comparable to certain nightmares). In terms of image-repertoire, the Photograph (the one I *intend*) represents that very subtle moment when, to tell the truth, I am neither subject nor object but a subject who feels he is becoming an object: I then experience a micro-version of death (of parenthesis): I am truly becoming a specter.[10]

At the moment of the photograph the subject is dematerialized. The photograph is a representation of an "I" which is "Not-I." The attempt to look "like myself" produces a self-counterfeit. This

[3]

inauthenticity — this gap — creates the sensation of fragmentation and objectification. The transformation by photography is the metamorphosis of a subject into an object. The copying of oneself (in the pose, in the reproduction) is a deathlike reification, a movement toward objectification, which gives the body the status of a carcass and the individual the character of a ghost.

And yet it would be a patronizing arrogance toward others and an unneccessary delimitation of our own powers as photo subjects if we were to typecast the figure in the photo as a specimen-like object of mastering regard. For even within the above analysis there remains the possibility of a subject, for whatever reasons, choosing mortification and accepting objectification. The figure in the photograph then becomes an agent, redeemed by an evident willingness to become someone else's "signified." Self-presentation is "negotiated" in two senses: navigating a threatening passage and also bargaining a contract. This is normally a strategic decision; and in acknowledging it we are also acknowledging an operating subject within the photographic discourse. In the "game" of the photograph there are several players, and the relation between them is shifting and uneven. In the "course" of a photograph, as the relations between players change, so will the position of the photograph change in the lives of the players.

Consider the passport photograph. The sitter is legally obliged to obtain a photographic portrait, and he engages a photographer (who is thus in a service position to the sitter) to produce the required image. At the studio, the photographer (for whom this work may be bread and butter — but also perhaps resented for being limited, dull and repetitive) directs and controls the sitter as to pose, facial expression and so forth. The photographer is paid, and the highly prescribed product (lighting, expression and cropping must fulfil certain guidelines, and the photo print itself must be of precise dimensions) becomes a bureaucratic document. Having satisfied the authorities, the sitter's citizenship is then officially acknowledged, and he receives the rights and protections due a passport holder. The community of viewers includes not only the functionaries in the passport office and at borders but also the friends and relations who will laughingly agree with the sitter that it is a terrible photograph.[11] (This attitude is not trivial; it represents a healthy distancing from state-delineated identity.) This description is about a photograph, but

[4]

not of a photograph. The passport photo is evidence of interactional meetings between figures physically co-present or absent, though actively influential. It illustrates, clearly and simply, how certain kinds of photo images can be understood as more than visual artifacts.

■

An older James Joyce left us with a picture (PLATE 1) taken by his friend C.P. Curran when Joyce was 20 years old: hands in his pockets, head cocked to one side, Joyce's expression is almost glaring. And we have more: asked what he was thinking at the time, he replied, "I was wondering would he lend me five shillings."[12] In the same way that Joyce turned elements of his life into his art, and his own career into the stories of his artist-protagonists (Stephen Dedalus, Shem the Penman), this photograph comes to stand for the young predatory artist and his relation to the world.[13] As portrayed by Joyce, the artist borrows and steals from the world to transform ("forge") the given material and make it his own. What the artist returns to the world is the celebration of his own genius.

To know that he was being read was more important to Joyce than he would have admitted. It was not that he demanded praise alone; he enjoyed dispraise too, and in fact all attention. He needed to feel that he was stirring an international as well as a Triestine pot, that the flurried life he created about him had somehow extended itself to the English-speaking world, so that everyone, friend or foe, was worried about him. He wanted to be commended, rebuked, comforted, but above all, attended to.[14]

Yet Joyce's notion of fame was archaic, and the lustre he sought would be won only through his work. As much as he enjoyed his portraits, their distribution did not contribute to the kind of prominence he would have considered important. To become, like Shakespeare, a radical shaper of the language itself, did not require photography. Photo fame would merely be the acknowledgment of his greater achievement.

Leo Braudy, in *The Frenzy of Renown: Fame and Its History*,[15] describes the change that overcame the notion of fame after the advent of technologies of reproduction and diffusion. Traditional fame was the immortal glory bestowed upon those who held an office (such as king) or achieved accomplishment (heroes and artists.) The technologies of photography, printing and broadcasting have increased the quantity, breadth and effect of fame production. Public awareness and attendance have been broadened. If fame was once the result of some status or action, the wider net of celebrity now catches and enhances figures of otherwise little renown. The phenomenon of someone "famous for being famous" has developed; and even those of high standing now obtain attention beyond their due.

> Of course, as Ben Franklin was one of the earliest to remark, the new power of visual media might also involve a new sort of entrapment for both the observer — under the sway of what he is so pleased to see — and the observed — imprisoned by the desire to be seen. [16]

In such a psychic environment, fame, success and photography become entangled. In discussing the photograph *Life Saving Attempt* (PLATE 2), Max Kozloff says that Weegee contributes "to the reportorial mode a libidinal depth of his own." [17] (For libidinal, read penetrating.) The woman in the photograph has been caught in a parapraxis, a gestural "slip of the tongue" provoked by the camera's own presence. Implicit in the reporter's attention is the command to smile. She was helpless to resist. In daydreams she must have rehearsed for this moment, and in pure stimulus-response her training showed. The extreme inappropriateness of her pose is a measure of the camera's determining power in setting a context that can violently conflict with the lives it enters. In the clash of contexts her relationship to the scene of the accident was overwhelmed by her spontaneous connection with the photographer.

Her mistake was wanting to please; and if a slip is still a choice, her decision to smile betrayed her desire for the nourishment of attention. The wish to show oneself is also a wish to "see someone looking at me," to have one's existence confirmed. Fame moralists tend to dismiss this sort of dependency as a pathetic vanity. But vanity itself, as *vanitas*, has a more profound history as the desperate manoeuvre to defy death armed only with temporal means. The immortality of great achievement is no different, for both petty and grand vanities are no more substantial than a wish.

When fame is domesticated and internalized in the fantasy world of the individual, pathological behaviour can break out. "Star" figures gain cult status while simultaneously becoming intimately (if artificially) familiar to their followers through the mass of detailed information provided about them. Braudy calls this the "democratization of fame" in the sense that fame becomes an experience potentially available to anyone and the celebrated become identified as the creatures of their audience. Claims upon fame and the famous become perceived as more broadly exercisable — and the resulting disappointment more widespread.

The phenomenon of the "celebrity stalker," such as Ronald Reagan's assailant John Hinckley or John Lennon's assassin Mark Chapman, illustrates how mass-media relations can recapitulate or be redesigned as direct and personal emotional relations. The celebrity stalker usually stalks in two ways, first by claiming the intimate attention of some famous figure. Considering all other fans so much ticket fodder, he attempts to force the celebrity to acknowledge the stalker's own specialness. He is, in his lights, both the biggest fan and, transcending that, the one who will save the celebrity from the distresses of fame. The stalker, more than anyone, "knows" the star and shares a destiny with the star.[18]

But he also seeks fame for himself. Fame will be the acknowledgement of his power and will give him the status needed to become the celebrity's consort. Hinckley's attempt to assassinate Ronald Reagan was a kind of love tribute to movie star Jodie Foster. It would both get her attention and give him a fame equal to or greater than Foster's own.

The celebrity figure in the photograph is, for the stalker, a split-off and idealized object. "Some people deal with their incapacity (derived from excessive envy) to possess a good object by idealizing it."[19] Melanie Klein's model of the envious soul provides us with a way to describe such media fixations. The celebrity, who is surely transformed into an object, can be manipulated symbolically by the stalker in any fashion he determines. Alternately loving and persecuting, the celebrity is particularly fit to be a split-off object because of the various ways in which media technologies create an illusion of closeness where really there is distance.

The damaged subject is caught up in psychotic projection and introjection, attempting to break through the pane of recognition against which his face is pressed. While desperately trying to cross over to the other side, he is also disparaging the figure of established acclaim. Apparently Chapman's principal complaint against Lennon was that he was a hypocrite and a phoney. Yet what Chapman found memorable about the few moments before the killing was that John Lennon was looking at him. Chapman had succeeded in vaulting the counter to join the famous figure of his obsession in physical co-presence and intersubjectivity.

This kind of confusion exists in the political realm as well. Mahmoud Mohammad Issa Mohammad is a Palestinian immigrant to Canada who faced deportation for having entered the country without revealing his conviction in Greece for an attack on an Israeli jetliner in which one person died. When interviewed, he described the incident as "an advertisement, just to publicize to the world, to make the world understand what was going on in the Middle East..."[20] It is an astonishing commentary on what currently passes for war and politics when death and destruction are considered merely the tools of publicity. Acting in front of and for the camera has become the contemporary mode of political representation, and the power of attention has become confused with the power to affect. Such confusion is not limited to outsiders. In a review of former White House Press Secretary Larry Speakes's memoirs, Nicholas Lemann wrote:

The allure of the White House is not captured accurately by the word usually used to convey the essence of upper-level Washington life, power. Speakes was not powerful, exactly....Fame comes closer than power to describing what Speakes loved about the White House (he mentions proudly that even Mikhail Gorbachev "knew me on sight"), and he also loved the sense of being at the center of things — the phone rings all day long, and whatever one is working on is of intense interest to hundreds of reporters who presumably reflect the raptness of tens of millions of readers, listeners, and viewers.[21]

The movement of photographic imagery into mass media, and the identification of media success with general success, power and enhancement, have fostered the belief that photographic representation is basic to nearly any form of enfranchisement. The camera, as a tool of empowerment, requires those who seek power to employ themselves strategically as photo subjects.

Andrew Danson's *Unofficial Portraits*[22] project is a curious attempt to short-circuit the process of political representation by establishing a "holiday" context in which the normal expectations of behaviour are suspended. He would set up his camera in the office of a Canadian politician, hand over the remote shutter release, and leave the room.

[8]

The politician was then to take eleven self-portraits. According to Danson, most politicians accepted his invitation, a few declined (René Lévesque, Jean Drapeau), and one actively courted him: Brian Mulroney. The terms of the situation invite the politicians to relax and have fun; it is almost commanded of them. The subtext calls for them to behave "out of office," that is as private individuals who have shed their official, and representative, mantles. But not all of them could (PLATE 3). The pictures occupy a zone that one might call "at home in the office," an occasion for people who, in varying degrees, are comfortable with their status as representatives. As Hans-Georg Gadamer elaborates:

> . . . it is because the ruler, the statesman and the hero must show and present himself to his followers, because he must represent, that the picture gains its own reality. . . . When he shows himself he must fulfil the expectations that his picture arouses. Only because he has part of his being in showing himself is he represented in the picture. . . . If someone's being includes as such an essential part the showing of himself, he no longer belongs to himself. For example, he can no longer avoid being represented by the picture and, because these representations determine the picture that people have of him, he must ultimately show himself as his picture prescribes. [23]

At first John Turner refused Danson's offer. But the photographer happened to meet Turner's wife Geills on an airplane, and she was able to convince Turner to take part. [24] Her own image appears in the lower right-hand corner of the photograph, where an authorial signature might go. Turner is often considered uncomfortably ambitious, as if his drive were coming from outside himself. One observer has described him:

> From nervous worry and excessive adrenaline, he was forever clearing his throat, adjusting the knot of his tie, licking his lips, barking at his own jokes, chewing a breath mint, and scrunching his eyes. . . . friends wanted to shake him by the shoulders and yell, "Come on, John, relax! You don't have to impress me." Yet Turner seemed incapable of relaxing because there was always his God, his mother, and himself to impress. [25]

Turner's initial resistance to the project and his stiffly suspicious appearance in the photograph can be understood in the light of his divided "impression management." [26] As a politician he must show and give himself to his public; but the satisfaction he obtains from

[9]

public life is to be shown and given to a smaller and more crucial audience: "his God, his mother and himself." Public success then becomes merely a means to something much more personal. While he dedicates himself to the public, that public must, in turn, serve him in meeting a quite private purpose.

There is also a shelf visible in the Danson picture, and on that shelf is a photograph of Turner meeting with Robert Kennedy. Turner reportedly had an entire wall in his former law office hung with such pictures,[27] common enough among politicians and others. However else the pictures are prized or employed, this practice suggests a trebly articulated self-display: look, it says, I'm being looked at (by the camera) when meeting with (and being looked at by) the renowned.

[1 0]

Danson's work affirms the necessity of politicians to be represented in ways acceptable to themselves. To read through the self-objectification of the photograph is to recognize the self-symbolization that the figure constructs. This construction occurs under conditions of conflict in which the figure is struggling for representation. The photograph provides a point of conjunction for a complex of strands in a web of intersubjectivities. Aside from questions of viewer empathy, or true or false identity, both of which are issues of trust, rests primary observation — to see the wanting of the agent who wants to be seen.

Joyce's aggressive artistic claims, the momentary flash of news-photo glory for the woman at Coney Island and John Turner's solemn obligation to sustain representation are all ordinary instances of the exhibitionist strategies of subjects within pictures. The pathological and the desperate are somewhat more extreme examples of those who, insufficiently nourished, will do anything to get into the frame — to become the objects of others' regard. For them, even notoriety is better than neglect. In terms of communicational hygiene, the tactical necessity or psychological compulsion for self-exhibition is countered by modesty (PLATE 4).

In the biblical tale shame also came from the crime of devouring, which in my interpretation was oral castration. Shame is opposed to exhibitionism. Language reveals the oral tinge of exhibitionism as a fantasy or wish to be devoured....Adam in developing shame did not protect himself so much from oral-sadistic voyeurism as from his own self-destructive wish to be devoured....The self-destructive *passive* element of exhibitionism tends to be more repressed than the oral sadism underlying voyeurism.[28]

The subject in the photograph enters into an accord: in exchange for being sacrificed to and absorbed by the camera, the viewing public (which may be as small as a family) offers significance to the subject. Barthes admitted one exception to the determining signification of being photographed: only a context of extreme love allowed his body to find its "zero degree" and erased the "weight of the image."[29] Perhaps only for his mother, he thought, could he stop posing. But then, perhaps only for his mother would he give up resisting.

[11]

1. Jacques Lacan, *The Four Fundamental Concepts of Psycho-analysis*, ed. Jacques-Alain Miller, trans. Alan Sheridan (Harmondsworth: Penguin Books, 1979), p. 208.
2. Ibid., p. 20.
3. Two related areas of photo subjecthood have been opened up. The first is the investigation of the subject as exploited victim within a system of image production, which, to use Walter Benjamin's phrase, turns "misery into a consumer good." The second is the historical study and ongoing monitoring of the application of photo-technologies for surveillance and identity processing by government, police and industry.

In another vein entirely, Jo Spence's "photo therapy" explores the possibilities for individual and social-health enhancement through the activities of the figure in portraits and self-portraits. See Jo Spence, *Putting Myself in the Picture: A Political, Personal and Photographic Autobiography* (London: Camden Press, 1986).
4. In sociology, the notion of co-presence is used to emphasize the interactive character of mutual physical encounter when the body of an experiencing self meets another. See Anthony Giddens, *The Constitution of Society: Outline of the Theory of Structuration* (Berkeley: University of California Press, 1984), p. 64.
5. Christian Metz, "Photography and Fetish," *October*, 34 (Fall 1985), p. 84.
6. Roland Barthes, *Camera Lucida: Reflections on Photography*, trans. Richard Howard (New York: Hill and Wang, 1981), pp. 10-11.
7. Martha Rosler, "in, around, and afterthoughts (on documentary photography)" in *3 works* (Halifax: The Press of the Nova Scotia College of Art and Design, 1981), p. 79.
8. As usual, there are the exceptions. For example, *Caught Looking: Feminism, Pornography & Censorship* is a feminist celebration of diverse smut. Yet, as the title suggests, it remains mostly concerned with observer rights. See Kate Ellis et al., eds., *Caught Looking: Feminism, Pornography & Censorship*, 2nd ed. (Seattle: The Real Comet Press, 1988).
9. Barthes, pp. 11-12.
10. Ibid., pp. 13-14.

11. "The photograph in Neil's passport was just like all such photographs, a gross caricature of his features taken in the kind of light used to take pictures of axe-murderers for circulation in public buildings. He glanced nervously around, half expecting to find his passport photo blown up to hideous proportions and hanging with those of other fugitives of justice in a prominent place not far from where he stood." Hugh Hood, *Five New Facts About Giorgione* (Windsor, Ontario: Black Moss Press, 1987), p. 45.

12. Stan Gébler Davies, *James Joyce: A Portrait of the Artist* (London: Abacus, 1977), p. 84.

13. The Curran photo, superimposed on a picture of a Dublin street scene, was used on the cover of the widely distributed Penguin paperback edition of *A Portrait of the Artist as a Young Man*. I must assume that it was intentional to leave ambiguous whether the image was meant to illustrate the author or the book. See James Joyce, *A Portrait of the Artist as a Young Man* (Harmondsworth: Penguin Books, 1960).

14. Richard Ellmann, *James Joyce* (New York: Oxford University Press, 1965), pp. 365-366.

15. Leo Braudy, *The Frenzy of Renown: Fame and Its History* (New York: Oxford University Press, 1986).

16. Ibid., p. 492.

17. Max Kozloff, *Photography & Fascination* (Danbury, New Hampshire: Addison House, 1979), p. 59.

18. "Man Who Shot John Lennon Examines Celebrity Stalkers," *The Gazette* [Montreal], February 5, 1988, p. C-6.

19. Melanie Klein, *Envy and Gratitude & Other Works 1946-1963* (New York: Delta Books, 1977), p. 193.

20. Zuhair Kashmeri, "Palestinian Regrets Violence of Youth," *The Globe and Mail* [Toronto], National ed., January 26, 1988, p. A-9.

21. Nicholas Lemann, "The Best Years of Their Lives," *The New York Review of Books*, June 30, 1988, pp. 5-6.

22. See Andrew Danson, *Unofficial Portraits* (Toronto: Doubleday Canada Limited and Art Gallery of York University, 1987).

23. Hans-Georg Gadamer, *Truth and Method* (New York: The Seabury Press, 1975), p. 125.

24. Ingrid Abramovitch, "Politicians Capture Inner Selves with Candid Camera," *The Gazette* [Montreal], July 30, 1988, p. E-4.

25. Ron Graham, *One-Eyed Kings: Promise & Illusion in Canadian Politics* (Toronto: Collins Publishers, 1986), p. 186.

26. The last chapter of Erving Goffman's *The Presentation of Self in Everyday Life* is called "The Arts of Impression Management." See Erving Goffman, *The Presentation of Self in Everyday Life*, Anchor Books ed. (Garden City, New York: Doubleday Anchor, 1959), p. 209.

27. Graham, p. 205.

28. Anton Ehrenzweig, *The Hidden Order of Art: A Study in the Psychology of Artistic Imagination* (St. Albans, Hertfordshire: Paladin, 1970), p. 246.

29. Barthes, p. 12.

Representing the Prairies

PRIVATE AND COMMERCIAL PHOTOGRAPHY IN WESTERN CANADA 1880-1980

KEITH BELL

This essay is intended to provide some suggestions for the study of the history of Prairie photography, which has traditionally been approached in two ways. On the one hand, modernist historians and critics have used biographical and formal (or "artistic") criteria to assess their subjects. Their critical writings have consequently tended to ignore the largely anonymous commercial (and later amateur) photographers who predominated in the region. Instead they have concentrated on photographers such as the Notmans and Alexander Henderson, whose work is described as "transcending" the commercial aspects of photographic production. Images selected from their oeuvre for reproduction tend to have been chosen for the relationships which they bear to painting.[1] Similarly, when critics do choose anonymous or commercial photographs for reproduction or exhibition, the selection is often informed by contemporary aesthetic tastes and by the formalist paintings of the Prairies by Tanabe, Rogers and others. In these latter circumstances, photographs are emptied of their original meanings and ideological purposes and are treated, according to current aesthetic values, as art — what Sekula has called a "cult of 'subjective experience.'"[2]

On the other hand, photographs of the Prairies are frequently discussed in terms of their assumed ability to present an authoritative visual record of the region's history. This initially came about, as I will demonstrate, from the way in which the work of professional photographers was used to promote a particular construct of the Prairies, an idea which eventually became ingrained in the national consciousness as the myth of Western development — a period of "struggle," "development" and "achievement," which combined to form the Prairie heritage of discovery and settlement.

The survival of this Prairie myth has been reinforced by the use of private and commercial photographs to provide "documentary" evidence in books on Prairie history, in exhibitions and in museum displays. This approach closely reflects the institutional situation in the West, where photographic collections are usually held in museum archives rather than by art galleries and are therefore catalogued as and considered to be anthropological or historical resources faithfully reflecting regional history.

As Sekula demonstrated in his essay "Photography Between Labour and Capital," archives "constitute a *territory of images*," where the original purpose of the photograph is preempted by ownership and its meaning is left open to new interpretations.[3] For example: a photograph of a threshing scene originally used in a pamphlet to promote Prairie settlement is not catalogued under immigration propaganda but rather under farm machinery, with the date and model carefully recorded. Similarly, anonymous photographs of poor farm families (PLATE 5) are exhibited as examples of early immigration and struggle on the Prairies, a necessary stage in the neo-Darwinian "evolution" of the West. Other questions, such as the families' identities or the circumstances of their poverty are set aside for a wider agenda: we are invited to feel proud of our predecessors' achievements and of the Western identity "forged" during the early years of settlement. As Sekula remarks (following Foucault): "…photographic archives by their very structure maintain a hidden connection between knowledge and power."[4]

This tendency for archives to follow the wider discourses of the dominant ideologies on the Prairies has tended to obscure the original site of photographic production and therefore the meaning assigned to the photographs by those who took or commissioned them.

I would like to avoid the pitfalls inherent in both the formalist and archival constructs by investigating some of the ways in which photographic representations of the Prairies have been historically created and sustained.

The earliest photographic representations of the Prairies were made by expedition photographers who accompanied exploration and survey parties to the West from the 1850s onwards. Their work, which was intended both as a record of the expedition as well as to provide "scientific" images of the landscape and peoples they encountered, was usually confined to established modes of representation: camp sites, surveying parties and picturesque landscapes.[5] However, the reputation of the West as a vast empty region was sometimes boosted by the expedition photographers themselves. Exploration in the nineteenth century was an inherently romantic activity, and images like Hime's *Prairie on the Banks of the Red River* (1858), were carefully constructed (with human bones as props) to create a suitable sense of empty space and imminent death.[6] The few dramatic images that emerged from the region were reinforced by an enormously popular expedition and adventure literature, of which the best known work was William Francis Butler's *The Great Lone Land* (1872). Butler's comment that there is "no other portion of the globe where...loneliness can be said to live so thoroughly," became the established image of the West — in both Eastern Canada and Europe.[7]

The decision in the 1880s to develop the Prairies as an agricultural region (the "Granary of the British Empire") brought about a rapid transformation in the manner in which the land was represented by photographers.[8] These changes did not take place simply because the new agricultural settlements altered the appearance of the landscape, nor did photographers only react to what they saw in front of them; instead they operated as mediators between those dominant powers — governments, the Canadian Pacific Railway (CPR) and the land companies — which sought to control and profit from Prairie settlement and those people whom these organizations wished to entice into occupying the land. While it had been acceptable for the expedition and survey photographers to represent the area in terms of its "emptiness" and "isolation," the requirement of the new ruling elites called for an image which was both reassuringly familiar and which also offered opportunities for wealth and status.

The developers' project was made simpler in the late 1880s by the invention of the half-tone process which, with its potential for mass reproduction, made photography a leading form of visual communication. As a result, photographs were increasingly used both in advertising and in manuals illustrating industrial machinery and management — a kind of "functional realism" whose concealed ideology was controlled by governments and monopoly capitalists. These organizations employed photography as a ready-made system to appropriate the representation of the West for their own purposes.[9]

The role of the commercial and advertising photographers in the construction and selling of this new image of the Prairies consisted of a number of interrelated discourses. The perception of the region as an empty vessel devoid of any significant settlement or institutions presented the Dominion government, the railroads and the land companies — operating in concert — with the opportunity to "create" this new land as nearly as possible in the form which best suited their purposes.

In pursuit of this strategy photographers were employed to provide images of the West that encouraged immigration and settlement. The new towns, regions and businesses appropriated the language of the larger institutions to promote their own, competing interests. While the forms of this language varied slightly according to economic conditions and changing immigration policies, its overall outline remained remarkably uniform throughout the period from 1880 to the outbreak of the Second World War.

This strategy took the form of extensive advertising campaigns using posters, newspaper and magazine articles, specially prepared publications such as *The Great Prairie Provinces of Manitoba and the North West Territories* (1881) and lectures, many of which were coordinated from the CPR's offices in Britain. [10] Publications were illustrated with reproductions of photographs and paintings, while lecturers used specially prepared sets of lantern slides. The CPR placed particular emphasis on the use of photographs, which were hung in the waiting rooms of the railroad's overseas offices, in window displays alongside samples of Prairie produce. In order to make the "reality" even more convincing, would-be immigrants who doubted the veracity of the CPR's claims were referred to the London offices of the Imperial Institute. [11] The perceived standing of this establishment as an apparently neutral arbiter of scientific (and therefore "true") information gave the CPR another layer of affirmation in their construct of the Prairies. The information at the Imperial Institute, however, was anything but neutral: the photographs contained in its Canadian section, for instance, came principally from the railway company itself. In this way the compatible interests of government and capital were served by an interlocking system, forming a virtual monopoly on visual and written information about the Prairie region.

The ability to enhance the apparent truthfulness of these photographs by placing them in as many different contexts as possible was further extended by the practice of making the photographic collections of the CPR and Canadian National Railway (CNR) freely available to those who were engaged in writing about Canada or in promoting settlement there. For example, *The Boy's Book of Canada*, written by Denis Crane and published after the First World War to encourage immigration to Canada by English boys ("Telling how the home of the bison, the redskin and the fur-trader has become a land of up-to-date romance, where a thousand things are 'doing' that appeal to the heart of a British boy"), was extensively illustrated with photographs supplied by the CPR and the CNR. [12] These were accompanied by captions such as "Gold that needs no refining" and "A homesteader's hay harvest," which closely followed (or simply reproduced) the captions provided by the railroads. [13]

Similarly, when James Lumsden wrote *Through Canada in Harvest Time, A Study of Life and Labour in the Golden West* in 1903, he illustrated the book with the "Canadian Pacific Railway Company's splendid series of photographs... freely placed at the author's disposal by Mr. Charles Drinkwater, Montreal, Secretary to the Company." [14] How flattering such "splendid" views were in the re-creation of the Western landscape becomes apparent only when they are compared with a group of snapshot views taken by the journalist Frank Carrel when his investigative expedition to the West was interrupted at Kamsack, Alberta. Carrel's images of the new Prairie town were later printed alongside several "official" views (supplied by the railroad and other organizations) in Carrel's book *Canada's West and Farther West*. Traditional art-historical comparative analysis of these photographs would only draw the conclusion that Carrel's abilities with a camera were "inferior" in quality to the work of the professionals employed by the railroads. However, Carrel's long views toward the sparse, shabby buildings set on flat, treeless land actually have far more to say about life on the Prairie for most of its inhabitants than the CPR's artful and carefully cropped images. [15] Any doubts which might have been raised in a reader's mind by Carrel's photographs would have been quickly dispelled by the way in which his text meshes with the CPR's photographic construction of the region.

Among the photographic campaigns used to promote the Prairies (of which the books of Lumsden and Carrel form a part) it is possible to identify at least two recurrent emphases: the construction of the region as a well-populated and hospitable environment where

[17]

farmers, businessmen and their families could find a life of opportunity and wealth; and the related concept of an efficient and technically advanced agriculture supported by an infrastructure of railroads, elevators and conveniently sited towns.

The first of these emphases was essential to the initial settlement schemes for the Prairie region developed by the Dominion government, the CPR and the land companies. As I have pointed out, the earliest photographs of the Prairie sought to reinforce the construct of the West as the "Great Lone Land" of Butler's 1872 account. This image proved difficult to dispel and was reinforced by extensive reports on the American "wild" West in the British and European press. As late as 1930 the British journalist Marjorie Harrison remarked that to most of her compatriots Canada seemed a romantic country with "god-like young men, thundering herds and galloping horses, lone figures on the skyline." She observed a "touching faith that most Canadians lived in picturesque shacks or log cabins."[16] In order to attract farm and farm-related settlement, however, this perception had to be reversed so that the lonely, even dangerous, landscape was re-presented as exciting (certainly) but also as settled and reassuringly familiar — what the advertising booklets called *The Last Best West*, *The Wondrous West* or *Western Canada: The Granary of the British Empire*.[17] The Prairie, these accounts declared, was no longer a "lone land," but was now passing through a neo-Darwinian process of development and civilization described by Dominion government promotional material as the "Evolution of the Prairie by the Plough" where *Prosperity Follows Settlement* in the *Land of Opportunity*.[18]

In order to carry out this campaign, the interested parties employed a wide assortment of professional photographers including Wm. Notman and Son, Alexander Henderson and Professor O.B. Buell, all of whom worked for the CPR; a number of Prairie establishments including the McDairmid Studios in Edmonton and the Central Photographic Studio in Calgary; and smaller operations like the J.F. Atterton Portrait Studios of Cardston, Alberta, J. Jessop of Gladstone, Manitoba, and the Cameron Photograph Studio of Lacombe, Alberta.[19] The supply of photographs from these establishments was supplemented in 1892 when the CPR set up its own photographic department. While the work of Wm. Notman and Alexander Henderson in particular has been valorized for transcending the more standard promotional views of the West through their "artistic" abilities, the requirements of the government, railways and land companies in fact imposed a remarkable uniformity on photographs used for display and publication.[20] It was the ability of these organizations to control how the comparatively isolated region appeared to the outside world that enabled them to rapidly establish a commonly accepted idea of what the region "really" looked like.

The photographs used to provide visual evidence of the new official construct of the Prairie were carefully selected to exaggerate both the extent of settlement there and the potential for prosperity. Views of the empty landscape were replaced by busy harvesting scenes with grain stooks apparently extending as far as the horizon. The implications conveyed by these photographs were clearly of a land of limitless wealth and opportunity, while the vast fields ("one crop pays for the land"[21]) were an obvious attraction for would-be European immigrants accustomed to agricultural operations on a much smaller scale. In case the reader should miss the point, the images were mediated by explicit captions such as "Where once the buffalo roamed," "boundless undulating fields of oats," "his second year's crop" or "fifty bushels to the acre."[22]

Moreover, the Prairie was invariably shown in a constant state of human occupation and activity, either at the time of spring ploughing or just before or following the harvest. This choice of the most favourable and visually attractive seasons was also selected by supporters of immigration like the journalist James Lumsden. The account of Lumsden's trip, *Through Canada in Harvest Time*, provides a clear indication of how the photographs were meant to be read. "Copious as the vocabulary of our language is," he declared,

> … it contains no diction adequate to communicate the impression produced by days spent in exploring the Imperial Granary. Over the vast horizon radiant with sunlight…you gaze upon oceans of yellow grain…until the vision is entranced, and the senses are well nigh overpowered by Nature's lavish exuberance.[23]

As we have seen, Lumsden's extravagant praise of the Prairie was supported by the CPR's "splendid" series of photographs as well as an itinerary which took him to selected model farms during the harvest season.

These images of an abundant landscape basking in a perpetual golden glow were reinforced by repeated suggestions that the western provinces were the ideal home for "ambitious men and women" seeking prosperity and the "opportunities which are...no longer had in countries of close settlement and high land prices."[24] Illustrations on the cover of *Canada West*, the official publication of the Ministry of Immigration and Colonization in Ottawa, showed a landscape peopled by happy farming families, with abundant produce and comfortable farm houses conspicuously served by power and telephone lines.[25] Electricity and the telephone, together with the radio and the automobile, were offered as important symbols of Prairie affluence. Cars featured prominently in views of farm homes and agricultural operations. Where photographs were used in the immigration literature, they were specifically designed or selected to provide both a sense of a "new and exciting life for all the family," as well as enough familiar looking landscape to reassure the prospective immigrants that the landscape was not too alien or uninviting. For example, the back cover of the 1921 *Canada West* shows a drawing of a farmer pointing to a series of photographs of the West arranged in a tier, like building blocks or cornerstones, each accompanied by an appropriate descriptor: "Contentment" shows a ripe wheatfield, "Affluence" a large house surrounded by buildings and livestock, and "Abundance" a sweeping view over a fertile landscape punctuated by farm buildings. The first letter of each of these words combined to spell CANADA WEST. Another view, on the cover of the 1913 edition of the magazine, shows a photograph of a mixed farm, framed like an altarpiece by Ionic columns whose bases are labelled "160 Acre Farms in Western Canada Free" — the same slogan displayed in the window of the Canadian government immigration offices in London.

Photographs of vast fields of grain were never shown without the presence of people who usually appeared engaged in harvesting and threshing, an impressive image which, according to the CPR's London office, particularly influenced prospective immigrants.[26] Other photographs, particularly those of houses and towns, were carefully cropped to avoid revealing how isolated they could be and how uninviting the surrounding landscape looked to the eyes of a European farmer used to small fields, trees and settlements close to one another. Together with the construction of a settled and populous landscape, the immigration campaigns also presented a landscape which seemed to be in a perpetual state of summer. Children (who never appear to work) play among the corn stooks, and it is always seeding or harvest time. All intimation of winter was carefully avoided (rumours of its severity had reached Europe), and the press together with other influential visitors were carefully scheduled by the CPR and the Dominion government to arrive at the best time of year (usually harvest time), when the landscape was at its busiest and most attractive.

The second recurrent emphasis in the photographic presentation of the Canadian West was that placed on technology and industrial efficiency in agricultural production. Railroads and the telegraph had been prominent symbols of progress in paintings and illustrations of the American West as early as the 1860s.[27] In Canada the promotion of technology as an important motive for settlement was applied to the whole economic system of the West. In effect the empty region, like a new industrial site, was open to the imposition of an integrated system of farm units and services mainly organized around the efficient production of grain, a scheme based upon the newly developed scientific industrial management theories of the type published by Frederick Winslow Taylor, Frank and Lillian Gilbreth, and others after 1880.[28] Photography on the Prairies, often regarded as an industrial process, provided the promoters of the new system with the most utilitarian and scientific means of presenting the "reality" of this construct to would-be settlers.

The photographic discourse which emerged from these requirements was based upon two pre-existing industrial types: the illustrated catalogue of farm machinery and the use of photographs to valorize industry: men and machinery combined to "overcome" natural and technological difficulties. Photographs were used on the Prairies to promote the possibilities of large-scale mechanized operations (usually ploughing, seeding or threshing) made possible by large farms and the open, treeless terrain. These, it was implied, resulted in economies of scale and labour which offered the opportunity for profits far beyond those possible in Europe.

These images, often provided as promotions by farm equipment companies like Case, were mediated by captions such as "Twentieth Century Methods of Cultivation in Western Canada," "Plowing with a Steam Engine," or "Sowing 250 acres daily...near Plenty, Saskatchewan...[on] one of the most up-to-date farms in Canada."[29]

Others showed wagon teams "on the way to the elevators" with record loads of grain or carefully arranged on farms to exaggerate both the number of wagons and the extent of the surrounding fields. Threshing outfits (PLATES 6, 7) also were recurring subjects, shown either in operation or drawn up in a semi-circle for a panoramic photo. The farmer and the owner (or manager) of the outfit were normally included in the scenes, usually set to one side of the activities and accompanied by a horse, buggy or car, visible symbols of their superior status.[30] The camera was often placed in the same privileged position, and the viewer was invited to read the photograph from the standpoint of supervision and ownership and thus to participate in the dominant ideology of industrialized farming provided by the Dominion government and the land companies.

Government and CPR photographic propaganda was also repeated or imitated on various levels by the land companies and individual towns and districts seeking settlers. For example, the Saskatoon and Western Land Company's elaborate handbook *The Heart of the Famous Saskatchewan Wheat Belt* was careful to include only those photographs which showed the Prairie as a busy agricultural landscape at the height of the summer season.[31] Views such as the inevitable "Fifty bushels to the acre" (PLATE 8), showing five men up to their necks in wheat, "A typical threshing scene" and "A familiar scene on a great Saskatchewan farm," constructed a highly favourable view of the SWLC's block of land for sale.[32] These images were accompanied by a text outlining Saskatchewan's "exceedingly attractive climate" and offering the prospect of "appreciating land values, beautiful farms, comfortable homes, thriving cities and towns, and evidence of general prosperity...."[33]

The promotional material used by individual towns also reflected the dominant ideologies, modified to suit their individual requirements. Driven by intense competition for settlers, businesses, or the need to attract the railroad companies, even comparatively small towns sought to represent themselves as attractive, prosperous and civilized. Consequently, large sums were spent on expensive brochures based on the souvenir-book format more commonly associated with large cities.[34] Saskatoon, for example, produced or was the subject of a large number of picture books, each designed to present the town as an important centre of Western development. In *Facts and Figures of the Fastest Growing City in the Empire* (ca. 1912), the city was promoted as a profitable site for investment with "no old inhabitants to hinder progress." The location possessed "exquisite natural charms," the consequence of its position on the North Saskatchewan River.[35] These advantages were summed up on the book's cover by a photograph of a large house with a columnar porch located on the most expensive street in town.[36] Another booklet, *Saskatoon, Western Canada*, issued by that city's board of trade in 1919, called the town the "Commercial Centre of the Most Famous Wheat Growing Territory in the World" and provided proof of prosperity through photographs of the more substantial (usually brick) buildings in town as well as an optimistic view of a "typical" farm home, the latter to demonstrate what "the average man might expect after three or four years, commencing on raw land."[37] These "typical" farm houses and their urban counterparts (invariably substantial two-storey structures) were common in promotional literature. The houses were usually depicted with the formally dressed owners and their buggy or car standing in front to indicate prosperity, but the photographs were carefully cropped to conceal the frequently bare windswept sites upon which most Prairie farm houses were built.[38]

A number of towns were also careful to design their brochures around specific class and ethnic requirements. *Gladstone and District Illustrated*, published by that town's board of trade in 1906, contained a preface remarking that the district was "particularly fortunate in the class of settlers who have already made it their home." They were "all English-speaking... natives of Eastern Canada, and the United States and British Isles, where habits of industry were bred into them."[39] This statement was followed by a remarkable series of photographs by J. Jessop of Gladstone illustrating the business and social advantages of the town, beginning with a series of views of "Galloway Bros.' Departmental Store," the largest establishment in town, then proceeding down through the hierarchy of the town's businesses to the barber shops and rooming houses.[40] After viewing the opportunities for trade and employment, prospective immigrants were enticed with photographs of town amenities: the best solid-looking brick houses, churches, schools, parks and, to conclude, a ploughing scene. In each case the photographic image was carefully constructed to emphasize (or exaggerate) the scale and prosperity of the community, as well as to give it an air of permanence (vital on the Prairie) comparable to that of a well-established town in Ontario or Britain.

The photographic projects of the Dominion government, the CPR and the land companies to re-present the Prairies were, for a time, very successful. This was largely the result of the systematic supply of appropriate photographs to any individual or institution wishing to make use of them. Thus, photographs made specifically for promotional literature were also provided free of charge for publication in encyclopedias, geography texts, souvenir albums and as lantern slide sets. In this way the official image of Prairie settlement widely gained further "factual" or "scientific" credibility. This might, in turn, be enhanced by the status of the text in question: for example, encyclopedias and geography books appeared to provide safe and respectable sources of disinterested or unbiased information where the promotional photograph could assume a new meaning, free, it seemed, from any suggestion of vested interest.

The extent of this influence is apparent throughout the contemporary literature on Western Canada. When immigrants or visitors arrived on the Prairies, their response was almost invariably one of surprise or shock. When Marjorie Harrison visited Canada in 1939 to research her book *Go West — Go Wise! A Canadian Revelation*, she reported that the country "to most of us is an illusion — a 'deceptive apparition.'" This was especially true of the Prairies, where her account pinpointed the source of that illusion:

The only thing that, thanks to emigration posters, we do realize, is the great sea of gold that is the prairie harvest. But we know nothing at all of the blood and the sweat and the heartache that has gone to the making of that harvest. And that is the most serious matter of all. We hear that on the prairie they have Ford cars, telephones and wireless. But not all the clamour of a rattletrap Ford, the din of the radio and the call of the circuit telephone will ever drown, in my ears, the quiet words of a prairie farm woman. "Most of us," she said, just stating a fact, without resentment or bitterness, — "most of us don't live — we only exist."[41]

Harrison left the West with the "impression" that Prairie farming was "a gigantic hoax" in which the "great land-owning concerns must sell; the grain markets must be supplied." This remark disturbed the Conservative politician Harold Macmillan, a supporter of the Empire "breadbasket," who wrote in his introduction to Harrison's book that "some readers will think that too much stress is put upon the severer aspects of Canadian life!"[42] But Harrison's attempt at intervention was completely subverted by the book's frontispiece: a photograph from the CPR collection showing one of the company's favourite propaganda images, a farmer standing in an apparently limitless, newly harvested field, with sheaves of wheat in his arms and around his feet. This despite her recognition of the influence of the official photographic construct of Prairie agriculture. She observed that, "the average farmer, with his quarter or half section of land and his little frame-house, provides an eye-opener for those of us who only see Canadian farming through the pictures in Cockspur Street [the Canadian government's immigration office in London]."[43]

[25]

There were, however, other photographic representations of the Prairies existing outside official settlement campaigns and corporate advertising. These were the products of small-town and itinerant photographers and the growing number of individual camera owners. For the most part, the work of these businesses and individuals reflected the prevailing discourses of the established institutions controlling the publication of photographs. Small-town photographers often made a living through the production of views showing threshing outfits, farm machinery and shop interiors for both local advertising and newspapers, and sometimes to sell to the CPR or other organizations for wider distribution.

At the lower end of this hierarchy, however, small-town and itinerant photographers provided a service to those Prairie residents who, at least until the Depression, were absent from the official photographic discourse on the region. There were the smaller farming and business concerns, often established in scruffy, isolated towns, sometimes in sod huts or unpainted shacks on the open prairie. The photographs made of and for these groups generally followed the established format used by the major studios. However, because the subjects of such work (with their poor living and working conditions) failed to conform to the appropriate image of Prairie life, they were excluded from representation in publications and exhibitions outside their immediate districts — an exclusion made more complete by the domination of the wider markets by the big studios like McDairmid and the preference frequently shown by the CPR for imported photographers like Wm. Notman, A. Henderson and O.B. Buell.[44]

By the turn of the century the production of these small photographic businesses was increasingly complemented by the work of amateur photographers, who took advantage of new developments in hand-held cameras and roll film. Their photographs generally reflected the prevailing conventions of the professionals and their clients: farm machinery, portraits of farm families and their property, and important events like weddings and harvests all formed a significant part of the photographic discourse of the Prairie photographer. However, in the absence of the specific financial and ideological requirements affecting professional establishments, amateurs often expanded the boundaries of the official photographic construction of the Prairies. In the process they included subjects in their work that were normally considered inappropriate or even unacceptable to government or business interests.

Among these works by amateurs were photographs of farming operations, such as stone-picking and small-scale agriculture on marginal land, representing aspects of day-to-day activities on the Prairie almost completely absent from the work of the big photographic organizations. In these photographs the carefully constructed image of the Prairie as an endless succession of fields, neat farmhouses and large-scale mechanized operations was radically altered. Where the official construct showed the landscape as humanized, controlled, secure and prosperous, many amateurs showed the country to be only precariously settled: farm buildings often appeared to be dumped at random on the land, fields were not always open and easy to cultivate and, above all, winter views showed a landscape devoid of the comfortable, homey conditions purveyed by the land companies.

The expanded access to representation which new modes of photography gave to Prairie people was even more evident in photographs of the region's residents. As we have seen, promotional photographers normally used large-scale farmers as their subjects and were careful to emphasize the hierarchy of power — owner, manager, workers — within these operations, which in turn reflected larger business and political units. Poorer farmers, who found that the Calgary Land Company's 1905 slogan "Just Like Picking Up Dollars" was less than the truth, were not considered appropriate subjects — a policy applied with particular care to the representation of women and children. [45] When women did appear in photographs and posters, they were portrayed either as well-dressed residents of comfortable Eaton's-catalogue homes or as the providers of pleasant picnics for male harvesters. Similarly, children were shown to live a carefree life playing among the stooks in the wheatfields on the "healthy" and "sunny" Prairie. By contrast, amateur and small-town photographers showed another Prairie altogether, where families were often poorly dressed and dirty and where even the youngest children worked. Women's work was particularly hard and, as Marjorie Harrison reported in *Go West — Go Wise!*, "A man's wife is his helpmate indeed, and on her falls the brunt of the first cruel years, and the greatest shock of the transplanting."[46] The carefully constructed images accompanying the immigration campaigns were directed toward women as well as men; it is thus not surprising to find that the controlling institutions were careful to present only an abstract ideal of the Prairie "woman," while seeking not to reveal the many levels of her experience — isolation, poverty and sickness — which represented the other realities of life in Western Canada.

The spread of amateur photography on the Prairies meant that the monopoly on representation held by the dominant organizations was challenged, at least on a local level. But the prevailing ideologies remained engrained in the emerging photographic tradition of the region. Commercial and press photographers sought out or were directed to the larger, more successful, agricultural operations, and a growing mythology of Prairie life grew out of the imagery which continued to be used to promote the region.

This controlling construction was only seriously questioned during the droughts and the Depression of the 1930s. Images of hardship, which had previously only appeared as the incidental products of private photographers, now emerged in the wider national context of newspapers, magazines and books. The questions which Marjorie Harrison raised about agricultural and social conditions in 1930 now began to receive visual representation as well. However, while the photographs of "hard times on the Prairies" were in part the result of public concern, their dissemination was also an element in the wider political campaign by farm organizations and provincial governments to obtain federal relief. Photographs of a less-than-ideal existence therefore briefly became part of a dominant ideology, before being relegated to archives and history texts.

After the Second World War the durable image of the Prairies as a prosperous and attractive region of comfortable small towns, rolling fields and industrious farmers continued to be the controlling discourse of photographic representation. This was not purely the consequence of better economic conditions; it also was due to the need to recreate an image of prosperity and stability of the type so carefully constructed by the land companies before the crisis of the 1930s. The difficult experiences of settlement and the Depression were dealt with in two ways: photographs taken at the time, particularly those of amateur photographers showing the more unpleasant aspects of the period, were now collected in museum archives where, emptied of their historical specificity, they became "documents" illustrating a carefully composed representation of an episode in the development of the Prairie; but contemporary photographers also made reference to the period of "struggle" and "hardship," using the deliberate juxtaposition of leaning barns and abandoned homesteads with prosperous looking fields, modern machinery and comfortable homes — the past treated as an era of romantic sentiment with the present accorded an image of optimism. Those early difficulties, the photographers suggested, had been overcome and a new era of stability achieved.

This past/present dichotomy was further emphasized through the preferred use of colour photographs, which were sometimes printed alongside earlier black-and-white views for further emphasis. Like the work of many Prairie landscape painters, this form of photographic production, which often appeared in an anthology form similar to early souvenir albums, was largely intended for markets outside the region (in Eastern Canada and elsewhere), thereby continuing the precedent established in the early years of Prairie settlement when, as I have shown, photographs were an important means of controlling outsiders' perceptions of the region.[47]

The representation of the Prairies expanded during this period to include the work of increasing numbers of photographers trained in, or at least informed by, art schools. Among these were modernists who, like their painter counterparts (Tanabe, Rogers, Knowles and others), developed the discourse of formalism along lines established by Greenberg and by the Emma Lake workshops, often minimalizing evidence of human settlement and exploiting the abstract forms and delicate tonal variations of the Prairies, for example in the work of Richard Holden in the late 1970s.[48] In their hands the West was once again treated in the terms of the "Great Lone Land," an inherently romantic concept in which the individual, like a character in a

Friedrich painting, confronts apparently fundamental truths underlying nature.

Formalism played an important role in reworking perceptions of the Western landscape and at times even became partly absorbed, as in the work of Courtney Milne, into the "official" vision of the region.[49] Other photographers, however, notably Randy Burton, Don Hall and (for a time) Grant Arnold, have sought to combine their formal concerns with documentary and "commercial" representations of the Prairie in a way which keeps their work accessible but free of the self-censorship which often affects contemporary images of the West. Burton, for example, sometimes uses early photographic constructs in the composition of his modern prints of Prairie life, notably in his work for the *Finders Keepers* exhibition,[50] which drew attention to the durability of the settlement myth. In a slightly different way, Don Hall presents images in photographs like *House in Humboldt* or *Lumsden, Saskatchewan* that provide the surface familiarity of the commercial genre but that on closer investigation often create a sense of isolation or disturbance, which questions the imagery through a form of internal subversion.[51]

In a similar manner other photographers, including Sandra Semchuk (in the 1970s) and Frances Robson, have sought to represent people (particularly women) and activities of the region which were usually marginalized in "official" constructions. Using elements of documentary practice, their photographs of rural families and women's groups reinterpret the work of early small-town commercial photographers — not only by giving these people a presence in photographs of the area but also by allowing them a certain freedom in the way in which they wished to represent themselves. This other Prairie provides an important voice in the region where vested interests in the control of "reality" through photography have such a firmly established tradition.

1. See, for example, Dennis Reid, *Our Own Country Canada: Being an Account of the National Aspirations of the Principal Landscape Artists in Montreal and Toronto, 1860-1890* (Ottawa: National Gallery of Canada, 1979). Reid only reproduced photographs by Wm. Notman which showed the Rocky Mountains, not the Prairies. These works, in their painterly qualities, seem to accord more closely with paintings by John Arthur Fraser and others.
2. Allan Sekula, "Photography Between Labour and Capital," in Leslie Shedden, *Mining Photographs and Other Pictures 1948-1968: A Selection from the Negative Archives of*

Shedden Studio, Glace Bay, Cape Breton, ed. Benjamin H.D. Buchloh and Robert Wilkie (Halifax: The Press of the Nova Scotia College of Art and Design and the University College of Cape Breton Press, 1983), p. 200.

3. Ibid., p. 194.

4. Ibid., p. 198.

5. For example, the extensive work of the Royal Engineer photographers during the British North America Boundary Survey of 1873.

6. Made on the Assiniboine and Saskatchewan Exploring Expedition. Reproduced by Edward Cavell in *Sometimes a Great Nation: A Photo Album of Canada 1850-1925* (Banff, Alberta: Altitude Publishing Ltd., 1984), Plate 41.

7. W.F. Butler, *The Great Lone Land: A Narrative of Travel and Adventure in the North-West of America* (London: Sampson Low, Marston, Low, and Searle, 1872), p. v.

8. This project is described from the CPR point of view by James B. Hedges in *Building the Canadian West: The Land and Colonization Policies of the Canadian Pacific Railway* (New York: The Macmillan Company, 1939).

9. For an excellent discussion of photography and industry, see Sekula, "Photography Between Labour and Capital," pp. 193-202.

10. See Hedges, Chapter 5, for a discussion of the CPR advertising campaign.

11. Ibid., pp. 101-102.

12. Denis Crane, *The Boys' Book of Canada* (London: Wells Gardner, Darton & Co., n.d.). Crane also published *John Bull's Surplus Children*, in 1915.

13. Crane, *Boys' Book*, both facing p. 140.

14. James Lumsden, *Through Canada in Harvest Time: A Study of Life and Labour in the Golden West* (London: T. Fisher Unwin, 1903), p. xiii.

15. Frank Carrel, *Canada's West and Farther West: Latest Book on the Land of Golden Opportunities* (Quebec: The Telegraph Printing Company, 1911). Carrel was one of a group of 13 journalists whose trip west was sponsored by the railroads and by settlement booster organizations. Carrel acknowledged the use of "many" CPR and other photographs in the preface to his book. Authors rarely used their own photographs because the railroads supplied high-quality images promptly and without charge.

16. Marjorie Harrison, *Go West — Go Wise: A Canadian Revelation* (London: Edward Arnold & Co., 1930), p. 2. This book was written mainly to provide advice and information to British women considering immigration to Canada. It formed part of a new genre of investigative studies by authors not satisfied with official accounts and tours of the Prairies.

17. *The Last Best West, The Wondrous West*, and *Western Canada: The Granary of the British Empire*, George Shepherd Library, Western Development Museum, Saskatoon. As well as being illustrated, these booklets contained immigration information and lists of "facts and figures" regarding the West.

18. *Prosperity Follows Settlement* and *Land of Opportunity*, George Shepherd Library. Similar slogans can be found in American settlement literature.

19. Information about Prairie photographers can be found in Hugh Dempsey's unpublished manuscript, "Nineteenth Century Photographers on the Canadian Prairies" (Glenbow-Alberta Institute, 1978).

20. In Stanley G. Triggs, *William Notman: The Stamp of a Studio* (Toronto: Art Gallery of Ontario and Coach House Press, 1985). Triggs commented that Notman's Prairie photographs appeared "raw and rough," as though he were "searching for a style" (p. 71). In fact, Notman was probably trying to fit his work in with the format already established by Prairie photographers working for the CPR and the land companies.

21. Slogan on a Calgary Colonization Company advertisement for land for sale along the Calgary and Edmonton railway, in *Farm and Ranch Review*, September 1905, p. 44.

22. From *Acres of Selected Lands: The Heart of the Famous Saskatchewan Wheat Belt* (Saskatoon and Western Land Company, n.d.).

23. Lumsden, pp. 119-120. Lumsden visited the farm of Mr. Greenway, the ex-premier of Manitoba.

24. *Canada West: Canada the New Homeland*, 1930 ed., p. 32.

25. For example, see the back and front covers of *Canada West* for 1913 and 1921, respectively. The photographs used for the magazine articles conformed to the standard promotional type. Illustrations of winter scenes were avoided.

26. Hedges, p. 101.

27. See Dawn Glanz, *How the West Was Drawn: American Art and the Settling of the Frontier* (Ann Arbor: UMI Research Press, 1982), Chapter 3 and Fig. 35.

28. See Allan Sekula, "The Emerging Picture-Language of Industrial Capitalism," in *Mining Photographs and Other Pictures*, pp. 203-268.

29. The names of equipment companies were often retouched on the negative to make the letters sharper.

30. These photographs were also used for advertising purposes by the threshing outfits.

31. *The Heart of the Famous Saskatchewan Wheat Belt*, Glenbow Archives, Calgary. The company was based in Montréal.

32. Ibid. This booklet was of particularly high quality, with numerous full-page photographic reproductions. As in nearly all cases, the name of the photographer was not listed.

33. Ibid. Also included were a list of thirty reasons for settlement in the SWLC land block, testimonies from farmers on the quality of the land and a promotional article on the West written by Emerson Hough and reprinted from *Outing*, January-February, 1907.

34. For example, see *Illustrated Souvenir of Winnipeg* [ca. 1905]; *Regina, Saskatchewan: Know Our City*, 1927; and *Views of Saskatoon, Saskatchewan* [ca. 1910], collection of the George Shepherd Library, promotional documents numbers 169, 16 and 120, respectively.

35. *Facts and Figures of the Fastest Growing City in the Empire* [ca. 1912], George Shepherd Library.

36. Houses illustrated in such booklets were invariably the property of important residents and clearly signified the potential for wealth in the town concerned.

37. *Saskatoon, Western Canada: The Commercial Centre of the Most Famous Wheat Growing Territory in the World*, George Shepherd Library.

38. For example, see "Charles S. Noble in Harvest Field, Nobleford, Alta.," anon., collection of the Glenbow Library.

39. Photographs by J. Jessop of Gladstone, printed and engraved by Winnipeg Printing and Engraving, *Gladstone and District Illustrated*, George Shepherd Library.

40. Ibid. Galloway Bros.' was represented by five views of the store and its employees as well as other views showing the homes of the two Galloway brothers and that of the store manager.

41. Harrison, pp. 7-8.

42. Ibid., pp. 9, vii.

43. Ibid., p. 126.

44. The varied work carried out by small-town photographers can be seen in the photograph of the Cameron Photograph Studio in Lacombe, Alberta, Glenbow Library. On the wall of the studio can be seen advertising copy for Deering and McCormick as well as threshing and harvesting scenes and photographs of new buildings.

45. Advertisement in *Farm and Ranch Review*, p. 44.

46. Harrison, p. 134.

47. For example, see Hans S. Dommasch, *Prairie Giants* (Saskatoon: Western Producer Prairie Books, 1986); and Gene Hattori, *Saskatchewan: The Color of a Province* (Saskatoon: Western Producer Prairie Books, 1987). Similar examples can be found in Alberta and Manitoba.

48. This was an important aspect of the photographic production of some members of the Photographers Gallery in Saskatoon during the 1970s.

49. Courtney Milne, *Prairie Light* (Saskatoon: Western Producer Prairie Books, 1985).

50. See Randy Burton and Grant Arnold, *Finders Keepers: A Photographic Survey of Saskatchewan Museums* (Regina: Saskatchewan Museums Association, 1982).

51. Both works are in the collection of the Photographers Gallery.

3

The New Photographic Order

Serge Jongué

Photography today is in an uneasy state that demands analysis of the relationships between the various practices that cut across its inherently diverse landscape as well as the associated new discourses that are vying to define if not determine the direction of its development.

During the 1980s, the rhetoric of criticism took on a dogmatic tone that was particularly surprising given its origins in the academic milieu, which is usually more open-minded. A new photographic order seems to have emerged in which the critics, art institutions and the commercial galleries are like the points of a Bermuda Triangle where artists written off as non-conformists can soon find themselves condemned to the watery depths.

The status and acceptance achieved by this dialectic of disapproval have helped to establish a hierarchy in which the fine-art photograph — the speculative image[1] — ranks superior to so-called realistic or representational photographs, which are readily dismissed by their detractors as "street photography."[2]

This concerted attack on the documentary school raises a number of questions involving both social and aesthetic issues.

Behind a façade of modernism, the neo-pictorialist approach — now favouring the analytical seriousness of academic thought, now preferring the romanticism of the "artist's statement" — indirectly revives the dubious debate between the fine arts and photography. Even more significantly, it sets up a theoretical opposition between communication and expression, between the prosaic and the aesthetic. It may seem surprising that a controversy many hoped had been laid to rest should come to life again. But we have to realize that the new theoretical romanticism, although apparently a direct reaction to the post-structuralist restraints of the 1960s,[3] is really a symptom of the confusion and moral exhaustion of the late twentieth century, a period when the proliferation of images and media has effectively short-circuited the dynamics that traditionally governed the relationship between reality and its representation, between the artist and society.

Boundaries between fact and fiction,[4] between the real and the reproduction, have become blurred, mainly because events can now be expressed as images the instant they occur. The effect has been to produce a kind of emotional immunity or desensitization while sharpening our awareness that the language of classical philosophy has lost its ability to signify and place in perspective the continuing contradictions between the various modes of perception operating in the contemporary world.

An almost inevitable response to this cultural uncertainty was the emergence of an art at once theoretical and theatrical that would give material form to the essence of this conflict. As an after-the-fact physical replica of reality, photography (which fine arts has never forgiven either for its mixed parentage as the offspring of art and science or for the spiritual aura of its substance) has become the favoured medium for the metaphorical expression and ongoing dramatization not only of the image but also of the processes by which images are produced and displayed, and the intention preceding their creation.

Seen from this perspective, the current contempt for realistic work and the cold, arid, even morbid[5] feeling typical of much recent experimental photography are attributable not so much to some fresh quarrel between the classical and the modern as to a combination of strategies for working out, through fantasy, an anxiety fuelled by the history of aesthetics and by unprecedented social pressures.

The silent questioning of a fragmented reality, the insistent investigation of the nature of our connection to the world — an inquiry in which the chosen instrument today is photography, or rather categories of photography — are simply extensions of the concerns that preoccupied the world of painting in the 1950s and 1960s: Warhol, with his awareness of the artistic potential of endlessly reproducible images and the strange effects they can produce; Rauschenberg, who emphasized the mysterious and symbolic qualities of photographic representation; the figurative narration movement, which, despite a family resemblance to photomontage, is the expression of an essentially painterly reaction to the profusion of images and messages produced by early post-industrialism; and, finally, the birth of the hyper-realist movement at the very time when an attitude downplaying the real was becoming prevalent.

The fine-art approach to photography, aside from its heavy reliance on such features as giant formats and colour (whose merit only the test of time will determine[6]), emphasizes the "photographic effect," giving substance to McLuhan's dictum that the medium is the message. But it also reveals a freedom of attitude and a willingness to see the medium as an instrument of expression rather than a restrictive straightjacket. This is undoubtedly the most important contribution the speculative image has made to the intellectual history of photography.

However, we still have to question the mindset of a school of criticism so completely taken with the most seductive aspects of the "photographic effect," and this applies as much to the academic milieu as to the "parallel" and commercial galleries. We must also weigh the impact of the current vogue for privatization and rapid commercialization of the photographic image — tendencies which in the long run are likely to produce dull and short-lived works. (Richard Baillargeon[7] and Pierre Guimond[8] have sounded the alarm on this subject in recent articles.) Finally, moving beyond the arcane conflict between those interested in the outside world — outward-looking photography — and those who prefer to look within themselves — the introverted approach — we need to analyse the recent history of photographic ideas and practices in order to discover what has provoked this renewed animosity towards the documentary image.

Here a study of the functional roles of representational photography would seem to be the most promising avenue, since it is impossible to separate the aesthetic and the social dimensions. Thus from the perspective of social communication as a whole — when we consider the public image of photography — we find that, with the exception of purely commercial practices such as amateur photography (in which any possibility of creativity is effectively stifled by the spiralling inflation of new technologies) and its close relative, studio photography (whose output, from portraits to wedding pictures, lends an official character to photography), the only forms that have been truly integrated into the fabric of society are fashion and advertising photography, and this pattern was established long ago. It is hardly surprising that in the new *Life* magazine, the stories are almost indistinguishable from the advertisements that grace its pages. At the other end of the scale, within the sheltered environment of the art gallery, free from the obligation to appeal to a mass audience, the speculative image is now trying to establish a higher profile and vying for space traditionally reserved for the fine arts. A challenge if ever there was one. After the near-failure of efforts to establish a market for photographic art, it is clear that the interest of prospective buyers is slow, to say the least. Meanwhile, documentary photography, particularly the branch devoted to photojournalism and social investigation, is paying a heavy price today for a role that has been traditionally, and perhaps inevitably, ineffective. At the centre of historical and political battles, this field of photography has been handicapped above all by the lack of autonomy it has always experienced and by its subjugation either as naïve prostitute to the press or as jaded mercenary in the service of ideological causes.

Although documentary photography has been deprived of its traditional public function — information — by the predominance of television (which suffers from all the same weaknesses), this does not preclude the possibility either of finding other uses for it in daily life or, now that it has been freed from the requirement to be topical, of developing a philosophy of communication that would go beyond mere observation to encompass a capacity for reflection.

We must go back to the 1920s and 1930s in Europe, specifically to the Bauhaus, to find a golden age of photography: a time when there was a fertile exchange of ideas between photographic art and other artistic disciplines; a time when freedom and innovation were the watchwords of photography.

This photographic self-sufficiency, this ability to develop new styles in response to the diversity of daily life, diminished as the Second World War broke out. There was a general change in attitudes at that point. By force of circumstance, photography became almost totally identified with news reporting and since then has alternated between propaganda and humanist testimony. At the same time, there has been a stylistic shift towards a social naturalism drawing on historical sensationalism and elements of the travelogue, now filled with local colour, now with international overtones.

After the historical upheaval of the war, photojournalism sought to liberate itself, at least physically, from the dictates of the press barons through the creation of the Magnum agency in 1947. This was the first effort by a group of photojournalists to assert their independence — a bold and isolated venture that foreshadowed the appearance, twenty years later, of the French-style photo agencies such as Gamma, Sygma and Viva, which relied on the magazine format in their efforts to continue the great tradition of photography-as-information, which TV with its ubiquitous presence was threatening to monopolize. The idea of the photographer as author was now gaining ground. But despite the romantic aura surrounding the new generation of Carons and Depardons — the spiritual heirs of Eugene Smith, Robert Capa and Henri Cartier-Bresson — the medium was still a slave to its contexts, and remains so to this day. Susan Meiselas has given an excellent analysis of the complex issues raised by the publication of photographic images in a print context and the exasperating distortions that can accompany this practice.[9] Faced with this new invisible obstacle, some photographers simply gave up: François Hers, formerly of Viva, who believes that photojournalism has nothing new to say and is merely repeating itself;[10] Donald McCullin, whose silence following his foray into advertising cannot erase the deep compassion of his early war photos. Other photographers from other lands, such as Sebastião Salgado,[11] continue to create works in which aesthetic tensions struggle with the compelling need to "bear witness" and still aspire to universal communication. All of them believe — though few have been fortunate enough to put this belief into practice — that the book is the ideal vehicle for photographic works dealing both with the real and with the spiritual. Thus, after decades of a makeshift approach during which books of photography were often no more than retrospective anthologies, documentary photography is finally taking a new direction, inspired by the concept of the independent voice afforded by the photographic project (described by Gilles Mora,[12] among others).

In Canada, where the documentary tradition has been particularly strong thanks to such bodies as the National Film Board (NFB), we are now seeing a reversal of values that is much more pronounced than in France. There, photojournalism is still supported to a certain extent by the press and benefits from that country's location at the crossroads of the continent. The situation is very different in this country: here the growth of photography has been almost entirely due to institutional influence, and the resulting exclusiveness of the distribution system has had a marked impact on the form of production.

Within Quebec, the historical trend away from photographic realism has been greatly accelerated by the unique linguistic and social character of the province. In an astonishingly short time, less than two decades, the seething documentary activity of the early 1970s has subsided, and the speculative image has almost completely taken over the exhibition spaces of the commercial, parallel and public galleries. With essentially no transition period, Quebec photography has moved from the public places it adorned — the traditional church basements and the walls of smoke-filled taverns — to the structured but confining space of the gallery. At the same time, group activities have given way to individual enterprise, and the preoccupation with a global vision of society has been replaced by the pursuit of introspective questioning.

In this respect, the development of photography in Quebec closely parallels the socio-political evolution of Quebec society, from its blossoming following the onset of the Quiet Revolution, through the Marxist tendencies of the 1970s (closely linked to the independence movement), to the ultimate failure of all these projects in the 1980s. During this turbulent era, Quebec documentary photographers opted for involvement rather than observation, choosing to work for political change rather than exploring the complex social reality surrounding them until in the end they realized the foundation of their work was crumbling away beneath their feet. The documentary silence that reigned from 1976 to 1980 was the sign of a deep malaise, punctuated not only by the departure of a number of practitioners who turned to more direct forms of social action but also by the appearance of open disagreement among those who remained in the field as to how their work should be circulated (the *OVO* affair). The year 1983 marks the approximate date of the reversal of power: since then, the keepers and dispensers of photographic "truth" have been players influenced by painting concerned primarily with the "photographic effect" and members of academia engaged in the exploration and redefinition of a territory in which the only critical thought (hitherto the preserve of self-taught practitioners) has been ideological rather than photographic. The product of a formative period (1971-1976) characterized by spontaneous political activism and a group spirit too often imbued with the intellectual prejudice typical of post-1968 politics, social documentary in Quebec was destined from its earliest days to be a subjugated practice, serving more often as a tool of ideological pronouncement than as an instrument for the free, reasoned, independent exploration of reality.

There was, however, one notable exception to the chorus of tame expression: the solitary and uncompromising work of Michel Saint-Jean, who examined the deeply Americanized Quebec of the late 1960s. The cultural ambiguity of a "Belle Province" blessed (or cursed) with the "advantage of historical delay,"[13] which took it in one leap from the rural society of the 1950s to the everyday experience of post-industrial society, was revealed in his perceptive interpretation: a vision of material obsolescence set against the ersatz culture of the fast-food phenomenon. Saint-Jean's work visually deconstructs the two complementary facets of a lifestyle whose thin veneer barely conceals the true nature of a Quebec most often relegated to the traditional role of the colony: that of supplier of raw materials. A harsh and painful truth accentuated by his dramatic style. Apart from this one discordant voice, photographers turned their backs on reality and this, paradoxically, contributed to the explosive burst of documentary of the early 1970s, the whole thrust of which was the search for a mythical and populist image of the Québécois community. In its own way, this movement reflected the sense of cultural crisis dictated at the time by the legitimate aspirations of a society under siege.

With the Disraëli project ("Disraëli, une expérience humaine en photographie"), this image began to take shape under a twofold influence: the ideas of the hippie movement, whose back-to-the-land philosophy fit in perfectly with the nostalgia for a rural Quebec that people subconsciously realized was lost forever; and an ideology reflected in an approach to photography that was based on immediacy of contact with the subject through a sympathetic confrontation in a manner directly drawn from the tradition of European photojournalism (Kertesz, Doisneau, Izis, Capa).

The two extremes of this society in transition were to be defined and illustrated by two photographers of European origin who came to Canada during the waves of migration of the early 1950s: Gabor Szilasi, who was the first to make character studies and to document rural interiors in the Charlevoix region and the Île aux Coudres, and Pierre Gaudard, who photographed the world of the urban worker with an equally straightforward directness. A spirit of emulation developed which found its first concrete expression in 1972 in the Disraëli project, the first extensive documentation of a specific environment by young Quebec photographers. The project was originated by Claire Beaugrand-Champagne, Michel Campeau, Roger Charbonneau and Cedric Pearson, all of whom spent a summer photographing in Disraëli, a community in the Eastern Townships where the rural way of life was gradually disappearing, and it was revealing in many ways. With its stamp of eclecticism and the "photographic happening,"[14] it created an immediate though unintentional storm on the quiet waters of Quebec's concept of photography, which had always considered Notman's urban middle class and Tessier's romantic peasantry[15] as two separate worlds hermetically sealed off from each other. The Disraëli project revealed the extent of social and political cleavages then operating in Quebec; but even more importantly, the Disraëli incident and the controversy surrounding it — which pitted the members of the municipal council against Pierre Vallières, spokesman for the left-wing separatism of the day — gave an indication of the psychological and behavioural directions that this young movement would take in the future.

In fact, the Disraëli project's faults had far more to do with its unconsciously exotic treatment of society than with the exploitation of poverty of which it was accused. Its founders, all of whom were very young, were committed to "zero degree" communication — an ideal that was also being pursued at that time by the *cinéma direct*. They expected to find a state of grace that would give them a magic power to transcend social differences and express the family-like cohesion of a society they believed was perfectly symbolized by rural life. Convinced of the inevitable harmony between their essentially urban ideals and a complex reality that had to be understood, not merely recorded, the Disraëli project members made a naïve and premature arrival on the intellectual minefield of a changing Quebec and soon found their hopes of a universal nirvana crushed. But on the other side of the political purgatory to which they were subjected lay the promise of a providential national renewal and the tangible possibility of once again being back within the family fold.

Today, with hindsight, we realize to what extent the photographic discourse of the period was bound up in politics. It is now hard to believe that while Alain Chagnon enjoyed a good press — and rightly so — for his photographs of the Francophone taverns of Montréal, Vittorio Fiorucci (exploring the same theme in the bars of Montréal's west end) was totally ignored. It was as if some edict had been issued denying Truth a place on Crescent Street.[16] And yet, this essay by Fiorucci — quite apart from its celebration of women characteristic of his sensibility — addressed a range of subjects from the Bohemian atmosphere of the day to motorcycle gangs. The very possibility of exploring the tensions between social ideals, which is essential to understanding any society, was denied by the photographic language introduced by the Disraëli project. The Disraëli group did not seek to identify and express differences; their objective was rather to exalt an ideal. As a result, the activities of both the Groupe d'action photographique and the Groupe des photographes populaires bogged down in a constant populism,[17] though to varying degrees. Their original well-meaning intention — to set themselves up as "press agencies for ordinary people"[18] and to "tell the other side of the story"[19] — in fact led them to the opposite extreme, trapping them in the kind of media sensationalism they had set out to fight and preventing them from investigating aspects of reality specific to the period. Parallel to this dogmatic narrowness, the new documentary photography adopted a style that reflected both its inexperience and its ideological mission, combining a plain, eye-level manner[20] with a direct approach that sought to name "the world"[21] (an approach that it equated with a complete denial of esthetic considerations). This apparent disregard for style has been an enduring dividing line within the Montréal photographic community. From 1970 to 1972, a whole generation of Anglophones at Loyola College, following such figures as John Max and Charles Gagnon, set out to question the inner meaning of images and engaged in highly personal explorations, while the Francophone community was totally preoccupied with the search for a social identity centred on the goal of an independent society.

This conjunction of forces — the political (the rise of Quebec nationalism), the economic (the availability of distribution channels such as *Perspectives* magazine, and government support programs such as Opportunities for Youth and the Local Initiatives Program), and the philosophical (the outlook of a young generation searching for a social ideal that would express their desire for freedom) — ultimately doomed the documentary school and deprived it of any opportunity for creative rapport with an existing photographic community.

During the late 1950s, a Bohemian group of photographers had naturally evolved out of artistic clubs such as l'Échouerie — among them John Max, Guy Borremans, Vittorio, Robert Millet and Jeremy Taylor. These "individualists" — and the list could be extended to include Sam Tata and John Gibson — became the ambassadors of modern Montréal photography. In 1957, for example, Max and Vittorio took the initiative in establishing contact with Eastman House in Rochester, and Max was the one who introduced Lorraine Monk of the NFB to the expressionist school of photography in Montréal.

Efforts to form groups in the early 1970s took place in a very different climate of marked hostility and extreme coolness towards anything from outside the milieu. It was symptomatic that one of the first resolutions passed by LADAP (les Ateliers d'animation photographique du Québec)[22] following its creation in 1974 was a recommendation to boycott *Exposure*, the pan-Canadian exhibition organized by the Art Gallery of Ontario.

The year 1976 was a significant turning point; from then on there could be no doubt about how closely politics and photography were linked. Michel Campeau and Alain Chagnon became militant activists; others, including Jean Fiorito, André Sénécal and Roger Charbonneau, plunged into social action; and the Francophone photographic community split into camps on questions of a purely political nature. *OVO* magazine, considered "too right-wing,"[23] withdrew from the collective adventure and, in the lull between 1976 and 1980, sought to win the favour of readers and supporters from completely outside the milieu.

By an ironic swing of the pendulum, the same magazine was accused of leftist leanings[24] in the post-1980 photographic renewal because it felt photography should be "plugged in," connected, a participant in a variety of political and social debates[25] — in short, because it favoured continuation and extension of the practice of social involvement so ingenuously inaugurated by documentary photographers not long before.

A schism developed between a group of photographers involved with the short-lived newsletter *Gélatine* and the codirectors of *OVO*, Jorge Guerra and Denyse Gérin-Lajoie, focussing on two major issues. The first was the way photographs were used in the magazine: the photographers felt the integrity of their work was being diluted or even destroyed by the piecemeal publication of their pictures as illustrations of editorial positions in which they had no say.[26] They demanded control over their production and insisted on personal visibility, while *OVO*'s directors argued that the magazine's thematic formula was popular with its readers. A corollary, of course, was the matter of balance between local and international content, always a thorny question in Quebec. *OVO*'s bias on this point had long been established and was well known: photography was to be an instrument of communication and social change. What is perhaps more surprising is the new attitude adopted by the photographers, and it deserves examination here. The *OVO* dispute, apart from the deep frustrations and enmities it created, marked an about-face by the former champions of social documentary. As indicated by the bitterness of the polemic that ensued, the dispute was a symbolic form of parricide, a settling of accounts, as artists desperately tried to free themselves from the political constraints of the 1970s. The resentment caused by these still too recent memories was catalysed by the affair and fuelled by the fact that the major outlets for photography in the Quebec press — *Perspectives, Le Jour, Week-End Magazine* — had disappeared, leaving *OVO* as the only vehicle available to an art form struggling for a new lease on life.

The obvious deficiencies of the Quebec documentary movement's selective exploration of reality were masked by the bitter disputes that surrounded not only its beginnings but also the political renewal that it supported and its tacit acceptance of the critical complacency bestowed on it. It is true that the Disraëli model encouraged the desire for self-expression, launched careers and spurred numerous artistic achievements (such as *Transcanadienne, sortie 109*[27] and Michel Cloutier's photo essay on truckers working at James Bay[28]) but because the photographers unconsciously refused to take part in the difficult battle of ideas over the now hybrid nature of Quebec society, it also led into an ever-narrowing spiral in which the choice of subjects for investigation seemed governed by the conviction that social micro-climates were perfectly self-contained and could be described without unleashing any debate of fundamental issues. Instead of seeking out a controversial reality, the young documentary photographers chose to maintain the comforting illusion of social cohesion; above all, they wanted to avoid rejection, and this explains their continuing desire to depict a homogeneous group and their unwillingness to address the increasing disparities in a society undergoing rapid transformation.

[4 4]

Thus, with varying degrees of success, Campeau decided to photograph the blind, abandoning his project on Montréal's Italian community; Claire Beaugrand-Champagne turned her attention to senior citizens (1974); and Jean Lauzon later focussed all too briefly on the mentally handicapped (1981). Beaugrand-Champagne's work on the arrival of Vietnamese refugees in Montréal (1980-1981) was the first real sign of change in a photographic discourse whose main thrust until then had been "osmosis" and unification. Indeed, an insidious anxiety — a kind of blind spot — can be seen in the inability of so many photographers to come to grips with Quebec reality. Astonishingly, the contribution of European immigrants of the 1950s and 1960s — which not only gave the photographic community the voices of Gaudard and Szilasi, but also brought the committed support, the know-how and the talent of people like Claude Haeffely at the Cinémathèque québécoise and Guerra at *OVO* — did nothing to make them more aware of the changes in their society; nor did the increasing flow of immigrants from the Third World in the years following 1975, although it was transforming the everyday life and cultural landscape of Montréal.

Michel Campeau's series *Week-end au "Paradis Terrestre"!*, produced between 1973 and 1981, is particularly telling in this respect, both for what it reveals — the gradual erosion of a reality mediated by the language of public relations (the predigested culture of all kinds of "salons") — and for what it omits: the presence of Neo-Quebecers.

Paradoxically, the reason why the crucial issue of immigration has generally been avoided is the very fact that it is so highly explosive, raising as it does the whole question of the major reshaping of the face of Quebec society. Few works deal with this issue, although one is Serge Clément's work-in-progress on the Portuguese community. Another is the work-in-progress by the VOX POPULI collective (Marcel Blouin, Sophie Bellissant), although this group's ethnocentric strategy of comparing conditions in the "old country" with the experience of the new land could easily lure them into the old pitfall of exoticism and distract them from their immediate objective of expressing the contact between cultures. It is as if Quebec photography, caught between curiosity and shyness (to paraphrase Rauschenberg), had not succeeded in piercing the complex realities of a changing society to integrate them into that family album cohesiveness that seems to be one of its deepest motivations.

Since 1980, few documentary projects have been undertaken. Their small number, however, has been more than offset by the independence of each photographer's approach: Beaugrand-Champagne's photo essay on military personnel at the Saint-Jean base (1984); Chagnon's work on women in non-traditional jobs (1980-1983) and his studies of the youth of Verdun; the collaboration by Marik Boudreau, Suzanne Girard, Gilbert Duclos and sociologist Kwok Chan on Montréal's Chinatown (summer 1983); and Edward Hillel's immigrant journey up the Main (1987). All these projects reveal a livelier interest in contemporary social change.

This classical documentary stream is now reaching maturity after an uphill battle: typically working under difficult conditions and ignored by museums and galleries alike (Dazibao is a prime example, despite the fact that it was originally set up in 1980 to bring together the various currents of contemporary photography), its practitioners have been hindered in their development by the time they must spend on paid assignments (their only guarantee of material survival). Among initiatives recently taken to organize the milieu are the creation of the STOCK agency in 1988 (Robert Fréchette, Jean-François Leblanc) and the efforts at modernization on the part of the Association photographique de Montréal, which is working to define Montréal's current photographic potential, promote market development, organize events and make the city part of an international exchange network.[29] There is also hope for new leadership from the VOX POPULI collective and the magazine *Ciel variable*.

Quite apart from these developments, an alternative documentary trend is now emerging, characterized by an inward-looking vision of reality; its interests lie in the areas of autobiography, narration and the aesthetic possibilities of formats. These interests, quite novel for Quebec, are being explored for the most part by the generation of 30- to 40-year-olds who are trying to work out on a personal level the antagonism between individual and collectivity which was such an issue in the 1970s. Their approach shows the liberating influence of fine-art photography — a cross-fertilization of ideas that holds the promise of an eclectic practice of photography.

The new directions taken by Campeau, for example, stress the need for a tactile, loving universe and focus on his never-ending search for human warmth and certainty in relationships (elements that are certainly pervasive in his work) in a course that has taken him from *Chez Georges* through *Disraëli* and *Tremblements du cœur* to *Love Test*. In Normand Rajotte's work, the trends can be seen in the working out of his dance of indecision between city and countryside. Urban essays (his photostory about the children of Montréal's south-centre neighbourhood) and rural subjects (his coverage of agricultural fairs) have been replaced by a quest for a religious symbolism, an incantatory questioning of the landscape and the earth in which man's being is anchored; a questioning accompanied by an exploration of the stylistic possibilities of format and, especially, sequence. His project also emphasizes the urgent need for an environmental policy. As for Serge Clément, whose documentary photography shows an exemplary continuity, his work has taken him in a few years from the physical to the mental voyage. *Les Québécois en vacances* (1982), a series still featuring the exotic appeal of travel, was followed by the first parts of his *Notes urbaines* project, which gradually introduced a broader concept of the forms reality can take (reflections, shadows, symbols) in the urban context, but also revealed a subjectivity that found expression in an international sequence (Montréal and New York, but also Portugal, Italy and South America). A fresh wind is beginning to blow, one that was missing from the earlier style of Quebec documentary photography. Examples of openness to the world on the part of individual photographers are increasingly frequent: Beaugrand-Champagne's travels to Thailand (1980) and Italy, Campeau's visit to Poland (1985), Carrière's trip to France (1983-84). All are finally becoming part of the international photographic scene.

Two contradictory and diametrically opposed approaches towards documentary prevail today in Quebec: one involves struggling from the inside against the emasculating ghosts of the

1970s to reach a sensibility in which the individual is in harmony with the universal — what Campeau calls a "subjective realism"; the other, influenced by a revival of the "eyewitness" tradition, aims to pave the way for acceptance of the new interpretive assessment of reality required by social change.

At the moment, it is impossible to predict whether the latter school will be content to follow in the footsteps of old-fashioned documentary photography (made obsolete as much by the endless technological opportunities for computer manipulation of the image[30] as by the jaded eye of a society saturated by a photographic "pratico-inert," to use J.-P. Sartre's phrase) or if it will produce a new way of expressing the current rhythms of society.

Having said that, we must remember that the Quebec documentary school is young — barely twenty years old — and is now going through a serious identity crisis. Its continued existence is threatened on all sides: by an uninformed conservatism that consigns photographic images to a supporting or service role; by its own growing inability to comment upon reality; and by the disappearance of the concept of craftsmanship. The idea of the artist-craftsman who combines intellectual purpose and technical resourcefulness has gradually been replaced by a division of labour in photography, in which conceptual and technical aspects are separated. Certainly during its years of growth, documentary photography in Quebec has been devoted almost exclusively to illustration, and this has prompted some to say that it has exhausted itself through repetition. There is a grain of truth in this. And yet it would be wrong to conclude that it has nothing left to say: that would be to accept a narrow, rigid and legitimist view of the world as if it could embrace all aspects of reality.

Similarly, to exclude an artistic practice which by its very nature must come directly to grips with social problems would be to renounce one of the few instruments for preserving the collective memories of a society. The task of imaginative recreation clearly cannot be left to television, for this medium, as the writer Jacques Godbout has pointed out,[31] is more concerned about how its commentators look and the way they speak than with giving shape and meaning to the events of the day. Nor can today's practitioners rely exclusively on the strengths of experimental photography, which encompasses both profound explorations and the most transient of works, or they would soon be caught up in the short-sighted opportunism of stardom and careerism which currently mar this photographic movement; and those who practice photography as a communication art and who are committed to the aesthetic quality of everyday images would find themselves asphyxiated before long. Beauty would be sent off to an early retirement in the museum or prematurely confined to the harem of the gallery, and the public would be deprived of the opportunity to understand and enjoy a new art form which is taking shape before our very eyes. We cannot wish upon the art of our time the status of a private art.

Commenting on the future is always a risky business, but we can restate the obvious fact that the categorical opposition between aesthetic and documentary photography must come to an end. We can also point out the incongruity of a terminology totally unsuited to the photographic medium, which is essentially subjective and which necessarily documents the physical fact, unless its nature is deliberately subverted by some intentionality. In terms of their approaches, the two streams should be thought of as communicating vessels, not as isolated entities. Those working in documentary should be aware of the need to continually modulate the harshness of reality, just as artists continually rework the forms in which they express themselves. Documentary must be spared the fate of Sisyphus so that it can attain the ideal of poetic expression (to paraphrase Miguel Rio Branco[32]) and so that the senses can enthusiastically combine aesthetic exploration with the approximation of reality. Observation of the world will then nourish spiritual sensibility rather than stifle it. And there will be an end to inhibitions, at least in photographic images.

1. This term is used by Régis Durand in "Les images spéculatives, ou «l'art comme photographie»" in *Catalogue général du mois de la photo à Paris* (Paris: Audiovisuel, 1986), pp. 120-124. It encompasses the many efforts to combine photographic work with the plastic arts, as well as the challenging of the methods through which the image is perceived (quotation, reappropriation, etc.) and finally the questioning of the photographic act itself. All of these are completely separate from the act of representation.

2. Gilles Toupin, "Culte du coin de rue et nouvelle photo," *La Presse* [Montréal], January 15, 1983.

3. During the 1970s, the theoretical openness engendered by structuralism was fashionably transformed into a dogmatic system of thought.

4. "J.-G. Ballard croit-il encore au futur?" *Actuel* [Paris] 105 (March 1988): 122, 127.

5. These terms are not intended as censure in the name of some illusory canon of beauty; on the contrary, they describe the physical reality of a number of current photographic strategies. See, for instance, Roy Adzak, "La modification" (Paris), or Cindy Sherman, "Dead-Head" (New York).

6. The "bandwagon" effect must be taken into account — that inevitable tendency to imitate and to follow in the search for new angles to exploit in the marketing of art.

7. Richard Baillargeon, "Pour la photographie," in *La photographie et l'art contemporain — Actes du colloque*, Esse [Montréal], Special Issue No. 2, 1988, p. 25.

8. Pierre Guimond, "Les arts, la photographie et le chocolat chaud," *T.S.F. Magazine*, 5 (undated, 1987-88): 95. (This magazine is produced by M.A. students in the Communications Department, Université du Québec à Montréal.)

9. Don Snyder, "Mixing Media," *Photo Communique*, 9,1 (Spring 1987): 28-36. This article deals with the traditionally uneasy relationship between photographers and the media, the former claiming the right to approve publication of their pictures, the latter approaching the matter primarily from a commercial angle. For Meiselas, the importance of communicating outweighs the risk of distortion by the media (dispersing the elements of a photo essay, problems of misleading captions, etc.) which is inherent in the publication process. Basically, she says, what matters is to extend the photograph's life span and make the work accessible to the widest public.
Jodi Cobb — quoted by Vicki Goldberg in "The Well-Examined Life of Jodi Cobb," *American Photographer*, January 1987 — also raises questions about the identity and moral responsibility of the "visual interpreter."

10. "Agences et photographes — Les reporters victimes du reportage," an interview with François Hers by Hervé Guibert, *Le Monde Aujourd'hui* [Paris], January 27-28, 1985, p. vi.

11. "Pour que les images ne meurent," interview with Sebastião Salgado by Patrick Roegiers, *Le Monde* [Paris], October 18, 1986, p. 13.

12. Gilles Mora, "Le projet photographique," *Les cahiers de la photographie*, 8 (Association de critique contemporaine en photographie, France): 14-25.

13. Interview with Pierre Guimond, Montréal, April 1988. This concept was borrowed by sociologist Marcel Rioux from the philosophy of historical materialism.

14. Interview with Michel Campeau, Montréal, March 1988.

15. Pierre Dessureault, "Documentaire/Commentaire," introduction to a catalogue for an exhibition of the work of Michel Campeau (*Week-end au "Paradis Terrestre"!*) and Pierre Gaudard (*En France*), (Ottawa: National Film Board of Canada, Still Photography Division, 1982).

16. Interview with Vittorio Fiorucci, Montréal, June 1988.

17. The Groupe d'action photographique (GAP) and the Groupe des photographes populaires (GPP), which came into being in 1971 and 1972 respectively, were part of the general renewal of Francophone culture that accompanied Quebec's political effervescence in the 1960s and 1970s. These two spontaneous groupings, based on personal friendships, quite naturally reflected nationalist ideology but did not

subscribe to any particular political point of view. The GPP's attitude was the more trenchant: exclusively interested in the popular milieu, this group also did militant (and unpaid!) photographic work for the *Bulletin populaire* (1972-77) of the Agence de presse libre du Québec (APLQ). GAP, on the other hand, was caught between an alternative practice and the traditional fine-arts approach to photography. Both groups fell apart in 1975-76. A parallel group, Photocell, was formed by English-speaking Montrealers, including Clara Gutsche and David Miller, with an emphasis on urban and community images.

GAP: Michel Campeau, Roger Charbonneau, Serge Lorrain, Claire Beaugrand-Champagne, Gabor Szilasi, Pierre Gaudard.

GPP: A group of about ten people, including Alain Chagnon, André Sénécal, Jean Fiorito and Marc Brosseau.

18. Interview with Michel Campeau, Montréal, March 1984.

19. Interview with Normand Rajotte, Montréal, May 1988.

20. Interview with Michel Cloutier, Montréal, June 1985.

21. Tod Papageorge, *Walker Evans and Robert Frank: An Essay on Influence* (Yale University Art Gallery, 1981), p. 7.

22. Individual interests with their eclectic tendencies would soon destroy the unity of this group, which was incapable of conceiving a more specific organizational focus than its commitment to the unique nature of Quebec culture.

23. Personal interview with Jorge Guerra, Montréal, May 1988.

24. *Idem. OVO* magazine probably made a fundamental error in perspective by failing to recognize the nature of an intellectual movement that was more interested, at that particular time, in protecting the Francophone enclave than in raising the general level of political awareness.

25. *Idem.*

26. Interview with Serge Clément, Montréal, May 1988.

27. Jean Lauzon and Normand Rajotte, *Transcanadienne, Sortie 109* (Montréal: les Éditions *OVO*, 1978).

28. Michel Cloutier, "L'automobile," *OVO* Magazine, 30-31 (1978).

29. Interview with Robert Hébert, Montréal, May 1988.

30. "When Seeing Isn't Believing: 150 Years of Photography," *Life*, Fall 1988, p. 160.

31. Jacques Godbout, "Quand les médias enterrent l'Histoire," *L'Actualité*, March 1986, p. 133.

32. From a letter to Carole Naggar, quoted in the entry for Miguel Rio Branco, *Dictionnaire des photographes* (Paris: Éditions du Seuil, 1982), p. 339.

(Translated from French)

4

Verum Factum

MICHAEL MITCHELL

It would happen on the way home from school. I'd be out there on the street with a couple of friends, slowly circling round a clutch of girls from my class. The girls walked with arms wrapped tightly around binders and flat across their chests, an arrangement that produced a sort of armless gait that made them wiggle and their hair bounce. They had it pretty well worked out. We'd just be thinking we were getting somewhere when our little adolescent universe would come slowly spinning around a corner and there'd be my mother sitting in a ditch, her sketch pad propped up against a culvert and her watercolours laid out in the dry bottom. Her concentration was absolute — she'd never see us — as she worked her formidable technique learned at the feet of Comfort and Carmichael in the Ontario College of Art of the late thirties. It used to embarrass me, this business of picture making. Nobody else's mother did it. I didn't understand the compulsion.

If I had any theory of art then, it was little more than a crude notion about mimesis, and what Mother did wouldn't quite fit. Sure she was a realist, but only by the broad stroke. She cheated. My mother wasn't above adding gables and people; she dematerialized power poles and trucks. Later, after I left home, her pictures became less idealized, and now that she's old she paints only the exorcised material of the past. The paintings are devoted to plastic bags, car wrecks and obsolete circuitry, perhaps in homage to, and in atonement for, all those decades of exclusions that had been suggested by her masters and encouraged by our culture.

This business of picture making proved to be catching. I ended up in Fine Arts at the University of Toronto, watching thousands of badly made slides flutter across a screen between studio classes in historical technique. In my second year I worked for weeks on an assigned still life: some fruit and a bottle standing on a velvet-draped pedestal. I soon got the objects under control, but the drapery eluded me. After I had spent weeks pushing muddy oil paint around, trying to make it look like cloth, my instructor finally came over for a look. Peering over his glasses he allowed that while I'd done a wonderful job of resolving the representation of draped cloth, he would have to fail me for leaving out the bottle and the pears. I knew then that I was not to be a painter. A case of beer and 48 hours later I was registered in Anthropology.

This work eventually took me to Latin America, where our research team hacked its way through the thorn forest and swamps of the Mexican Pacific Coast almost to Guatemala. The country was hot, inhospitable and largely uninhabited, but occasionally something wonderful would happen. I once rode off into the mountains for several days accompanied only by a very old and taciturn campesino. For months we'd heard rumours of an abandoned mountaintop city. The old man claimed to have seen it. Together we rode our mules round and round through the trackless bush, down into empty valleys, up over crumbling ridges. We had no food, the mules stumbled. On the third day my guide indicated the top of a mountain. It was so steep we had to drag the mules up behind us. At the summit was an immense overgrown ruin — ceremonial mounds, a ball court and a vast plaza — a virtual inventory of Meso-American civilization. Exhausted, I sat down in front of a large stone stele covered with elaborate carving. I knew what I was supposed to do — copy and translate the glyphs and calendrical signs, tot up the bar and dot numerals, and thus figure out which people had built the place and when they did it. Instead I found myself simply staring at the whole thing, lost in a reflection on the human mind. The day, the month, the year no longer mattered — I didn't care if they'd been Zapotecs or Mixtecs. But as I sat there — the first person like me who'd ever been there — my professional credentials seemed pathetically inadequate to deal with this message from the past. I unpacked our expedition's camera, a tool that I barely knew how to use, and spent the day photographing. Finally, as the day declined, a superstitious and frightened old man made me come down from the mountain.

No one since has set foot on that mountain. In a chance encounter with my old crew more than a decade later I learned that several attempts to retrace my steps had ended in failure. The old man was gone, and all that remained of my wandering were the notes that I'd made, some potsherds and what now were valuable photographs. The pictures were not just information, they were proof. Through them the site was accepted and inserted into the historical sequence, neatly linking one era and a people to another. And I got something as well. The experience started me on a path back to that painting studio, through it and beyond. This time I had the right medium.

Once, in an Art History class, a lecturer had quoted Daumier on photography — it described everything and explained nothing. In my nineteen-year-old mind, that pretty well finished off photography. Now that half a dozen years of social science had culminated in the old man and the mountain, a detailed description seemed to me to be the most that one could do. All theories were subject to revision and obsolescence, all interpretations were merely that; but maybe a clear, intelligently seen description might last and be useful. Perhaps it was enough.

This, of course, is a simple apprehension of photography. With a decade or two of working, reading, looking and thinking, one's notions become more complex and historical in perspective, placing photography within the larger development of image making.

When we compare ourselves with the other species on this planet, we conclude that we are the most intelligent. Yet we remain flummoxed by the size and complexity of our world. We still inch our way along the path to some workable knowledge by modelling the little that we understand. We scale it down and create a model that will fit in the hand. These models omit everything that is not visible to the naked eye and the acculturated mind. If it doesn't fit the current schemata, then it doesn't exist. These models take many forms. The Inuit tell tales, aborigines in Australia sing their maps, the Indian avatar makes drawings in the sand. But here in the West we prefer material things — objects and images. We have been drawing and sculpting our notion for centuries. Recently we have begun to demand more efficient production — model making takes too much time. By the late eighteenth century we were hard at work on what would be the basis for the ultimate system. Near the middle of the nineteenth we finally got the foundation system right. Point and shoot — simple. Now we could catalogue and control everything.

This new modelling system teetered on a pivotal point in the evolution of Western culture. The method and the hardware were of the past — Renaissance experiments in perspective, camera-based drawing aids and ancient observations of the effects of light on various materials. The camera itself was based on our own bodies. Like most of our buildings and tools, it had the bilateral symmetry of the human figure. This culminated in the radial symmetry of the lens which, of course, modelled the eye. The light-sensitive plate at the back was an extremely simple analogue of the part of the brain that decodes the impulses from the optic nerve into a picture of reality. And photography's treatment of time modelled memory.

The camera, so often turned on buildings, was itself architecture. The central space of Western culture was the room, the Latin *camera*, from which one looked out onto the world on which one acted. The greatest of these rooms, the interiors of the great Gothic cathedrals built across Europe in the Middle Ages, manifested the apogee of Christian belief and aspiration. They were colossal metaphors — darkness penetrated by light. Mediated by coloured glass, diurnal light became divine light that beamed down upon icons and altars embellished with beaten silver and leafed gold that shone in imitation of the source. With each new construction the windows got larger, the colours cooler, thus driving out darkness. However, this progression proved to be not the triumph of the divine, but the slide into the secular. We left the room, reduced it to portability, gave it one clear window, and utilized the precious metals for their light sensitive properties rather than their lustre. The metals became grey deposits on paper. The image was no longer within. It was no longer sacred. It was solely of the world, fixed and removable. The old world of myth and magic disappeared in the hard light — all that was left was raw, physical reality, which photography took on directly.

Photography, like printing, is a technology; and just as the book destroyed the oral tradition by weakening our oral/aural memory, so photography has damaged the visual tradition by crippling our visual memory. We have become dependent on paper, our concepts limited to the seen and recordable, our notion of fact limited to what can be recorded and rerecorded, filed and retrieved. Yet these technologies, born of the secularization and science which they have radically reinforced, are not quite what they seem. Despite their resolutely material foundation, they share a quality with music: they are more events than objects. Painting and sculpture, the old technologies, were resolutely physical objects. To effectively experience them you had to stand before the original. They resisted reproduction. Photographs, as we all know, can be experienced in a perfectly satisfactory way in reproduction. In the nineteenth century a Woodburytype in the hand obviated the need for a silver print. During the twentieth, photographic images have spread like rumours and whispers through the wire services. Now, in the age of laser scanners and edge enhancement, the most laboured piece of darkroom work looks like a simulacrum of the reproduction.

As this dematerialization is extended through electronics, photography becomes a multi-edged sword. Once, following an all-night drive to Florida, I pulled into a dark motel on a sleazy strip in Miami. After pulling down the blinds against the approaching dawn I went to sleep. Awakening hours later in the dark air-conditioned room I was disoriented. Since I had no watch I stumbled across the room and turned on the television. As every channel was carrying the Orange Bowl parade I finally gave in and watched. In time the sound on the set seemed to go out of sync with the picture. It actually doubled itself like the marching bands in Ives's exuberant pieces. The more I fiddled with the set the worse it got, until the music and commentary became a cacophonous canon that didn't work. Frustrated, I dressed and went outside to ask the time. And there it all was — the TV trucks, the commentators' stand, the crowd. I had been watching the transmission of an event taking place on the other side of the door.

Television is photography in extremis. Even the paper is gone. Now light replicates light, sound replicates sound, reality and image are confounded. The medium extended no longer models — it merely transmits. We now have a vehicle as insubstantial and evanescent as the original recorded moment.

If television seems mindless to most of us, so does photography to many artists and critics. The images produced by the medium are so directly tied to the world in front of the lens that even the medium's more thoughtful practitioners have taken to lamenting the absence of any significant ideas among their fellow photographers. Most photographs are made so quickly that they don't seem like considered images. Without brush strokes and hand marks to signal the autographic origins of the image, we are not led back to the maker. An image that fails to insist forcefully that it is the product of human intelligence is an image that fails to encourage consideration.

In a medium in which the maker hides the hand, the output seems a mere stare or glance, a printout from the back of an eyeball, at most the production of a mind whose clutch is disengaged.

Yet for all these perceived limitations, even the medium's harshest critics have found it difficult to deny the photographer's ability to generate handsome images. This is the medium's high ground; and it is here, irrespective of theoretical and critical debates concerning photography's potential as an art form, that the medium's most persuasive apologists have built their houses. From Emerson's *Naturalistic Photography*, through Stieglitz, down to Szarkowski and the modernist position, the rhetoric has been based on notions of purity, form and aesthetics. Literal content, context and history have become marginal glosses to the image.

Such elegant and persuasive pronouncements notwithstanding, photography received one of its most compelling, albeit oblique, endorsements in the 1960s. The source was a surprise and the message ignored. In the mid-sixties we concluded that we had too many things. Big yard sales, a kind of street-level divestment, became obligatory cultural events. Having escaped from their possessions, the newly lightened and liberated took to the road. Artists, those inveterate makers of things, joined the odyssey. Sculptor Robert Morris announced that "the static, portable indoor art object can do no more than carry a decorative load that becomes increasingly uninteresting";[1] and in farmers' fields, on deserted mesas and on mountaintops artists cut grass, arranged stones and dug trenches into works that were neither static, portable nor decorative. Some people sniggered when gritty photographs documenting this ephemera began appearing with price tags on gallery walls. But the strategy was shrewd. It showed a good understanding of the photograph's ambiguous objecthood: it was there but it wasn't, it had transparency, it was disposable and wasn't valuable unless it was signed like a urinal or a bottle rack. The visual arts needed a good housecleaning, and the objectless quality of photography was politically perfect.

The artists, of course, soon abandoned their position. They had to eat. But the program — cut down on stuff, get out into the world, communicate with economy, be a general practitioner — was valid and timely. Now that most artists are back to busy object making, it seems that photographers are the natural heirs of the forsaken program. Moreover, the obnoxious aspects of the artists' activity —

the violation of the landscape and the elevation of the artist into a seer or a hairy-chested mud wrestler — were obviated by photography. Photographers could take without leaving a mark, and the best of them strove for a kind of transparency. When they did their job well, only the picture was visible.

The problem was that the photographers generally didn't see it that way. They didn't see at all because their noses were stuck in dusty back issues of *Camera Work*, and their ears were still ringing with the delphic utterances of the old *Aperture*. This visionary and expressionistic tradition in photography collapsed for want of any substratum other than a few charismatic personalities like the late Minor White. While their heads were down, time and technology — and the news departments of television networks — effectively, if inadequately, snatched away photography's documentary tradition. Henceforth documentary photographs would only be seen in picture frames. There still remained the medium's great central tradition — the line from Western exploration photographers down through Atget to Walker Evans and Frank, where photographs balanced between the affective and the informative, where pictures could resonate without cant — but by the end of the sixties this tradition was in trouble. Its masters were either in their declining years or had moved on to other interests. Great work requires confidence and faith. One has to believe in the possibilities of the raw, pure medium, have confidence in the future, a sense of an audience and faith in the essential rightness of one's culture. One has to believe that one's medium is truly important. All this had suffered serious erosion by the close of the decade.

The uncertainty was very evident in the photographic work of the period. In 1969 Nathan Lyons organized the exhibition *Vision and Expression* at Eastman House. While more than half of the 150-odd images selected were, in technical terms, pure photography, many of them exploited marginal effects — blurring, eccentric formats and tonality, extreme lenses, multiple printing or theatrical set-ups. The traditional work that was included looked mannered and stale. The show's real focus seemed to be on images that looked toward printmaking rather than photography. Far from being the seminal exhibition of the period, *Vision and Expression* was symptomatic. Photography was entering a period of confusion; a hard-won confidence was disintegrating.

Of the many directions pursued during the seventies, the serious exploration of the expressive possibilities of the rapidly evolving new colour materials seemed to offer the greatest potential for a revitalization of the medium. Much of the new colour work that emerged drew its inspiration from traditions that had evolved in black-and-white photography earlier in the century. Steven Shore's pictures reflected a close examination of Walker Evans's and some recognition of Friedlander's. That the work of Shore and his contemporaries should build a house for colour photography upon such foundations was natural enough — there were no acceptable building blocks from colour photography's past, which had been largely commercial. What has proven surprising is that, despite its early emulation of classical models, colour photography's new edifice has proved to be very badly built. In less than a decade it has declined into a neo-romantic, mannerist pile, a kind of false-fronted pictorialism. The colours are of the late afternoon, the locations are nostalgic or exotic, and all too often that which is brutal has been beautified. Despite some exceptional pictures, the general impression is one of a house that has been decorated before the frame has gone up. Everything Morris had condemned when he examined the work of painters and sculptors in the sixties was now being produced by photographers in the eighties.

If conventional photographers didn't apprehend what was happening, the rest of the visual arts community certainly did. In their hands photography became not a prime medium of expression but a material to exploit in hybridized work. To the dismay of photographers this work has been celebrated in the critical press and has triumphed in the marketplace. Moreover, its practitioners developed a series of deceptively simple strategies to address or obviate the issues that had dogged fine-art photography for years. By bonding text to the images, they brought to heel the frustrating ambiguity of photographic images and sharpened their meaning. Photography's slavish and, to many, tedious obeisance to the medium's traditions and masters was exposed by artists who recycled classic images in composites or presented rephotographed masterworks neat. Applied colour, over-drawing, scratching and chemical manipulation restored the presence of the hand. Many of these artists kept the commercial labs busy making enormous prints that aped the scale of contemporary painting. At last photographs looked like art.

At the end of the seventies photographers had enjoyed a moment in the sun — surveys in the popular press, an unprecedented number of commercial-gallery openings, record auction prices and some serious critical attention. But it seemed that no sooner had Ansel Adams made the cover of *Time* than it was all over. Galleries closed, magazines folded and everybody went home. Photographers were left in their basements with Solander boxes full of prints and a lot of questions.

While it was exhilarating finally to have been discovered, the expectation was that the door that had just been opened would lead to a succession of ever bigger rooms. Instead, photographers discovered that they had become doormats for a new generation of artists who used photography rather than worked within it. Why did this happen?

Is photography inherently a modernist medium, a practice destined to go down with the great idealist and formalist vessel that has carried much of twentieth-century art almost to the millennium? While it may appear that there is a kind of modernist photography — the work and workers promoted by John Szarkowski, for example — it would seem that modernism in photography is in reality more a critical context to be overlaid on certain kinds of work than anything intrinsic to the medium itself. In fact it would seem that many qualities and aspects considered absolutely extrinsic to modernism — realism, description, subject matter, even narrative — are an inextricable part of all photographs. The photograph is such a modest, almost mute, object that it can only be meaningful with extensive participation and completion by the viewer. Every photographer who works long enough discovers that his or her images are never stable texts. And if this is not dismaying enough, they also discover that not only is the author dead in photography — for most viewers of photographs the author never existed.

One could make the argument that photography in its purest form is the ideal medium for post-modernist work. From this perspective it would appear that many of the strategies applied to photography by the stars of post-modernism are actually retrograde and counterproductive. The function of texts and manipulations is to drag the medium screaming into the past rather than to bed it down in the post-modernist present.

Yet pure photography is still slipping into oblivion for reasons that are not entirely clear. We are certainly not living in a culture that enjoys contemplating reality — or its representations. Television, our central visual communications medium, by and large serves up material that is pure fantasy. These fictions are briefly interrupted by the most gruesome slices of reality — news of war, disaster and deficits. Commercially successful movies and magazines are seldom reality-based. Nobody wants to choke on the facts. Moreover, the visual structure of most television images is so simple and unsophisticated that the cumulative effect on the viewer is to lower, rather than raise, their visual literacy. Carefully constructed photographs may ask too much of the viewer while simultaneously not seeming to give enough back. Additionally, in a new-technology-loving culture, the increasingly horse-and-buggy status of conventional photographic means adds little to the luster of its images.

Photography was conceived in the climate of the commercial needs of Daguerre and served commercial and practical needs long before it became a medium for the making of art. Most of the means developed in photography have been under commercial auspices: practical colour materials, lighting technologies and working methods. In a sense, the artists who work in the medium have always been Johnny-come-latelies who in time have realized that there were aesthetic possibilities in what were essentially commercial procedures. This may be quite evident retrospectively; but perceiving the next technology to offer such possibilities is considerably more difficult from the vantage point of the present. Looking at my own working life I see what may be some of the possibilities. Many of the images I obtain on travelling assignments are put on-system, digitized and then adjusted as the end-needs dictate. We alter colours, add shadows and highlights, change the weather and excise the irrelevant. The final fiction looks just like a photograph. In other cases the final image is merged from old stock — a day on location and several in the studio. The seams are invisible in a mural-sized print. It goes even further. I take half the image with a camera and build the rest on a screen because it doesn't yet exist. It's rendered in 16,000 lines, the same definition as my photograph. You can't tell. In Toronto I no longer have to go to the streets to scout the best vantage point — we've got the whole downtown, every building, every window and floor, stored on hard disk. Drinking coffee in a comfortable chair I hop from rooftop to rooftop, take elevators down a few floors, turn around, point up or down. I look out windows from buildings yet to be built. Some of the structures I see from the non-existent window don't exist yet either. In this kind of world, you might well ask, Where is the ground? I don't know. And I don't need it, because I'm too busy in a helicopter, a polaroid of a computer model shot from a screen taped to the windshield so the pilot and I can hover on a non-existent floor, facing a non-existent window looking out onto a non-existent view.

Soon we'll all have access to such technology. Maybe we'll even make art with it, although it's a difficult way to make a personal statement. Those who stay with it will need the temperament of a Glenn Gould; not just the gloves, summer and winter, but also the willingness to be a hermit in all senses. More than 20 years ago, when he abandoned the concert stage for the studio and a splicing block, Gould got to where we soon will be. He made many beautiful recordings. He almost made the *Goldbergs* into a piece of Canadian music. But what did we hear when we listened? Was it just the sound of one mind talking to itself? Did we matter? Is that why he had to hum and sing along — to let us, and maybe himself, know that he was still there? What kind of discourse do we have when production and consumption become totally private experiences? When the performer kicks out the audience? And why did it flounder with any repertoire but the highly formal, near mathematical work of Bach? Why have musicians returned to recording through performances, using only a single mike? What are my answers? If I go out tomorrow with an old Rollei and some film, what do I think I can do?

I could say that I think that the world is a more curious and complex place than is any idea that you or I might have about it. Others had said that, before I realized it was true — a good enough reason to keep one's hand out of the process. And what of the assertion that photography can't be a vehicle for conscious and articulate statements because it's so inextricably, so slavishly, bound to the givens out there in the world — that fundamentally we lack the controls to keep all sorts of detritus from creeping in? I would say that here we have a great virtue, because the content we recognize, that spurs us to take a picture, is always conditioned by our times, inflected by models within and outside the medium. In the long term it is the junk we didn't see at the time that will be a picture's salvation.

And is it too easy, too generous, its triumphs gratuitous? Those of us who have worked at it for a while find the opposite — it's niggardly. Show me a brilliant photograph by a dabbler and I'll either show you that it's trash — a copy of a copy — or that it was earned. There's a breathtakingly beautiful and heart-rending photograph I treasure, made by Peter Pitseolak (PLATE 13).[2] Its nominal content is the wreck of a small supply ship, the *Nascopie*, off Cape Dorset in the summer of 1947. The ship, its stern canted up toward the viewer, appears high in the frame where sky and water of the same value meet. There is a faint blush of light beside the ship. The rest of the photograph is water. It looks thick and viscous and gets gradually darker as it washes down the frame. The lower third of the image is entirely black. Although intellectually we know that this dark formless mass was probably just the shallows by the shore on which Pitseolak stood, emotionally we experience it as the ship's last destination — the lightless bottom of a cold dark sea.

Peter Pitseolak was an Inuk amateur photographer, of which there are many in the Arctic. He took photographs throughout his life; and while his subject matter for us was exotic, the photographs are not. They are basically just family snapshots. His one transcendent image was made when he was in his forties — his prime. The *Nascopie* was a ship that he normally piloted into Cape Dorset when it made its annual visit. The year it sank it had a new captain who rejected his services. Pitseolak was left high and dry to watch a disaster from the shore — a disaster that cut off his people's traditional lifeline and signaled, he was intelligent enough to realize, the end of the ways they knew. His response, the photograph, is his summa of the event, both fact and emotion. The Indo-American art historian Coomaraswamy once remarked that "the secret of art is found in the self-forgetfulness of the artist — the true artist says, 'It did it.'"[3] After years of rehearsal, Pitseolak for one brief moment became not a snapshooter but a true artist with a camera.

Still photography is the perfect medium for "It-did-its" — for images that seem to make themselves. The early years of photography gave us many of them. They are often photographs of very little — Niepce's backyard, Talbot's sun pictures or Hime's empty Canadian prairie. There was not yet a canon of suitable subjects nor a self-consciousness about making them. The nominal content of these pictures is so unassuming and so minimal that we almost have to accept that simple sight and light are their real subjects. Despite their modest pretensions they continue to insist upon our minds. They have a quality of pure presence — not the presence of the plate or paper print, nor the presence of an art object, but the presence of something seen, of consciousness. They remind us of what it is like to be and to have eyes.

Recently I got a call from those girls that I used to follow on the street. Twenty-five years had passed since we all walked out of high school, and they wanted to get together. I agreed, but when the time came to get into the car to go see them I couldn't do it. One of my old friends did go and said that they, he and a dozen women, had had a wonderful time. But I have no regrets. I couldn't bear to see what a quarter century had done to us — the collapsed relationships, the small progress, the pull of gravity and the deaths among us. It was not that I wasn't interested in the facts. I was just not concerned with the current ones. It was the old ones that I was interested in. What had made them so desirable? I much preferred our graduating photographs.

And my mother, still absorbed in her painting, at this moment likely making her ten thousandth watercolour that will eventually fade and crumble like my photographs? Which one of us is confused, or right or wrong? We live 3,000 miles apart and seldom talk. Our silent dialogue comes from a mutual devotion to appearances. She still fixes things up, and I am still trying to accept things as they are. I don't find it easy. I go through months when I do no camera work for myself. In those times I turn to the typewriter and the delicious experience of a blank piece of paper, the freedom to do whatever I want and not be a slave to the visible world. However, it's a comfort that soon tires me, and I'm out once again lugging my hardware around the world.

There it all is, swimming on the ground glass, all the better for being upside down and backwards because it reinforces the strangeness of all that "isness" and "thereness." Slowly the insistent chatter inside one's head stops. Then the world slows, floats and stills. Nothing is left but the brilliance of phenomena. Then I want to show the unborn what it once looked like. I want them to see what we once saw and what we thought was significant. I want them also to see all our mistakes and omissions — our failure to see what was in store for them. At those times it seems like a calling both noble and humble.

I'm then content to see myself as a kind of shoemaker — someone who makes something we all need but don't think about much — something that quietly helps us get from here to there.

Vico, the first modern historian, observed over 250 years ago that we know only what we make — *verum factum*.[4] What would he have made of photography, that medium that gives us the illusion that we have made whatever we have photographed? Does the act of recording lead to knowledge, or is it just acknowledgment? It would seem that when we make a photograph that hasn't been made before, we have converted phenomena into fact. It has been recognized and inventoried; but its meaning is like oil upon water — shifting, iridescent and beautiful but ultimately immiscible with its carrier, a slick that doesn't belong. A painting, a novel, a piece of music, is always wholly a product of its time. Each is always the synthetic product of a culture no matter how brilliant or seemingly advanced the mind of its maker. While photographs always will reflect the formal and stylistic ideas, the technology and concerns, of their times, they also always will reflect the world outside of culture. For all its limitations, its firm grounding in Western culture and science, photography (compared with drawing, painting or sculpture) is still our least inflected tool for describing that which is outside the self. Photographs made out there, in the world, will always record more than their maker recognizes, hence their quality of acquiring, rather than shedding, an aura with the passage of time.

We live in a culture, and increasingly in a world, that is concerned with control. A reality-based medium like photography inherently denies us a total hegemony over content and form. This is the real genius of the medium and why it will never have the security of the other arts, nor their obsolescence. The invention of photography was a cataclysmic event because, for the first time in human history, we took on something that carried us outside ourselves and beyond culture. One hundred fifty years after that event we find ourselves in a world that is overpopulated and poisoned with garbage. Faced with similar problems in the past, Europeans responded by colonizing other continents. Now that the planet is seemingly full, we eventually may seek space on other planets. The shock experienced by the European mind upon contact with the Orient, the black world of Africa and the native cultures of the New World will seem very small when we confront the utterly alien.

Irrespective of race and culture we, as a species, have always expressed ourselves anthropometrically and modelled the universe from the base of ourselves. We don't really "see," we just experience ourselves and our culture. While the traditional arts are wholly the product of this limitation, photography is not. Photographs have always shown us the unnoticed and, in some applications, the unseeable. We accept photographic information because, no matter how strange the result, the medium is familiar. It is our creation, and we are learning to live with the strange messages it brings. A world that can embrace and understand the implications of photography, its derivatives and the sights that they bring is a world that is rehearsing the eventual evacuation of this planet.

[65]

1. Quoted in Harold Rosenberg, *The Re-definition of Art* (New York: Collier Books, 1973), p. 11.
2. The photograph has also been reproduced in Peter Pitseolak and Dorothy Eber, *People from Our Side* (Edmonton: Hurtig Publishers, 1975), p. 134.
3. Quoted in Dorothy Norman, *Encounters: A Memoir* (San Diego: Harcourt Brace Jovanovich, 1987), p. 82.
4. Giambattista Vico, *The New Science of Giambattista Vico* (Ithaca, N.Y.: Cornell University Press, 1984).

In Camera

THE PHOTOGRAPHY OF DONIGAN CUMMING

GEORGES BOGARDI

Reality and Motive in Documentary Photography, the title chosen by Donigan Cumming for his monumental, three-part cycle, recalls the dualities in Jane Austen's titles (*Pride and Prejudice*; *Sense and Sensibility*), as well as the distinctions drawn by Balzac between the "zoological species" and "social species" which populate the *Comédie humaine*. Closer to us in time and more explicitly relevant to the nature/culture or nature/nurture dichotomy that obsesses the modern spirit — including the spirit of Cumming's work, which might as well have been named "The Lived and the Posed" — is the title of Roland Barthes's collection of essays, *L'obvie et l'obtus*, in which Barthes's post-structuralist, semiotic analysis is applied to works of visual art, to works he called "l'écriture du visible."

The *obvious* and the *obtuse* are categories invented by the later Barthes in an attempt to transcend traditional, structuralist readings (including his own) of the visible text — and perhaps, in the end, to transcend semiology itself. To the transparent foundation of *information*, the communication of the readily perceived, are added two more constructions: that of a network of symbols (*significations*) which constitute a common currency of exchange among literate members of a given culture; and an extra meaning (*significance*) in a work of art which resists easy codification but is, nevertheless, its most gripping feature of all. This "extra" meaning is the one that compels us to return to the work, the one that somehow makes us know it matters. It makes the work of art an obscure and irresistible object of desire, transforming the knowing reader into a hapless detective endlessly ruminating over motifs and motives.

One more dichotomy appears to constitute the core of Cumming's project which, by now, includes not just the body of photographs and their title, but also the critical polemics that have

surrounded *Reality and Motive* since its first (partial) showing in
1983.[1] Cumming's work is, at heart, an illustration of the troubling
dichroism of the photographic medium itself: it exhibits properties of
documentary fact when viewed from one angle, those of narrative
fiction when seen from another. Neither angle is adequate for
bringing the content into sharp focus; from picture to picture, we are
forced to shift ground and negotiate the uneasy terrain between
photography and art.

Such manoeuvring ought not to be so difficult, not today.
"The distinction between art and photography, historically fraught
with anxieties, has ceased to be one of definition," Nancy Foote
wrote in *Artforum* in 1976.

"Nevertheless," she noted, "it continues to bug us. Though the post-modernist
revolution has (as in many other disciplines) eradicated traditional boundaries and
brought about a tremendous increase in 'esthetic mobility,' photography's status in
the art world remains problematic. For every photographer who clamors to make it
as an artist, there is an artist running a grave risk of turning into a photographer."[2]

Foote's essay pertained to a time before everything old had
become "Neo-" again. It was about the conceptual art of the seventies
which then appeared to represent the ultimate rejection of traditional,
formalist studio practices: painting, sculpture — and photography.
Lived experience — palpable, extended and durational — replaced
the unique form and, with it, that unique (and uniquely modernist)
instant in which a still, immutable construction offered the gaze the
promise of an immutable fact, an immanent Truth.

In his introduction to *Structures for Behaviour*,[3] a seminal
exhibition of post-modern sculpture held at the Art Gallery of
Ontario in 1978, Roald Nasgaard spelled out the new rules inherent
in the perception of durational, hybridized art, rules that clearly
apply as well to grasping the extreme "esthetic mobility" of
Cumming's project. The new sculpture's horizontality and
architectural structuring look back to modernism, Nasgaard observes;
in the same way, most of Cumming's individual images refer overtly
to the subject matter and compositional strategies of famous
documentary photographs of the past.[4] The aura of violent
commitment that emanates from *Reality and Motive* — and especially
from the critics' analyses of it — is in large part due to this

entanglement with the past: it is the jaundiced gratitude of the hopelessly indebted.

Post-modern art's links with the past are undeniable but, notes Nasgaard:

> …to an increasing degree the art, as such, of these works is not very readily found in the objects or structures by themselves…These constructions may or may not be of special visual interest but it quickly becomes apparent that what the eye alone can see is not sufficient to reveal what the sculptures are about. In an unprecedented way the works seem to demand to be physically traversed, to be walked round, through or over. The eye by itself is insufficient to understand what they are because it cannot always encompass them and the spectator is made aware of broader requirements of behaviour in order to raise the works from their inertness.[5]

If we substitute "photographs" for "sculptures," then Nasgaard's description is an uncanny anticipation of the problems presented by *Reality and Motive*. What the eye can see in any single picture of Cumming's is already a polymorphous amalgam of information and strategy. There is copious description of the models and their surroundings; explicit (and frankly didactic) demonstrations of how the photographer's directorial role is an intrusion into the models' lives; and the unfolding of some kind of dramatic action whose central conflict is the "extra" meaning of the work. In this dramatic action we observe the model becoming a *character* through a reenactment of two parallel scripts: one composed by a photographer in full possession of all the hackneyed conventions of the documentary genre, the other inspired by a private impulse of wish fulfilment but still dependent on the artist's collaboration because it's clearly the camera's presence that releases the "player" in the model.

Installed in a fixed sequence,[6] the 70 photographs of the first part of *Reality and Motive in Documentary Photography* (R.M. I) are double-hung in the gallery, so that the horizontal development of character transformations is qualified and annotated by a vertical reading (PLATES 14, 15); R.M. II comprises 45 pictures hung in a single row (PLATE 16); R.M. III is an installation of six mural-sized photographs, each accompanied by a sound track (PLATE 17). This auditory dimension means that R.M. III must be displayed in a space of its own, which effectively cuts off any single vision we might hope to have of the work as a whole. The added medium of sound also signals what the previous parts only hint at: that Cumming's project is something other than the purely photographic meditation the title promises. Martha Langford has likened it to Artaud's existentialist theatre;[7] Robert Graham, while locating it within the documentary tradition, notes nevertheless that "Cumming's work appeals to encounters outside of documentary's usual channels."[8]

It could be that those "broader requirements of behaviour" Nasgaard demands of the postmodern viewer include the admission that work like Cumming's presents us with a multisensory, polysemic experience that simply cannot be fitted into convenient categories, and that no single interpretation, no matter how rigorously reasoned, can ever be entirely apt. This is the very nature of the new art advocated by Barthes in *The Death of the Author*, where he dismisses the neatly turned plots of traditional *écrivance* (an art in which the author is in charge of all production of meaning, reducing the reader's role to that of a passive consumer of received ideas) and proposes, instead, a new *écriture* which, "…by refusing to assign a 'secret,' an ultimate meaning, to the text (and to the world as text), liberates what may be called an antitheological activity, an activity that is truly revolutionary, since to refuse to fix meaning is, in the end, to refuse God and His hypostases — reason, science, law."[9]

It is quite possible that this notion, or at least the sentiment behind the idea, and the metaphor that shapes both, were first awakened in Barthes by the Paris showing of *The Family of Man*, the exhibition of documentary photographs organized by the Museum of Modern Art in 1955. The leaflet introducing the show to the French public intoned: "This look over the human condition must somewhat resemble the benevolent gaze of God on our absurd and sublime ant-hill"; and this inspired one of the most bracingly iconoclastic of Barthes's "mythologies."[10]

Barthes and Cumming share the same enmity: they despise the blind idealism inherent to the documentary tradition, the blinkered smugness which presumes to "sum up" some aspect of the human condition and having done that, with a single click, implicitly assures the viewer that something has now been accomplished, simply by attention having been paid. This is the shameless complicity on which the "humanistic" spirit of documentary is based: the photographer and the viewer align themselves with whatever ideological power rules by holding out "hope."

Barthes unmasks this complacent, "we are all one family" code, and Cumming destroys it by refusing to settle for the comforting closure of the single, decisive image. Duration created by sequence, and narrative equivocations within the sequence, undermine any fixed notions of what his characters live or "what they are" — robbing the viewer of the essential optimism that is the poisoned apple proffered by the documentary ideology: the intimation that culture is a scheme in which everyone has a secure place. And if that place is an uncomfortable one, never fear: "Concerned photography" is already at work, right there, being God's right hand, quickly repairing the damage some careless swipe of His left hand has caused. No man is an island after all, the "concerned" reason; and just by looking at the Other, we are looking out for each other. The notion of an artist "running the grave risk of turning into a photographer" takes on special meaning in this context: it is the risk of Pygmalion turning into Pollyanna.

■

Like a hard-boiled detective who has trained himself to look at the facts and expect only the worst, Barthes's semiology can at times appear to be based on some principle of creative paranoia. The "indisputable image" that is the photograph when discussed as "myth" is the empty container of the *signified* that is enveloped by a *concept*, which is itself a subterfuge: "the motivation which causes the myth to be uttered."[11]

For all his attachment to the amorous discourse of art, Barthes seems to treat the photographic icon not as an equal but as if he were a lover for whom the text is an all-powerful, mysterious Other whose every utterance must be decoded. The clarity of face value, of indisputable presence, is not to be taken for assurance of fidelity: realism, Barthes seems to argue, is a code like any other — and perhaps the most dangerously treacherous of all.

The same iconoclastic misery hovers over *Reality and Motive in Documentary Photography*: it engenders the work's title (which, in turn, arouses in the viewer a vaguely corresponding mood of skepticism) and inspires the double-rowed syntax of R.M. I. But for all their congruencies, there is a crucial difference between Cumming and Barthes. Barthes's methodology permeates his *style* as well, and style, Barthes reminds us in *What is Writing?*, is more than a mere device. It is the unconscious manifestation of a temperament: biological or biographical in origin, "style is…the transmutation of a Humour."[12]

[70]

Cumming's skepticism, in contrast, is restricted to functioning as a strategic device and is never allowed to permeate the work itself. The victory of *Reality and Motive* is that Cumming's troubled relationship with the photographic medium, a personal dilemma that might easily have become "style," is transformed into a driving force for a fully realized work of fiction. Doubt transcends being mere method, and the photographs are allowed to transcend the function of merely illustrating attitude and method. Cumming's doubt is a dangerous undertow, but it is also a source of immense energy, animating the characters as well as the photographer. It releases the artist in the photographer and allows what might have remained a mere critique of the documentary ideology to bloom into a full-blooded, creative work of fiction.

■

Once liberated from photography's treacherous code of realism and allowed to move to analysis of narrative fiction, Barthes, too, seems released. His codes multiply, and his previously reductive semiology blooms into an almost alarming luxuriance. In *S/Z*, his book-length investigation of Balzac's *Sarrasine*, he identifies five "signifying systems" or codes that construct the text, each code a multiplicity of systems in itself and constantly interacting with the others. [13]

Barthes works his way along the text a few phrases or actions at a time, each step bringing him closer to the revelation of a code; and this is how we, too, may attempt to read *Reality and Motive in Documentary Photography* — except in reverse, by simply trying to locate the seminal elements that motivate Cumming's work. [14]

Brazenly simplified (and possibly mangled by having been wrested from Barthes's thicket of prose), his five codes are as follows:

1. THE PROAIRETIC *or* CODE OF ACTIONS. "The main armature of the readerly text," this propels the narrative. It is not a set of major movements meant to develop a plot but any and every gesture, as trivial as opening a door.

2. THE HERMENEUTIC CODE *or* CODE OF PUZZLES. Barthes names ten consecutive strategies designed to keep the reader's attention by delaying the revelation of the "truth" the reader seeks. This is a series of riddles.

[7 1]

3. THE CULTURAL CODES. There are many of these, all referring to contexts (and texts) already familiar to the reader. They assure contact and, at their basest, *realistic* level, do not create meaning but reaffirm conventional wisdom.

4. THE CONNOTATIVE CODES. A series of suggestions that encourage the reader to cluster connotations into a "theme." These are the messages most expressly addressed to the receiver. They do *not* exclude obvious denotation.

5. THE SYMBOLIC CODE. Rhetorical devices, based mainly on the conflict of binary oppositions (of situations, actions, images or codes themselves), that elevate a mundane event into the realm of the mythologically essential. Though Barthes does not say this, he leaves the impression that this is the privileged code of art.

Following the Barthesian clues, we can locate some elements of each code as found in *Reality and Motive in Documentary Photography*:

1. CODE OF ACTIONS

Four major narrative lines converge in Cumming's work. The tripartite sectioning of the project records movements: from overcrowded rooms of the inner city in R.M. I, to the more spacious suburban settings of R.M. II, to, finally, the chapel-like construction of R.M. III, which can only be installed in a pristine, high-ceilinged art gallery.

The characters who inhabit these spaces (several of them appear in more than one part of the work) also move. In a psychic evolution that follows the changes of location, they move from quotidian domesticity to symbol-laden self-dramatization to quasi-religous ecstasy: from acceptance to escape to transcendence. Intersecting with the symbolic code, they also follow a gruesome trajectory that is the economics of faith in our society: they replace the desperate materialism of the functioning poor with the narcissistic self-involvement of the mobile middle class and finally leap over the edge — into the cult-worshipping self-abnegation of the underclass.

A second narrative focusses on the peripatetic photographer. His actions are always visible: Cumming visits people's homes, has them pose, arranges their possessions (or the props he brings with him) in a way that will direct our reading along this d/evolutionary plot. The frames of R.M. I's photos fairly burst with the possessions of their rooming-house tenants, while R.M. II's compositions are much less crowded. Rather than a teeming space, the surroundings in R.M. II are neutral backdrops, and objects seem less like accumulated possessions, hoarded and jealously preserved, than disposable stage properties: props chosen only because they are useful to the construction of a phantasy image of the self.

A third action, minor compared to the others, narrates the lives of those characters who appear several times in sequence; that of two elderly men, for instance, whom we first see in their shabby-genteel home (their dressing gowns make it clear that they share this room). In a later picture we see one of these men again in an antiseptic hospital room, now alone. This thematizes the connotative code of decline and loss.

But Cumming's most overt code of action is *posing*. His models are hyperactively involved with the camera. Unlike the traditionally passive or unaware subjects of traditional documentary, they are full participants in the creative project. They play out multiple lives rather than living one, and the camera reanimates them with every shot. Each posed gesture serves to point an accusing finger at the cultural codes of documentary reduction to Truth, at the gaping chasms underneath the fragile link between cause and effect.

The link seems solid in traditional documentary because the "still" lends it an aura of immutability, the finality of closure. Duration, as Cumming uses it, allows us to observe the self in mutation, or at least in its contingent states of temporary compromise between the wished and the endured.

2. CODE OF PUZZLES

This is the central code of post-modernism and the most powerful arsenal in Cumming's attack on the documentary. The paradigmatic strategy of equivocation — the title's dichotomy, the double-rowed hanging, the contrapuntist's use of sound and image in R.M. III — is used to frustrate the viewer's desire for closure. All the codes converge in this one, the dominating element of Cumming's discourse.

"Photographs furnish evidence," Susan Sontag writes. "Something we hear about, but doubt, seems proven when we're shown a photograph of it."[15]

When Cumming photographs a frail old woman sitting on her bed, our immediate impulse to thematize quickly files her under L/S/D — lonely, sick, dispossessed. But in later shots we see her in other guises, appearing variously as a vamping bathing beauty, as a pensive-regal figure standing by her fridge (which is full), and as a porno queen.

What "evidence" has been furnished? Only that the reductive code of realism cannot account for the multiple personalities that hide within each of us; and that decline, while inevitable, does not inevitably follow a straight path clearly signposted with thematic directions.

The hermeneutic code dominates *Reality and Motive in Documentary Photography* because, for all our passionate interest in the characters, we can only thematize the multiple clues they project, we can never know "who they are," even as fictional entities. The models are neither free agents (subjects unaware of the camera) nor paid impersonators (they *collaborate* with the photographer and therefore are beyond the total control of the artist's imagination). And they are beyond our own. Faced with these spectres looming behind the inviolably smooth surface of the photograph, our relationship to them comes to resemble the self-projection in Proust's terrifying definition of love:

It irradiates toward the beloved, in whom it encounters a hard surface whence it rebounds to its point of departure. It is the ricochet of our own affection that we call the other person's love for us. [16]

So powerful is Cumming's use of mystification that at least one viewer seems to have been persuaded, photographic evidence notwithstanding, that the models don't exist at all. Commenting on the picture of the two men in dressing gowns, here is how Clara Gutsche describes the models: "Organically bound to their natural habitat are two unsavoury male specimens, one receding and shriveled, the other aggressive and bloated." [17]

One might reasonably describe in this way the figures painted by Bacon or invented by Sade, but surely not people who, the photos make clear, are our contemporaries living in Montreal. That a viewer — especially one who is a partisan of the "concerned" school — can be trapped into this level of insensitivity is some kind of tribute to

Cumming's mastery of the codes of puzzles: his viewer cannot possibly believe that the models exist as other than characters, that they might possibly read the magazine in which their description appears. Having been photographed, they may be called specimens: they cannot be alive because they can't be hurt.

3. CULTURAL CODES

R.M. I is a virtual compendium of the already known: each picture is a reference or quote, if not an outright parodic homage to some of the best-loved images of the documentary genre. The various conventions of the snapshot are also well represented: the portrait, the couple, the family, the group of friends gathered around a table.

Two codes are conspicuous through absence: Cumming does not use close-up head shots, and he rarely ventures outdoors, thus dispensing with two of the privileged clichés of documentary: the celebration of Power, in the manner of Karsh, and the veneration of Nature, in the tradition of Adams. (Clearly, neither of these myths fits into the scheme of "concerned" photography which, as a rule, mistrusts the sublime.)

When Cumming stages scenes outdoors, placing models in a garden or at a lake's shore, nature seems as still and artificial as a painted backdrop. The models keep perfectly still, and nature itself seems to be posing for the camera: no wave dares to splash in these photographs.

Landscape is mostly glimpsed indoors, not even through windows but in the paintings and photo-murals of the models' rooms. (Sometimes we also see one of Cumming's own photographs on the wall: this is a negation of the cultural code of the unique event but a powerful code of action of repeated visits by the photographer.)

These interiors are also filled with trinkets of pop culture — Elvis Presley memorabilia dominate — and with newspapers and documents expressly presented to the camera. All these signs situate the viewer in a specific time and place.

4. CONNOTATIVE CODES

Cumming does not rely heavily on connotative codes. While the whole of *Reality and Motive in Documentary Photography* certainly provokes thematization (in our discussion of the previous codes we have done hardly more than reposit suggestions of decline, social status, transcendence, etc.), it is only in R.M. II's repeated display of Freudian symbols that we might begin to recognize a "common nucleus" of connotations.

These codes, however, are not reiterated from picture to picture. While each individual photograph can be read as a metaphor, the sequence does not develop into allegory, no single connotation is strong enough to engender a system of reading.

Many critics have remarked on the affinities between Cumming's photographs and those of Diane Arbus, and it is not impossible to read R.M. II as an extended meditation on the art of Arbus. They share similar themes of antithesis: incongruous couples, the bravado of the defeated, the defiant narcissism of the outcast.

There is an important difference, however. In Cumming the connotative code is semiologically dormant. It laconically points out certain patterns of behaviour without pointing toward a possible scheme of relationships that might be responsible for generating these patterns. (This absence is less noticeable in R.M. I, where the double-rowed structuring and the frequent reappearance of familiar characters seem to constitute a series of plots.)

In Arbus, on the other hand, the connotative code is stridently active: the photographs' captions denote for the viewer social and psychological schemes operating within her images.

In the photograph *A Jewish Giant at Home with His Parents in the Bronx, N.Y. 1970*,[18] Arbus portrays one specific caprice of nature and then extends this situation into a more universal metaphor through the explicitness of pointing out the components: Jewish — giant — home — parents — New York. The tiny couple is all parents who have ever stared disbelievingly at their child, trying to fathom what beloved monster to which they have given life; the giant is every child whose growth of self-esteem results, inevitably, in a concurrent shrinking of the parental figure, the increasingly suffocating love within the parental home. This Freudian reading is suggested by the image and expressly *dictated* by the caption which sharpens the focus of universality into a specific world's view: the Freudian complexes of Alex Portnoy. The connotative code is strong in Arbus because it works in tandem with a cultural code.

Cumming's connotative code, in contrast, is subsumed by his privileged code of puzzles. A Freudian reading is possible, in some images it is even suggested, but it is never dictated. In his own gripping photo of a family[19] the triad is inverted: two healthy young people kneel by the bed of an old woman so frail that she is fading away before our eyes. Freud's temporal Darwinism of family life *might* be a reading here, but not the inevitable one.

Compared to the low, confining ceiling in Arbus, which locks the trio into a dark box, Cumming's ceiling is barely present, permitting our gaze to move upward, beyond the frame. Neither is Cumming's trio locked into a circle of stares: the couple face the camera, the old woman turns her back on it; she is elsewhere, on her own.

Cumming's family is framed, instead, by two pictures of Christ aligned with the vertical edges of the photograph. The two pictures frame the composition, *implying* that the family unit is bracketed by Faith. But this implied reading is put into doubt as soon as we notice that in the picture on the left Christ is blindfolded, his eyes covered by a streak of light which is a reflection produced by the camera's flash. Faith is undone by artifice, connotation of documentary evidence dissolves into puzzle, meaning is dis-solved by the hermeneutic code.

5. THE SYMBOLIC CODE

Throughout this contemplation of *Reality and Motive in Documentary Photography*, I have tried "naming" the work by locating the astounding number of dichotomies it features and implies. If the privileged code of narrative fiction is the differentiation of binary conflicts, then we must conclude that Cumming's work is photographic fiction of a kind unprecedented in the history of the medium. R.M. I is a manifesto on the dual roles of art and photography; R.M. II is a novel about being and becoming; and R.M. III — which resists semiology because, once it has been dismantled and its sound track silenced, it simply no longer exists as text (it cannot be mechanically reproduced) — is a passion play in which all the conflicts are reenacted.

Elvis sings:

You saw me crying in the chapel
The tears I cried were tears of joy...

Barthes says, "No sooner is a form seen than it must resemble something: humanity seems doomed to Analogy, i.e., in the long run, to Nature."[20]

By exposing the duplicity of photographic evidence — the tears we see in his pictures could be tears of joy or sorrow, or they could be make-up — Cumming releases us from doom: his refusal to fix pat analogies inverts into the liberating tap of Art's wand.

1. See Martha Langford's essay "Donigan Cumming: Crossing Photography's Chalk Lines" for an analysis of the critical reaction to Cumming's work. In Martha Langford, *Reality and Motive in Documentary Photography* (Ottawa: Canadian Museum of Contemporary Photography, 1986), pp. 14-35.

2. Nancy Foote, "The Anti-Photographers," *Artforum* (September 1976), p. 46.

3. Roald Nasgaard, *Structures for Behaviour* (Toronto: Art Gallery of Ontario, 1978). The exhibition comprised sculptures by Robert Morris, David Rabinowitch, Richard Serra and George Trakas.

4. Langford, pp. 20-23, traces the source of these "quotations."

5. Nasgaard, p. 9.

6. See Langford, p. 25, for the physical specifications of how the three parts of the work are installed in exhibition.

7. Langford, pp. 31-32.

8. Robert Graham, "Donigan Cumming: Undoing Documentary," *Parachute* (March, April, May 1984), p. 24.

9. Roland Barthes, *Image, Music, Text*, trans. Stephen Heath (New York: Hill and Wang, 1977), p. 147.

10. Roland Barthes, *Mythologies*, trans. Annette Lavers (New York: Hill and Wang, 1972), pp. 100-102.

11. Ibid., p. 118.

12. In Roland Barthes, *Writing Degree Zero and Elements of Semiology*, trans. Annette Lavers and Colin Smith (Boston: Beacon Press, 1970), p. 11.

13. Roland Barthes, *S/Z*, trans. Richard Miller (New York: Hill and Wang, 1974).

14. A similar application of Barthes's method is used to analyse a story by James Joyce in Robert Scholes, *Semiotics and Interpretation* (New Haven and London: Yale University Press, 1982), pp. 87-104.

15. Susan Sontag, *On Photography* (New York: Farrar, Straus and Giroux, 1973), p. 5.

16. See Marcel Proust, *À la recherche du temps perdu* (Paris: Gallimard, Bibliothèque de la Pléiade, 1954), Vol. I, p. 609. Translation used here was taken from *Marcel Proust, Aphorisms and Epigrams from Remembrance of Things Past*, ed. and trans. Justin O'Brien (New York: Columbia University Press, McGraw-Hill Book Company, 1964), p. 143.

17. Clara Gutsche, "Open Parody, Hidden Agenda: Donigan Cumming," *Vanguard* 13,4 (May 1984): 23.

18. Diane Arbus, *Diane Arbus: An Aperture Monograph* (Millerton, N.Y.: Aperture, 1972), unpaginated.

19. Reproduced in the catalogue *Reality and Motive in Documentary Photography*, p. 56.

20. Roland Barthes, *Roland Barthes*, trans. Richard Howard (New York: Farrar, Straus and Giroux, The Noonday Press, 1977), p. 44.

The Manipulated Photograph

DENIS LESSARD

No suggested reading is offered; just follow your instincts.

CHANTAL BOULANGER

Linear continuity, where one thing follows another in logical sequence, is no longer an appropriate model for describing our relationship to the world and to culture. Today the only adequate way of expressing this relationship is through the arrangement and combination of elements in space. When collage and related spatial techniques were introduced in the early twentieth century, artists rebelled from established concepts of painting and sculpture, renouncing the route of predictability and easy explanations. The medium of photography, because of its technical possibilities, soon became party to the process of questioning through its use of retouching and photomontage. But the achievement of effects unknown to traditional photography depended on redefinition of accepted notions of framing and focus.[1] At the origins of these photographic manipulations, then, lay both aesthetic and political motivations — reasons of the head and of the heart.

Because the photographer must frame, shoot, develop and enlarge the image, what the photographer did became almost as important as what was produced. From there it was an easy step to other forms of intervention, particularly of a creative type. The "constructed" nature of photography, its combination of mechanical and manual elements, also pushed imperceptibly in this direction.

DEGREES OF ALTERATION

Merely superimposing several images on a single negative, whether accidentally or intentionally, is enough to add an element of heterogeneity that alters the photographic image even before the final print is made. This can be seen in the work of Cheryl Sourkes, for example. She begins by collecting environmental images which she then combines with cultural images that she has photographed in libraries. A discreet but determined detective, she ferrets through the various departments of human knowledge — "history, cosmology, physics, religion, psychology, mythology"[2] — and reorganizes the fragments or "splinters" she finds there to recreate life's complex and variegated quilt in a way that could never be achieved with a seamless surface. But Sourkes leaves a few clues to help the viewer decipher and organize these picture puzzles.[3] This dynamic approach has something in common with mythology, which the artist has described as a "passage from disorder to order."[4] But her use of referential materials serves essentially to suggest directions. Sourkes explains, "I think that anyone who takes the trouble to look at the work without being intimidated by not knowing the sources of all references will be able to find something in there for themselves."[5] This is similar to the advice offered by Ezra Pound, whose poetic work also consists of fragments culled from the immense storehouse of international culture:

Skip anything you don't understand and go on till you pick it up again. All tosh about *foreign languages* making it difficult. The quotes are all either explained at once by repeat or they are definitely of the things indicated. If the reader don't know what an elefant is, then the word is obscure.[6]

There is a kind of centrifugal effect that pushes the reader or viewer to go beyond the words or the photographs to ponder the source of the materials and their intrinsic value. This process is already embodied in the approach Cheryl Sourkes takes to her work: "...sometimes if I see something, it will remind me of another image that I have and I'll take it to accompany the other image. I wasn't looking for it in advance but images tend to evoke other images...".[7] Materials that are dormant — I like this word, because it conveys the idea that they are fated to come together at some future point in time — are also part of the creative repertoire of Raymonde April and Lucie Lefebvre.

Technically, Cheryl Sourkes's photographic collages are produced by juxtaposing negatives and "positives" (negatives transferred to positive transparencies or "Kodaliths") on a light table. The arrangement of elements on the light table is a crucial first step, and the final work bears its traces in many ways: the finished print preserves the latent potential of the disordered and provisional assemblage, and each completed photograph is imbued with a luminosity that seems to emanate from the images as if from a Cibachrome or a back-lit transparency. These collages are reminiscent of the photogram, which is made by placing objects directly on a photo-sensitive surface and exposing them to light. In her use of the technique, however, what Cheryl Sourkes exposes are not objects, but rather images that are already transparent (PLATE 41).

The luminosity she achieves owes some of its impact to the black surfaces that frame her often linear and delicate images, which she has recently begun to accentuate with colour tints. Accentuation of this type, part of the photographic process rather than an addition of lines or colours after printing, has also captured the interest of numerous other photographer-artists. The range of techniques currently being used to isolate and draw attention to particular details or elements includes découpage (Lucie Lefebvre), tearing (Marie-Jeanne Musiol) and highlighting (Lise Bégin).

What makes the black surfaces in Cheryl Sourkes's work so fascinating is that they seem to give material form to the gaps in our understanding of the world. In line with her reductive vision, the artist alters the photographic medium by scratching parts of the negative with a razor blade to achieve almost painterly effects. However, the intention here is quite different from that of Robert Rauschenberg who added colour to his photographic transfers to canvas and paper in the 1960s: what Rauschenberg was trying to do was to appose an abstract, expressionistic, pictorial shape with a repertory of images mined from various cultural strata. Cheryl Sourkes has a different purpose in mind:

I think that the roughness, the scratching, the abrasion of the surface is a mirroring of the rawness of feel that I wanted, that I looked for until I found a way to do it in the photographic process. The roughness was important to me. I found one of the things about photography that was alienating was the pristine surface and the illusion of an intact comfortable world, whereas the world seems to me full of discontinuities and abrasions, rough and unfinished edges...[8]

Angela Grauerholz, on the other hand, works within more restricted parameters. Her manipulation is limited to a slight shifting of the camera, a technique that she first employed for interior scenes and landscapes and has more recently used for portraits. The resulting softness is evocative of the "pictorialism" of some nineteenth and early twentieth century photographers, but in this case it is applied to everyday subjects stripped of their importance.[9] Her treatment goes beyond or restricts their specific reality, suggesting a presence that is also an absence, as though the artist were working on the fringes of photography, in a space that holds "the *maybe's*, the *what if's* and the *imagine's* within representation."[10]

RETOUCHING

Historically, retouching has been part of photography since its infancy, whether for the purpose of enhancing colour, correcting nature's imperfections, or compensating for technical shortcomings.[11] Application of colour highlights, phototransfers to canvas or paper, composite photography, retouching of negatives and photogravure are among the wide range of techniques that have been employed to alter the photograph through masking, découpage or painting.[12]

Originally, these procedures were supposed to leave no trace on the final print; but the methods used were less than perfect and blank spaces often occurred in the images. Photojournalists and photographer-artists alike soon realized that these in-between spaces could be used to advantage to construct fully convincing, coherent images of fictitious events and situations, or to dislocate the image in order to obtain a critical perspective distanced from reality.

Photomontage as practised by the Dadaists and later by the Russian Constructivists was an extension of these techniques in which aesthetic and political concerns came together.[13] While the Surrealists used photomontage and its potential for dislocation to create images that seemed to emerge from the unconscious, lettrism,[14] a movement founded by the Frenchman Isidore Isou in 1945, gave renewed emphasis to surface texture and treatment within the photomontage. First applied to painting, lettrist theory reduced writing in all its forms (imaginary or not) to little packages without regard to linguistic meaning and utilized them as a sculptural resource. Lettrism thus combined mechanical technique, a supporting medium, and artistic purpose. The lettrist approach also had an impact on photography, as can be seen in the work of several artists discussed here, including Lise Bégin and most notably Marie-Jeanne Musiol, for whom the photograph is a substance to be worked on. [15]

For the lettrists, writing was a "destructive force" [16] comparable to corrosion in the process of photography — photography itself being a combination of the mechanical and the artistic that breaks images into particles of light and exposes them onto a sensitized surface. It was in 1952 that Isidore Isou first made use of altered photographs, employing them as a base for his "metagraphic" [17] gouaches. Following his lead, a number of French photographers including Maurice Lemaître, Frédérique Devaux, François Poyet, Alain Satier and Roland Sabatier, began exploring the possibilities of lettrism. Isidore Isou, meanwhile, had by 1968 come to think of photography as a cutting edge or chisel.

> In the chiselling phase, when the element is taken under consideration, photography must give way to what it replaced and shed its apparent, immediate wholeness to splinter into the dots and dashes characteristic of painting. Fine art, cloaked in "cliché," reappears once the clichés break and shatter to pieces. [...] chiselling represents a visible *destruction* of the figurative object, because the system consists of a *series of pure chops and tears of a given, recognizable, figurative and still intact element of the image.* [18]

This photographic practice is characterized by the use of scratches, tears, lettering, drawing and painting worked directly on the image. Interestingly, the idea of chiselled photography first appeared in an experimental film directed by Isou entitled *Le Traité de Bave et d'Éternité* (1951), in the form of blanked-out faces. The technique was similar to that used in animation, where the artist works directly on the film.

It was also in 1968 that the Austrian artist Arnulf Rainer became interested in photography and began to take pictures of himself making faces in an automatic photo booth, altering the images only by signing them. *Face Farces* was made into a film in 1973. Rainer soon became aware of the communicative potential of these self-portraits. Wrapping nets and elastic bands around his face, he exaggerated the contortions, which he then emphasized by retouching the photographs with ink or oil paint:

In 1970, after experimenting with mescaline, I thought I could see spots of colour here and there on my photographs, faces with corrections. I followed these hallucinatory phenomena, typical of the drug, exactly as they appeared to me and imitated these psychic projection mechanisms in a normal state. Afterwards, I began to draw on my own photographs, feeling that I could not only reproduce myself more intensely, but also transform myself symbolically, and almost separate me from myself.[19]

Rainer's violent methods of accentuation could be considered an extreme example of a practice of retouching photography that dates back to the faint blush brushed onto the cheeks of our great grandparents in family-album portraits. Other examples can be seen in the series *Face Corrections…*, in which Rainer reworks photographs of expressionist art and self-portraits by Egon Schiele and Vincent Van Gogh, as well as studies of facial features by the Austrian sculptor Messerschmidt (1736-1783).[20]

The purpose of manipulation here seems to be to heighten the message of photographic images by *intensifying* them rather than destroying them. Once again, the titles are revealing: for instance, *Körpersprache* (Body Language), 1970-1975, and *Frauensprache* (Woman Language), 1975-1977. Rainer continued exploratory work in this vein until 1980, concentrating increasingly on the theme of death, as he "remade" the death masks of famous artists (*Totenmasken*, 1977-1978) and transformed a variety of death-related images (*Totengesichter*, 1979-1980).

In 1979, retouching took a new direction, when the American photographer Duane Michals began to paint over not only his own photographs but also images by Cartier-Bresson, Kertész and Ansel Adams, questioning the specific reality of the photograph. Overpainting in oils, covering almost the entire surface, is another way of exploring the limits to retouching and of probing the entire practice of photography and its historical achievements. Duane Michals uses overpainting not only to challenge the major periods and masterworks in the history of art, but also to capture a moment or state of otherness between the photograph and the painting of the same subject, one superimposed on the other. In *Richard Gere Awake and Richard Gere Asleep*, and in *Julia Bruck 1979 and as She Will Appear in 1987*, two works created in 1979, paint clings to the photograph like a bacterial culture, conveying the notion of sleep in the one case and ageing in the other. As in the work of Arnulf Rainer, a desire to *exorcise* or to complete the image is evident, a desire expressed in various efforts to alter the photograph.

As with Arnulf Rainer, the themes of identity and identification, of the need to communicate and the problems this involves are found in several series by Suzy Lake. Her alterations of the image, however, are less radical, especially in the 1979 series *Are you talking to me?* (PLATE 34)[21] The viewer is presented with a long sequence of large black-and-white self-portraits, each capturing an isolated gesture or a fragment of conversation that seems to go nowhere, like an insignificant moment or an awkward silence in a personal relationship. Expressiveness and a sense of uneasiness are achieved more discreetly than in Rainer's work: the negatives are stretched before printing, distorting the facial features like reflections in a house of mirrors, and then colour is lightly applied to parts of the face in an almost realistic way. In earlier sequences that date from 1974 — the famous exchange of faces with friends — Suzy Lake progressively deleted the features of her subjects, grafting them through photomontage onto her own face to create a subtly dislocated combination surrounded with an aura of disturbing strangeness.

In Lise Bégin's work, aesthetic motivations lie behind the blurred effect that she achieves through a deliberate erosion of the photographs by rephotographing and photocopying before working over them with drawing and painting. (PLATE 18)[22] The artist demonstrates a feverish intensity, an awareness of fragility and a responsiveness to pressure and emotion, as expressed in this 1983 text:

Quick, take photos of these photos.
Use these pictures by your procedures of the heart, of the spirit.
Precedent ... "For the Road." For the album. In colour...
Installed on the veranda behind the hills of sand,
I did paint all of that trembling in the breaths of wind,
Escaping this palette on the grass.
Everything leans to the left, to the blue side, to the heart side,
causing this image to pitch.
So badly framed.[23]

Poetry invades and shatters an image that can no longer be contained on a cold, hard surface. Alteration of the image becomes an imperative, as compelling as a brute force of nature. The point of departure, however, is often very close at hand, even familiar — as with Angela Grauerholz — but turned inside-out like a glove: "By suggesting a subjective inventory of every-day elements, she [Lise Bégin] diverts our consciousness into the realm of poetry." [24] Is this not an intention shared by Lucie Lefebvre and Cheryl Sourkes as well?

Ambiguity must be harnessed — although it can be unsettling — because it is a potent source of energy, especially when it crops up in unexpected places:

> The fortuitous, the contingent do not surface during the framing, nor in the selection of scenes to be photographed but rather when adopting certain signs that connote sentimentality and are meant to shape a composite non-unified mental world. [25]

> Her [Lise Bégin's] images often combine by montage the handmade gesture and the photographic gesture. It is the seam at the meeting of the two gestures which determines the status of the image. We would perhaps expect the division to fall typically, the photograph's referent placed in the real and the drawn gesture as representation. Bégin's procedures however often place the gesture "in front" of the image, intertwining the two, fusing them into a fundamentally ambiguous but single text. [26]

As Serge Murphy points out, Lise Bégin's work evokes "the absent presence of painting." [27] In each of her works or series, the marks she makes on the image convey a different meaning, perform a "new function" — from the claw marks around the portraits of friends in *La touche de la bête* (1979), to the coloured highlights on the drawing photographed in black and white in *Bacchus le chien* (1979) and her exaggeration of the ambivalence of the river images that form the basis of *La carte détériorée du tendre* (1983). Why add colour to black-and-white photographs when she could just as easily have taken a colour photo? But this is precisely the terrain where all the action takes place, with the artist's frightening and magnificent power to change the colour of things.

In *Bronze* (1982), a strip of photographs 250 feet long running the length of the stairways in an exhibition hall, Lise Bégin uses superimposition to break the medium's inherent linearity, mining the depths of memory and, like Cheryl Sourkes, creating an inventory of women's images: "Lise Bégin builds her work as journey through memory, layering level after level of life experience. Use of the overprinting procedure illustrates the ability of memory to perceive several realities at once."[28] Images appear like questions. Once again, there is more than one possible reading, and many things escape us as they escaped the artist, who leaves everything floating, vulnerable and unrestrained.

In artists' statements and in critical reviews, "fissure" and "crack" are words frequently used in connection with altered works. For example:

> Lise Bégin's work offers a glimpse at a crack where reality and its opposite mingle. Balance is always maintained, the artist stands in the shadow of the interplay, controlling the game so that it never ends, so that there is no winner (that is the sublime game where I can say everything and more).[29]

> My work comes out of the fissures or cracks in my psyche and it comes out of an exploration of those places. Those are my points of entry. That's where the energy is. Perhaps in some way, they're a process of healing and, in some way, they're a process of deepening those places.[30]

MULTILATION OF THE IMAGE

Lucie Lefebvre produces many photographic *mises en scène*, placing objects against backdrops made of cloth and crumpled paper and then juxtaposing them with slide projections, but perhaps the most intriguing aspect of her work is her practice of cutting out images and transforming them into photographic bas-reliefs (PLATE 19). The artist thus "works with the very matter of photography, moving beyond the closed frame imposed by the camera."[31]

Lise Bégin has adopted the same approach in several series, including *Un à un* (1982), where she started by photographing animals from the television screen, then blocked out the background, and set these images against photos of herself imitating the animals' posture. Suzy Lake also uses the découpage technique in *Confrontation with Shadow* (PLATE 20), where the cut-out photograph of the artist appears beside her shadow drawn in charcoal on the wall.[32]

Although the principle of photomontage enters into these works, the unifying surface dissolves to leave only the most resistant kernels of the image, the core elements needed to convey a multi-faceted meaning. Indeed, there is something here of the child's spontaneous approach to photography.

When they (children) too start taking photographs, the initial pleasure in traditional shots soon passes, and their irreverence surfaces, combined with a stubborn desire to express themselves. What happens then may astonish us, but in fact it is quite natural. The pigeon they wanted to photograph flew away and vanished; so they draw a pigeon. Here is a boy who looks like an Indian, but he has no feather; so they glue one on. [33]

Marie-Jeanne Musiol goes beyond découpage by actually tearing her photographs. But then the tear — a variant of the crack or fissure — could be classified as simply a more direct form of découpage. Yet there is nothing accidental about the way the artist proceeds (although a certain element of risk is always implicit in the act of tearing), for her purpose is to extract and isolate elements from the web of images and to give them emphasis. For the artist, tearing is an act of self-assertion and liberation, "an outward sign of inner change." [34] And while it does involve destruction, the act of tearing is ultimately a creative one. The resulting pieces are like scattered shards unearthed in archaeological digs and later patiently assembled to reconstruct history. Of course, we never find all the parts of the puzzle, but the fragments that are discovered serve as tools of knowledge to help us gradually understand the object under study. In *Le trou noir de l'histoire* (PLATE 21), for example, Marie-Jeanne Musiol features a series of temple doors, all of them portals to intuitive knowledge or, in the artist's words, "ritual entries": eroticism; spirituality; art in its broadest sense, including architecture; nature; chance or accident; and history. Sourkes shares the same concerns, because she too views history and culture as collections of fragments that seem to well up from a black hole.

In the series *Ombres* (1983), Marie-Jeanne Musiol tries to reclaim possession of her own image and contour by capturing shadows, those first fleeting photographs of the body that exist even before the images are fixed on glass or metal plates. The addition of drawing emphasizes her desire to define her being. Her approach pushes back the frontiers opened by modernistic photographers like Lee Friedlander who experimented with the indication of scale provided by their shadow falling in the field of vision, a "defect" in photography censured by all the "how to" manuals.

Musiol's choice of the Shiva motif in other works almost dictates fragmentation of the image, since the body of this Indian divinity lends itself to a "photomontage" of dancing arms and legs holding objects. The separation of the body from its attributes adds another dimension to the mythological character, a synthesis of several individual identities. We are thus taken back to the elements that make up the myth. *Shiva: vie et mort, mort et vie* (1986) is a work in three parts: on the wall, a photograph of a statue; beside it, torn fragments of the same image, with each fragment arranged according to its position within the image; and on the ground, various representations of the deity to give the iconographic and historical background. Pierre-Paul Cormier sees this as an example of painting and sculpture coming together within photography: "Addition and subtraction suggest a sculptural approach; the whole depends on pictorial organization (composition)."[35]

Through the découpage of Lucie Lefebvre's work and through tearing as practised by Marie-Jeanne Musiol, the photograph becomes a surface to be worked on like any other, as in the lettrist school. The reinstatement of the tactile quality gives the image and what it represents a very physical presence on the wall.

In the series *Le trou noir de l'histoire*, torn fragments are repositioned, sometimes slightly shifted, upon a wider shot of the same image. Another technique involves isolating the fragments in the darkroom by superimposing a mask with irregular, torn edges. Thus in *Le temple est ouvert* (1986-1988), the images loom forth with an almost ghostly presence, similar to that achieved in the stunning photographs of art and architecture produced in the nineteenth century.

TOTAL DESTRUCTION

In the late thirties, the French photographer Raoul Ubac also experimented with manipulation using the technique of burning:

La Nébuleuse (Raoul Ubac, 1939) was produced by burning: heat from a small torch was used to sear the emulsion of a negative showing a woman standing. The melting caused by this process wrinkles and twists the field of the photograph in an effect that has often been equated in academic and critical literature with automatism, that is, the creation of suggestive imagery by chance. But Ubac's title implies decomposition rather than creation of a shape, and the process with its line like a flickering flame is a means of deliberately producing this formlessness.[36]

This technique raises the interesting question of how far the artist can go before totally destroying the object-image. The ultimate in destruction was undoubtedly achieved by Hollis Frampton in his film *Nostalgia* (1971):

Frampton has laid each one [photograph] upon a hotplate that is situated like an animation stand directly below the camera's lens in closeup. The photographs begin to burn slowly and as they do, a voice-over commentary is read that provides information not about the burning image, but rather about the photograph that will appear next. So, for example, the film commences with a photograph of a darkroom with an enlarger and developing trays visible on the right. As the image begins to burn, a narrator (Michael Snow, though he is not identified in the film) delivers opening remarks: "These are recollections of a dozen still photographs I made several years ago."[37]

If a photograph represents one frozen moment in the lifetime of an object, a landscape or a human being that will undergo the inexorable wear and tear of time, alteration of the photo compresses the duration of this arrested moment and accelerates it. In *Nostalgia*, Frampton undertook the destruction of photographic work — the historical predecessor of film, as Bruce Lyn Jenkins observes — at the very moment when his interest was turning from photography to cinema. Thus, his retrospective and destructive look at one art form led to his adopting another, which makes him quite different from Raymonde April who for a time made a practice of cutting up her old photographs and reusing them to create new images.

MYSTERY

Our review of this shifting and disjointed terrain leads us to the brink of the mystery which undeniably permeates the creative process. Artists themselves claim their share of the ineffable, a range of *unknowns* that never rise to the surface. As Cheryl Sourkes says:

. . . of course I'm really drawn by the mysterious but I don't try to find a solution or a finality in it. I like to experience the mysterious, to evoke it. I think that our culture, our materialist culture, likes to deny it. Though when I walk through the streets and go through the books, it's that that validates my question. I take it as evidence that there is a long community exploration of those same questions in many different cultures and different ways and different practices, and I gather them.[38]

"Alchemy" is the term proposed by Chantal Boulanger to describe the work of Lise Bégin [39] — a different kind of chemistry that goes beyond science and defies it.

The manipulated photograph forces us to let go, to accept what is given and forget what is omitted; to accept the product, rather than the point of departure. Although we can see vestiges of the various stages of reworking, the only real connection that remains between them is the alchemy of creativity.

Interestingly, Arturo Schwarz chose to organize his exhibition for the 1986 Venice Biennale around the four phases of the alchemical process, a perhaps questionable decision, especially if his aim was to perpetuate the mystique that still surrounds the artist's personality. However there is no doubt that the practice of photographic manipulation shares the nature of alchemy, in the sense that it effects a transmutation of photographic material by bringing together fields often perceived as mutually exclusive (photography, drawing and painting) without fusing them completely. Indeed, all the elements remain visible, as though in suspension: the original photograph, the process of manipulation, and the final result.

Most artists working with photographic manipulation seem motivated by a desire to break through definitional boundaries and technical constraints by appropriating the image. They are driven by a need to "make and remake" [40] or, to paraphrase Marie-Jeanne Musiol, to "fragment," [41] in order to go beyond the confines of the photograph itself. All these considerations bring us back to the difficult question of the limits to intervention, and this applies equally to the process of creating works and to critical commentary. How much can an image be altered? How far can alteration of the image be taken? How far should interpretation go? Perhaps Proust was right when he said that we are always fascinated by things that hold a few illusions yet to be shattered…

1. See especially Patricia D. Leighten, "Critical Attitudes toward Overtly Manipulated Photography in the 20th Century," *Art Journal*, 37, 2 (Winter 1977-78): 133-138, part one; and 37, 4 (Summer 1978): 313-321, part two.
2. Interview with Cheryl Sourkes in the series "View: The Canadian Photographer," Canadian Museum of Contemporary Photography, 1987.
3. Cheryl Sourkes, from proceedings of "Marques et contrastes" colloquium, November 27-28, 1987, Université du Québec à Chicoutimi. (Jonquière: Éditions Sagamie, 1988)

4. *Ibid.*

5. Interview with Cheryl Sourkes by Irene Dual in *Cheryl Sourkes: Opening Up the Psychic Economy* (Vancouver: The Charles H. Scott Gallery, Emily Carr College of Art and Design, 1986), p. 5.

6. Extract of a letter from Ezra Pound to Sarah Perkins Cope, dated January 15, 1934, in Marie Hénault, ed., *The Merrill Studies in the Cantos* (Columbus, Ohio: C.E. Merrill, 1971), p. 2.

7. Sourkes, "View." Also, see article by Raymonde April in this anthology.

8. *Ibid.*

9. Cheryl Simon, "The Déjà Vu of Angela Grauerholz," *Vanguard*, 15, 2 (April-May 1986): 27-29.

10. Martha Townsend, *April/Davey/Grauerholz* (Kingston, Ontario: Agnes Etherington Art Centre, Queen's University, 1985), p. 31.

11. See, inter alia, Gilles Rioux, "Notman et les jeux/photomontages," *Vie des Arts*, 21, 83 (Summer 1976): 18-21; Ann Thomas, *Fact and Fiction: Canadian Painting and Photography 1860-1900* (Montréal: McCord Museum, 1979); and my commentary on the exhibit entitled "Les origines de la photo imprimée" (McCord Museum, 1981), in *Communication et information*, 5, 1 (Fall 1982): 235-240.

12. Michel Lessard, "Photographie, peinture et gravure," *Photo Sélection*, 7,4 (June 1987): 11-16.

13. See Dawn Ades, *Photomontage* (New York: Pantheon Books, 1976), 112 pages. Also Van Deren Coke, Bernd Lohse and Ute Eskildsen, *Avant garde Photography in Germany: 1919-1939* (San Francisco Museum of Modern Art, 1980), 104 pages.

14. Information on the lettrist movement was taken from the writings of Isidore Isou, *De l'impressionnisme au lettrisme, l'évolution des moyens de réalisation de la peinture moderne* (Paris: Filipacchi, 1973), 96 pages, from the collection "Le monde des grands musées," New Series No. 3 (July 1973). I would also like to thank Édouard Jaegle of the Galerie Jade (Colmar, France) for introducing me to Frédérique Devaux (Paris), whose assistance was very valuable to me.

15. Marie-Jeanne Musiol, text for the *Entrées rituelles* exhibit, 1987.

16. Isou, *De l'impressionnisme*, p. 80.

17. *Ibid*, p. 84.

18. Isidore Isou, "Nouvelles considérations esthétiques et éco-esthétiques sur la photographie du mouvement lettriste," mimeographed article, dated April 15, 1968, p. 1. [Our translation. Ed.]

19. Arnulf Rainer, extract from *Face-Farces* (1971), reproduced in *Arnulf Rainer : mort et sacrifices*, ed. Claude Schweisguth (Paris: Centre Georges Pompidou, 1984). [Our translation. Ed.]

20. Throughout history, artists, cartoonists and scientists have demonstrated an interest in physiognomy. For its role in the work of Arnulf Rainer, see the article by Wolfgang Hartman, "Face Farces von Arnulf Rainer," in the catalogue *Arnulf Rainer "Der Grosse Bogen"*, Kunsthalle Bern, 1977, pp. 17-28.

21. See Bruce Ferguson, *Suzy Lake: Are you talking to me?* (Saskatoon, Saskatchewan: Mendel Art Gallery, 1980).

22. See my text in the catalogue *Lise Bégin, Défolier* (Montréal: Musée d'art contemporain, 1984), n.p.

23. Lise Bégin, extract from a text reproduced in the catalogue *Lise Bégin, Défolier*. Tr. by Elizabeth Willing.

24. Serge Murphy, "Lise Bégin. Vienne l'âge d'or ! (ne vois-tu rien venir ?)," *Vanguard*, 16, 2 (April-May 1987): 18. [Our translation. Ed.]

25. Chantal Boulanger, "Lise Bégin: Galerie Jean-Louis Helstroffer," *Vanguard*, 13, 2 (March 1984): 34.

26. Stephen Horne, *Image: Double: Shadow. (Raymonde April/Lise Bégin)* (Halifax: Anna Leonowens Gallery, Nova Scotia College of Art and Design, 1986).

27. Murphy, p. 17. [Our translation. Ed.]

28. Chantal Boulanger, "Lise Bégin. Le corps imagé," in *Traces* (Québec: Réseau-Art-Femmes, 1982), p. 31. [Our translation. Ed.]

29. Murphy, p. 18. [Our translation. Ed.]

30. Sourkes, "View."

31. Extracts from a presentation by Lucie Lefebvre at the "Marques et contrastes" colloquium. [Our translation. Ed.]

32. See comments by Danielle Léger in *Vanguard*, 15, 3 (Summer 1986): 41; and by Jean Tourangeau in *Vie des Arts*, 31, 123 (June 1986): 78.

33. Anne-Marie Meissonnier and Elizabeth Amzallage-Augé, *L'enfant photographe. La photographie à développement instantané* (Paris: Centre Georges Pompidou, Atelier des Enfants, 1982), pp. 7-11. [Our translation. Ed.]

34. Conversation with the artist, January 17, 1988. [Our translation. Ed.]

35. Pierre-Paul Cormier, "Parallélismes," *Le Droit* (Ottawa), December 13, 1986, p. 63. [Our translation. Ed.]

36. Rosalind E. Krauss, "Corpus delicti," *Exposante-fixe: photographie et surréalisme* (Paris: Fernand Hazan and the Centre Georges Pompidou, 1985), p. 65. [Our translation. Ed.]

37. Bruce Lyn Jenkins, *The Films of Hollis Frampton: A Critical Study* (Ann Arbor, Michigan: University Microfilms International, 1983), p. 236.

38. Sourkes, "View."

39. Boulanger, "Lise Bégin. Le corps imagé," p. 31.

40. Gilbert Lascault, *Faire et défaire* (Montpellier: Fata Morgana, 1985), pp. 9-14.

41. Marie-Jeanne Musiol, "Noir Blanc," *Cahiers*, 22 (Summer 1984): 15.

(Translated from French)

Photoconceptual Art in Vancouver

IAN WALLACE

Photography and conceptual art have had a specific and special part to play in the history of Vancouver art over the past two decades. Since its initial appearance in the late 1960s, its flourishing in the 1970s, and its renewed significance after the challenge of the new painting in the early 1980s, photoconceptualism remains as one of the most vital genres of contemporary art. The development of photoconceptualism has proliferated widely and has had significant implications for regional developments in contemporary art, particularly in the Vancouver area but also in almost every other regional centre of importance. Specific individuals have certainly had an important part to play in this, but equally important is the relationship between the particular characteristic of the modern city dominated by "media culture" and the historical position that photoconceptual practice has had in the debate over modernism and post-modernism. It is within this nexus that the Vancouver artists, ranging from N.E. Thing Co. in the late 1960s to Jeff Wall in the 1980s, have made original and innovative work.

Strictly speaking, photoconceptual art does not necessarily refer to photography that has a conceptual intention, but rather to photographic work that originated in conceptual art and the late-modernist tendencies most closely associated with it. But even though photoconceptualism grew out of a modernist aesthetic, it simultaneously critiqued it, favouring a heterogeneous mix of practices and an emphasis on representation and subject matter. In opposition to the hegemony established by mainstream modernism, it counterposed heterogeneity and marginality. This is what made photoconceptualism from the very beginning also a "postmodernist" activity; and in this it identified with regionalist challenges not only to the domination of the art centre but also to the authority of histories conceived from those centres — the "grand narratives" so to speak.

It is not stylistic appearance that identifies photoconceptual practice, for in fact photoconceptualism has moved far from what conceptual art looked like. Rather, it is genealogy and methodology which establish the significant links and give them historical shape. Therefore, despite apparent differences, this work has maintained some of the core propositions of conceptual art: an emphasis on concept or subject matter over the medium and thus an openness to a wide variety of techniques; a basis in language, behaviourism, politics and mass media; a critical approach to traditional genres and institutions; an almost immediate international dissemination of its critical discourse through magazines, catalogues and exhibitions; and a unique link to the universities.

The relationship of language and theory to photoconceptualism is rooted in the problematic nature of conceptual art, its intellectual self-consciousness and the textual practice that was identified with it from the beginning. This is not to imply that pictorial concerns, whether related to painting or photography, play a secondary role, but that the emphasis is on the function of the image within all its linguistic parameters, both within and without the frame; that is, in terms of the total economy, its positioning within a world view, including the world of art and its institutions. It is specifically in the way the work positions itself and organizes itself as language, as a text of images as it were, that photoconceptualism asserts itself as a genre distinct from all other types of photography. This distinction therefore is not only formal; it is also paramountly ideological, and as such it questions its condition as a value. It positions itself as addressing the problematic of modernism in its current, most critical phases and thus disavows pure expression in favour of an investigation of the nature of the medium and, through its representational function, its contingency on meaning.

Any useful discussion of a defined practice must simultaneously acknowledge the limits of the medium and the open-endedness of its activities. The decisive edges of photoconceptualism inevitably overflow into a variety of other practices: sculpture, painting, performance, video, concrete poetry, etc., as well as classical photography itself. So rather than discussing the work at its limits, we can gain a clearer idea of its distinguishing features by looking at the problematic central to current developments of conceptual art, that is, its relation to the notion of the regional; not only that of medium itself, in this case photography, as distinct from the concept of art as a whole, but also the regional as a territory whose peripheral relation to a dominant centre conditions a specific set of immediate working conditions, social relations and the receptivity of the work in the local institutions that promote it. The role that photography and conceptual art have played in the politics of regionalism has given it a particular relevance to the development of the avant-garde in Vancouver art since the late 1960s. And since the Vancouver situation is similar to developments running concurrently in a number of other regional centres, particularly those areas where a strong tradition of modernism came into contact with liberal politics and mass media, general observations on Vancouver can apply elsewhere.

The shifting history of photoconceptualism over the past two decades can be briefly profiled in three stages: (1) the initial appearance of photographic imagery in conceptual art in the mid- to late-1960s; (2) the multiple developments of narrative and cinematic strategies in performative and theoretically based "semiotic" work of the 1970s; and (3) the critical and deconstructive "inhabitation" of mass-media imagery through the technique of the ready-made or "appropriated" imagery since the early 1980s. All of these tendencies are still active in one way or another.

Between 1965 and 1970, during what we might call "early conceptualism," photography appeared as the documentation of idea-works and their sites, as language games and thematic inventories and as a reflective investigation of the social and architectural landscape. Well-known examples of the original American conceptualists include Ed Ruscha's photobooks of 1965-66 and Dan Graham's *Homes of America* of 1966-67. In Vancouver, the direct influence of this work could be seen in the work of N.E. Thing Co. (Iain and Ingrid Baxter) and Jeff Wall in the late 1960s. The first major exhibitions featuring photoconceptual art in Vancouver were the *Photoshow* of 1969, curated by Christos Dikeakos, and the *955,000* show, curated by the New York critic Lucy Lippard in early 1970. These exhibitions included Vancouver artists along with a range of some of the most important and, at that time, still relatively unknown international conceptual artists, some of whom were just beginning to use photographic imagery. These exhibitions were comprehensive and advanced even for the time and consolidated the significance of photoconceptual strategies for Vancouver artists who were formulating original approaches to mainstream developments but from a regional point of view.

One of the earliest exhibited photoconceptual works from Vancouver, N.E. Thing Co.'s *Piles* catalogue of 1968 (PLATE 22), is a perfect example of this tendency. This was a published portfolio of photographs structured around a theme similar to Ed Ruscha's work, such as *All the Buildings on Sunset Strip* (1966). Consisting of photographs of piles of "found" objects from the industrial suburbs of Vancouver, Baxter's piece playfully and ironically mimicked a variety of modernist typologies latent in images of the industrial landscape. With a blend of minimal cool and pop-art humour, he appropriated the profane world through photography in order to make both aesthetic references and visual puns, but also as a form of homage to the beauty of the banal. Baxter's project was less absorbed in theoretical or critical concerns than in an affectionate and irreverent play with the camera as an extension of a new sensory apparatus — McLuhanism in its lightest moments.

This combination of modernist structural methodology and localized imagery is also reflected in an early piece by Jeff Wall from 1969 titled *Landscape Manual* (PLATE 23), which was included in the first, seminal exhibition of conceptual art, the *Information* show, at the Museum of Modern Art in New York in the spring of 1970. *Landscape Manual* was a publication consisting of photographs shot through the window of a car touring the suburbs of Vancouver, accompanied by a text which simultaneously reflects on the process of the making of the piece. Like Baxter's *Piles*, it examined the "defeatured" zones of the regional suburbs specific to Vancouver yet also typical of any other North American suburb. Following the model provided by the photographic "travels" of New York conceptualists such as Dan Graham and Robert Smithson, which established an allegorical link between the "defeatured" zones of the industrial and residential suburb and the radical "emptiness" of the minimalist aesthetic, Wall's *Landscape Manual* introduced a narrative political potential into the methodological structure of an apparently "objective" accounting of the environment, in this case an intentionally crude and provisional parody of a scientific manual.

The political implications of such early work were grounded in the notion that the objective mirroring of reality by the photographic document could reflect self-consciousness and therefore effect self-transformation. At this stage, however, the political concepts were only implied through the ironic distance that stood between everyday reality and the conventionalized codes and typologies offered by the aesthetics of minimalism. Yet above all this work marked a distinctive shift in the mood and function of the artwork, from an inner-directed to an outer-directed activity. The innovative possibilities of this way of working with the camera were simultaneously picked up and further developed by several other Vancouver artists at the time, and these developments were paralleled in almost every other major regional centre that came into contact with conceptual art.

The second phase, covering most of the 1970s, showed an impulse toward narrativity and performance which pulled conceptual art toward using photography as a medium of performative and pictorial representation. This often included film, video and sequential photographic constructions combined with text. This second phase registered the first important influence of conceptual art in an international context, in effect producing "second-generation" conceptualism. Although by the mid-1970s the profusion of tendencies existing in close proximity in Vancouver precluded the exclusive dominance of any particular style, the emphasis on narrativity, performance and text-oriented work led Vancouver photoconceptualists to experiment with large-scale pictorial installations with video as well as photography. The sense of the spectacular image that came out of performance and video went far beyond the minimalist or reductivist aesthetics which characterized the earlier phase of photoconceptualism in the late 1960s. These tendencies of the the 1970s to reject earlier reductive aspects of modernism gradually gave rise to a "post-modernist" analysis which will be described later.

Considering its importance as a subject of discussion throughout the 1970s, it is surprising that there was no significant engagement with a feminist critique in photoconceptual work in Vancouver until the early 1980s. The only exception might be the work of Marion Penner Bancroft, who came out of a background in classical photography, but who began in the late 1970s to introduce an autobiographical subject matter in which a predominately documentary photographic imagery was accompanied by text. This approach, already typical of the "narrative art" of the early 1970s, was also picked up at the same time by more tendentious feminist artists elsewhere and came to dominate feminist photoconceptualism throughout the 1980s.

There were, however, a number of significant lateral developments appearing in Vancouver in the mid- to late-1970s which departed from some of the more entrenched strategies of narrativity that had become established earlier. When Jeff Wall began constructing his large, back-lit Cibachrome images in 1977, he presented narrativity within the single unified picture space of classical painting and cinema, rather than in the serial or sequential shift of imagery typical of the period. Rodney Graham's work since the mid-1970s (in such pieces as *75 Polaroids* [PLATE 24], *Camera Obscura* and *Illuminated Ravine*), also moved away from narrative structures and instead emphasized the epistemological and informational aspects not only of the camera as an imaging machine but of imaging in general as a structural conundrum between the prerogatives of language, the limits of technique and the enigma of nature. Ken Lum had by the late 1970s begun using the photographic image as an emblematic representation that both appropriated existing imagery and mimicked conventions of commercial photography. From one of his earliest works, *Anonymous* of 1977 (PLATE 25), which was a mass-printed photographic self-portrait postered throughout the city, through to the appropriated imagery of *Architectural Digest Presents* and his *Portrait Logos* of the early 1980s, Lum's work has commented on the iconography of popular, generic imagery.

In any case, by the early 1970s the formal biases of the modernist avant-garde had shifted over to a new interest in subject matter. The emphasis on subject matter, all the while a general characteristic of regionalist attitudes, led to the first stage of a breakdown of the modernist hegemony characterized by the dominance of "Greenbergian" formalism which, being almost exclusively aesthetic and abstract, precluded any critique of representation or social subject matter. The radical reductivism of much early minimalist and conceptual art, which occupied a position at the "terminus" of modernism (this work I call "late modernism"), was also dissolved in this process. For the conceptual artists who used photography, this generally meant a shift from system to process to symbol; that is, from the factual information of the photographic document structured as a formal or systematic repetition, over to the symbolic potential of the image organized for an interpretive hermeneutic reading.

This shift of emphasis in linguistic theory from "structure" to "sign"—from the formal patterns of language to the semiotic or symbolic connotations of the image—, parallels the theoretical shift from structuralism to semiotics which also occurred in the 1970s. In photoconceptualism this was first reflected in what came to be known as "narrative" or "story" art by about 1974-75. And, as will be seen further in the argument, this development generally came from "second-generation" regional interpretations of conceptual art rather than the classical mainstream movement that originated in New York.

The textual references inherited from conceptual art and literary theory combined with an emphasis on process and performance. Although this imagery was usually arranged sequentially, thus maintaining the structural tendencies of earlier forms of conceptual photography, the influence of cinematic and performative models made it pictorially richer and less reductive than the earlier work. The new open-endedness of narrative art, which drew upon a variety of photographic genres, also allowed for a critique of the imagery and technology of mass media which became associated with forms of critical post-modernism. One of the most pervasive strategies of this tendency has been the use of the ready-made or "appropriated" image. Unlike the earlier "Duchampian" ready-made, which questions the status of the artwork itself, the new use of the photographic ready-made is as an instrument for intervention into the prevailing mode of production of mass-media representation and reproduction. As a deconstructive, socially progressive critique emerged between the late 1960s and the late 1970s, the political engagement with mass media began to open up new readings of photographic imagery in their narrative, emblematic, allegorical and connotative aspects.

This "semiotic" stage which developed throughout the 1970s is presently being played out in the debate around the notion of simulation and the "hyperreal" advanced by Jean Baudrillard and which questions the legitimacy of any meaning attached to a signifying symbol. The ready-made, which has until now played upon the decontextualization of conventional readings of the everyday object, now seems to present itself as a cipher for the arbitrariness of the sign. As a result, the "deconstructive" political critique has been diverted into a critique of the legitimacy of determinant meaning in the signifier itself. The present situation, now influenced by the subjectivist tendencies of painting in the 1980s (or possibly the opposite, that the performative character of 1970s photoconceptualism influenced painting in the late 1970s), has turned the sign of the image into pure gesture. The photographic image is read less for its symbolic, representational dimensions than for its ability to register a pure act. While formerly the tendency was to provide a pictorial image-structure for interpretation, as in the work of Jeff Wall and the recent work of Roy Arden, there is now a tendency to present the photographic image as an almost sculptural object that asserts pure presence and resists interpretation, as in the work of Ken Lum, Stan Douglas and Rodney Graham.

But whether the emphasis is on the pictorial or the sculptural object, these tendencies reverse the reductive character of the earliest stages of conceptual art, which turned the Duchampian gesture of indifference into a sign for the radical negation of the art object, in favour of an "allegorical" operation which intervenes in all the traditional institutionalizations of modernist art — to operate upon these institutions a "deconstruction." By intention or by default, this situation also therefore sets into motion the possibility for a new political critique, one which breaks out of the frameworks of traditional readings in order to reposition the image as "object" into a more problematic relation to the general economy of image-objects in society as a whole and thus call attention to their function within a system of values. Again, Ken Lum's work, particularly his *Portrait Logos*, comes to mind; but a more feminist critique along the same lines also appears in recent work by Kati Campbell.

Throughout each of these succeeding stages, and especially in the mid-1970s, new adherents were drawn to photoconceptualism, many coming from mainstream photographic traditions. By 1975 the effects of an active and expanded market in photography further stimulated and legitimated this photographic practice within or at the margins of conceptual art, even when it tended to reject the classical tradition of photography. It became widely discussed as an issue and was featured in a number of solo and thematic museum shows, often around the issue of the legitimation of photography as "art." The institutionalization of this work in the museums and academies had by 1977 brought forward a new generation of artists and critics who referred directly to the innovations of the earlier photoconceptualists. This second generation also benefited from the alternative institutions established by the generation of 1968-74 and which maintained a commitment to avant-garde attitudes and forms, including bookworks (often photo pieces), performance (photo-documented) and video. In all of these three areas photography has played a major role. Furthermore, the use of large-scale photography from the early 1970s on blended photoconceptualism with contextualist issues arising from installation art and its critique of the institution of the museum.

There are specific reasons why photoconceptualism has had a particularly strong development in Vancouver. Despite the repeated observations that Vancouver is an isolated community, Vancouver artists from the early 1960s on were relatively well-travelled and informed about a wide variety of international tendencies. They were constrained by the limited exposure to original works of historical and contemporary art, but this lack of direct and ongoing contact with the original nevertheless led to an intense appreciation of the reproduction, particularly the translation of the effect of the original through photography. It is not coincidence that such theorists of mass media and communication as Marshall McLuhan and Buckminster Fuller were appreciated in Vancouver (they were both present at the 1965 Festival of Contemporary Art at the University of British Columbia). Such theorizing on the conceptual and sensory dynamics of mass media and communication was synthesized artistically in the formation of Intermedia in Vancouver in 1968. Thus the appreciation of modernity in Vancouver was partly influenced by its dependence on information derived from media. But this ethos of information culture also came into conflict with the ethos of *genius loci* based upon a romantic valorization of "place" that still maintains itself in the cultural sphere even though it has largely been dissolved in the actual social world. The driving force of the modern "informational" city displaces the notion of the centre from "place" to "concept," from a specific geographic location to a dispersal of ideological effects. The notion of the regional is now not so much a peripheral territory as that of a molecularized network of competing hegemonic practices within widely distributed specialized fields. In the case of photoconceptual art in Vancouver, the regional field is currently the site for conflicting political critiques and questions of ideology that are reflected across the various territories of contemporary art, notably around issues of feminism, censorship and imagery in public places.

The long-established romantic tradition in Vancouver art meant that conceptual art never gained a wider acceptance because of its predominately intellectual, critical and "dematerialized" character, which was rooted in modernist reductivism and implicitly a questioning of the status of art itself. The anti-sensuous character of conceptual art, however, was appreciated on another more specifically political and intellectual level by those artists who came from the universities and whose background was in art history, politics and information theory. Coming out of the student movements of the late 1960s these more intellectual artists were attempting to bridge the gap between a political avant-garde (Marxism and situationism) and an artistic avant-garde (modernism). Since there was literally no regional market (at least for the intellectual avant-garde), the primacy of the art object as such was never a question—sales were rarely made anyway. The emphasis was on attitude, process, play and political content. Art was made out of a synthesis of theory and technique that had little relationship to the demands of the marketplace.

The upshot of this brief account is that Vancouver's relative isolation was compensated by artist-driven initiatives and institutions which consciously developed contact with (largely "underground") art scenes elsewhere through travel, theoretical literature, modern communications networks and magazines. The institutional dominance of traditional art forms, particularly painting which stressed regionality and generally held out against outside influence, were balanced out by avant-gardist and internationalist tendencies which formed in the alternative institutions such as Image Bank, the Pender Street Gallery and the universities, and, it is fair to say, the Vancouver Art Gallery from the mid-1960s through to the mid-1970s. In part, at least, what these avant-garde factions recognized in the ephemeral, performative text-oriented and media-oriented aspects of conceptual art were common techniques that overcame marginality and which were a strategy of survival for the active, communicative and self-sustaining avant-garde culture in Vancouver from the mid-1960s on. The variety of approaches embodied in these activities comes out of the complex attitude that Vancouver artists

[103]

held toward the already complex subject of conceptual art. This has a bearing on the position that what I call photoconceptualism holds not only in the local art community dominated by painters but also in the equally active community of traditional photographers. The detailed history of this development still needs to be written.

But the emphasis on "conceptualism" in photoconceptualism is fairly recent. In Vancouver, as elsewhere, conceptual art had for a long time been treated with suspicion. However, on the international scene an interest in conceptual art began to surface again in the early 1980s, as generations of students who had come into contact with conceptual artists teaching in the universities and academies developed what could be called in its broadest sense "late conceptualism" and which positioned photography as its dominant technique. Many of these conceptual artists from New York had visited Vancouver in the late 1970s and early 1980s. Direct contact with the work of these artists allowed for a reappraisal of the significance of conceptual art in the Vancouver context. The photographic innovations that had been developed locally over the past two decades and which had become consolidated and refined into an independent and original form also became integrated with the international scene, resulting in a renewed awareness in the regional context that something is at stake in this development: not just in the establishment of short-term career successes but in the building of long-term histories that form legitimations and opportunities for development across a broad front of activities. Thus conceptual art gained a totally different meaning in Vancouver in the 1980s than it had in the 1960s.

As a result, the deliberate cultivation of artistic and political discourse within the terms of photoconceptual art in Vancouver has some fairly precise ideological motivations and implications. Above all, despite the involvement of photoconceptualism in the controversy around post-modernism, Vancouver artists on the whole have maintained continuity within the modernist avant-garde; and along with the development of criticism and theorization of this work, the questioning of the presumptions emerging from the debate around post-modernism has given the Vancouver work a particular directed edge that distinguishes it from similar work coming from other regional circles. In relation to the post-modernist debate, the position that Vancouver holds on the periphery of mainstream modernist traditions has two contradictory implications: one is the effect that regionality or provincialism has in reifying decentralized or pluralist aspects of post-modernism; the other being that by virtue of its marginal position unaffected by dominant market forces, a more purist and critical modernist tradition, such as found itself in a small sector of the photoconceptualism movement in Vancouver, could simultaneously proceed with an independent and coherent development in tandem with mainstream histories and uninterrupted by market trends. The effect of regionality on Vancouver photoconceptualism comes specifically under this double condition which stresses both heterogeneity and purism.

Moreover, the early Vancouver work that was initially influenced by minimalism and conceptualism and thus a purist avant-garde tradition, was quick to reject the dominantly formalist tradition of modernism associated with Clement Greenberg while simultaneously recognizing the continuity of that tradition in its relation to avant-garde modernism. This consistently appears as an integration of abstract structures derived from formalism coupled with representations emerging from the application of photography to a political critique filtered through the strategies of conceptual art. That is, formalist structures such as repetition and seriality, which conceptual art inherited from abstract painting, were applied to radical conceptual critiques of ideology and language. Thus an emphasis on subject matter and extra-artistic concerns was introduced in the late 1960s which later came to be identified with a post-modernist outlook by the late 1970s. This was evident in some of the earliest attempts to interpret the notion of the post-modern. More accurately though, it has become clearer in recent years that this conceptual work was for the most part a critique of the limits of modernism from within the general terms of modernism. History and ideology then, have been concerns central (but not exclusively so) to Vancouver photoconceptualism since its beginnings in the late 1960s.

But even though they were ignored locally, the conceptual artists in Vancouver were aware of the implications of their work in a larger network and could act on immediate issues with a larger ideal in mind, one informed by an internationalist outlook but rooted in the reality of the immediate region. While the intellectual sources came from elsewhere, the documentary photograph was able, by its very immediacy, to ground theoretical and critical conceptual content in the representations of the regional social geography, that is as a local presence of the "idea." As already noted, it was by virtue of this combination of both a regionalist photo-document and an internationalist theoretical context that photoconceptualism was picked up by Vancouver artists in the late 1960s.

But meanwhile conceptual art was going through some significant changes that emerged not only from cross-referencing with other representational practices such as pop art and film theory, but also by other political ideologies, notably feminism and the ecology movement. Out of these new influences arose discussions about the problematic and institutionalized aspects of more traditional forms of avant-garde modernism, notably painting, which led to both a questioning and movement away from these practices as well as toward them. These questions led to a break-up of the modernist front, of which conceptual art was a part, and the consequent eclecticism of avant-garde photoconceptualism in this period (which dominated for the rest of the 1970s) attracted a pluralistic audience that ranged from the academic intellectual to the punk-expressionist. In this mixed context, the intersection of an academic bias with the alternative marginal spaces of the artists' galleries kept the discourse in the public realm and not limited to the universities alone. Thus through the combination of politics and pop art (what has in retrospect been identified as a "situationist" aesthetic), some of the radical momentum of the late 1960s was retrieved.

But it is fair to say that the performative models of the mid-1970s often ended up in a highly eclectic, introverted mood that led to a faltering of the avant-garde position of photoconceptualism. There was a break-up of purpose and a dependency on parody. Subject matter became more of a histrionic hook than a matter of conviction. The way out of this situation came from a reappraisal of the critical contextualist tendencies of conceptual art in the late 1960s, particularly by those photoconceptualists who accompanied their artwork with polemical writing. This practice has long been established by artists such as Joseph Kosuth, Daniel Buren, Dan Graham, Martha Rosler, Hans Haacke, Mary Kelly and Allan Sekula, as well as art historians and critics such as Benjamin Buchloh and Griselda Pollock. These figures had visited Vancouver from the late 1970s on and figured directly in the regional debates. The emergence of a generation of artists from the universities throughout the 1970s who were in varying measures influenced by conceptual art, particularly in its emphasis on critical theory as well as art practice, kept the regional variants of photoconceptualism from being dominated either by the market or the museum. It is also noteworthy that the recent interest in theory by traditional photographers has certainly brought the latter closer to photoconceptualism and conceptual art.

Moreover, by the early 1980s the art circles in Vancouver had become much more complex. The development of the audience for contemporary art had progressed greatly since the 1960s, and an intellectual, political and critical outlook, scorned throughout the 1970s in Vancouver, gradually developed an increasingly sophisticated understanding and acceptance. A variety of options, emerging from both regional and international outlooks, had created a number of micro-audiences and broken down the hegemony of the art centres. This situation was to be replicated elsewhere and is in part the outfall of post-modernist pluralism, the quick dispersal of avant-garde developments through the media and the fracturing and multiplicity of discourses in the art centres themselves. Again, this post-modern condition has led to a situation that shares the same conditions on a regional plane as well as on an international or "global" plane.

Insofar as it has worked under this dual condition for the past two decades, Vancouver is in many ways a typical or exemplary city of the post-modern condition. The two main discourses in this city by the early 1980s remained that of subjective, romantic painting and that of the more political analytic critique of photoconceptualism. The romantic expressionist painters (The New Romantics) looked largely to the media centres of New York and Berlin for the myth of modernist expressionism, even though their sensibilities were essentially formed by the long-standing expressionist traditions of regional painting (e.g. Emily Carr, Jack Shadbolt and Claude Breeze). Several moved away and found that their regional attitudes were not so far different from those of their counterparts on the international scene. As for photoconceptual art, since its first appearance in the late 1960s there has been a steady if sometimes uneven development that, while not being equally successful or rigorous in its aims, or even falling exclusively within the domain of photoconceptualism, has nevertheless assimilated, reinvented and dispensed with "pure" photoconceptualism in a variety of ways that has always kept it relevant and responsive to changing situations.

There was also a relatively original local development in the work of Jeff Wall that had few parallels elsewhere. This work, which carried on some of the tendencies of narrative art, was engaged primarily in critical/contextualist discourse through an emphasis on subject matter which combined theoretical, discursive, semiotic or iconological readings with an intensification of pictorial technique. Wall's work had a significant difference however. His pictorial techniques were now exclusively photographic and as such had implicitly formed a critique of painting. Although the implication of this critique has never yet been sufficiently engaged to become an overt issue, it colours the relations between the critical ambitions of photoconceptualism and all other forms of pictorial art, painting in particular. The critical edge of photoconceptualism therefore generally occupied that zone between painting and classic photography and sought its audience and legitimations elsewhere: in the discourse of politics, the institutions, architecture, feminism and language. In short, all of those subjects that were also of concern in the late 1960s and early 1970s and which were the driving force of the avant-garde and its commitment to an art of subjects over an art of forms. And now, instead of being on the margins as a regional research developing new tools of expressions, it occupies a place of centrality as a focus of questions of ideology, authority and representation; that is, at the critical point of modernism.

Therefore, in contrast to the tendency of post-modernism to disavow history and the contingency of language, photoconceptual art in Vancouver also identifies with the continuity of the modernist project in its rational enlightened aspect as discourse. This is not to claim that this work is necessarily wholly in command of such rationality — it is rather a working out of these objectives, with all of the contradictions implicit in them, within the space of public discussion given to the ideal of modernity and the avant-garde by the institutions of contemporary art, which are still, and perhaps even increasingly so, enlightened.

The modernist continuity spoken of here is far beyond the academic "Greenbergian" formalist modernism so popularly scourged by (equally conservative) critics today. Yet neither has formalism entirely been left behind. The concept that the evolution of plastic form and media of representation has its own consequences as a "content" of modernity has been internalized as a function of representation itself. In addition, since photography is innately a representational form in which abstract "substructural" forms still can modify the surface image, the content of its representation is not limited to the form of its representation but is in a reciprocal relation to its historical place in the positioning of its value as a political practice. This is precisely the significance of photoconceptualism, which has positioned photography as pure technique in a new relation to its function in the ideological operations of art.

Therefore, the question of photographic technique in this context is relevant. It appeared in some of the earliest examples of conceptual art for a number of specific and revealing reasons. Photographic work — especially in this early period—was generally minor in scale, technique and finish. In comparison to painting, installation and performance, which were often more spectacular, photoconceptual art was usually found in book-works or as a documentary footnote to other original productions, often positioned at the margins of the institutions. Foremost, though, photography had the look of modernity — especially when it referred to anti-aesthetic informational modes (such as found in the earlier work of Iain Baxter and Jeff Wall). By contrast, painting inherited history within its very technique. Photography also, unlike pure, minimal art, had the look simultaneously of the literalist structure of the document and of the open-ended suggestive readings of representational, albeit "industrial" or non-aesthetic, imagery. This combination of literalism and symbolism, of inert, objective fact and connotative reference, had the effect of joining the radical paradigm of minimalist abstraction found in certain aspects of conceptualism of the 1960s to the mass-culture motifs of pop art.

Secondly and perhaps more importantly, the structural use of informational photography had the effect of opening up within the terms of modernist formalism a narrative and ultimately tendentious political critique of the everyday and the superstructure. Information theory, language games and ideological critique were the three main discourses that conceptual artists could investigate through photographic practice. The ideological critique, which evolved into a critique of the image itself and of conditions of spectatorship and identity, led to a study of the film still as an extension of visual-art practice, largely through the presence of linguistics and feminism in film theory. Through the theoretical analysis of the image, the political critique of the avant-garde could turn its attention to mass-media and cinematic imagery. This led eventually to the so-called deconstructive work of the late 1970s.

This outlook of photoconceptualism has accepted the possibility of a structural metacritique that can intervene in the seamless flow of consumption by asserting contingency, urgency and thus determinacy. The prime distinction is in the relation of this work to photography as a technique and, by extension, the relation of this technique to ideology. Even though it is photographic technique at the margins of photography, its prime function derives from the position of the photographic medium as a value.

Photography has a specific place in the production of imagery and imaging. This position is modest in its relation to the ideological concept of art as a *value*, but it is monumental as an instrumental practice (that is, in its purely technical and commercial aspect) in forming and mirroring social and ideological *values* as well as in disseminating those *values* as reproductions. Without *valorizing* photography as a technique in itself, photoconceptualism, through the mimicry of a variety of forms of photographic genres and production, self-consciously concretizes the *value*, the ideological inflection of its imaging function in the social world. And in doing so, it draws attention to the *value*-constructs of this imagery in order to intervene in this order intellectually, conceptually as it were. This is its critical dimension as distinct from its purely expressive dimension.

Photoconceptual work links itself with the historical avant-garde in demanding its autonomy — an autonomy that asserts the political necessity of art not as a function of ideological demand but by constructing a critique of ideology and its immanence in the mediascape. While it inhabits the spectacular languages and forms of the mediascape, photoconceptualism also, through the self-consciousness generated out its genealogy as conceptual art, separates itself out of this immanence to assume an independent position, so that, despite its marginality, it does make a difference. That is, it poses itself as determining the fate of its affairs. Thus in the flow of its overall development, and considering the open-endedness and ambiguity of the situation, photoconceptualism has assumed (or has

[110]

inherited despite its intentions) a posture of allegiance to historical modernism.

It is also noticeably "of the world" and makes direct reference to the social constructions of the world in distinction to the expressive gestures of painting, which describe the subjective inner self. Jeff Wall's work is amongst the most advanced in regard to this development. His work goes beyond picture-making and subject matter. He positions the picture and its subject in direct relation to the continuity of the modernist polemic as a condition by which the picture and its subject assert a value in social discourse as a whole. This is the contingency of modernism from the perspective of photographic technique: what matters is not only the medium of expression in itself, but also what the picture is about. Wall uses photography in its most intense form as a transmission of spectacular subject matter: the back-lit Cibachrome transparency. Wall's work can thus never be isolated as an abstract, aesthetic sign — it always returns to the representation of the actual experience of the social scene. And this also means that the medium in all its intensity is also a contingency on its effect as meaning.

But most importantly what follows from this is that conceptual art stands in opposition to the current rhetoric of post-modernism, which promotes a general capitulation to the fragmentation, commoditization, and ultimate devaluation of language. It must be admitted, however, that even though photoconceptual art in Vancouver exhibits a unity of effect (one critic has called it "Judd-like"), in fact this serves a variety of purposes. Much of the discussion that surrounds the work of the Vancouver photoconceptualists is in fact a search for the common denominator in a plethora of options. There are many conflicts and individual developments, but there is a common language that grounds itself in the primacy of language as it winds its way through a multiplicity of discourses. This commitment to modernist contingency thus is opposed to post-modern arbitrariness, which posits that any "free-floating" signifier can be substituted for another.

But the logic of the arbitrary in post-modern art cannot be overlooked. It is a logic constituted out of the relative spatial difference between "things" or "signs" in a society dominated by the logic of consumption, mediation and indeterminacy. It operates on the principle that the subject must first be alienated from contingency, then integrated into an indeterminate flow of shifting, ahistorical processes. The logic of consumption demands that the object consumed be redundant, a cipher, in order that nothing be changed in the act of consumption. The object or image consumed has to be mediated into nothing more than a sign or cipher for the object of desire, so that there is no actual fulfilment and that the act of consumption is no more than a perfect acting-out of itself.

This logic of the post-modern condition of a technocratic consumer society is perfectly mirrored in contemporary art of all types; not only in post-modern art but in modernism as well. Contemporary art mirrors the essence of the whole system. It conditions the whole system of language of which modernist art is a part, albeit in tension with it, but it cannot be willed away by correct thinking. Photoconceptual art, through its calling to consciousness of the contingencies of representation, identifies this overdetermination and thus allows for critique. The arbitrariness of post-modern art only mirrors the symptoms and, through devaluing reason, forecloses on critique. It is only a passive response to the real conditions of signification in our society because it merely absorbs itself into the seamless flow of cultural consumption. Photoconceptualism in general and particularly in Vancouver, with its roots in the political critique of culture and language that came out of conceptual art in the late 1960s, has both embraced and rejected these conditions. It has entered into these conditions and identified the immanent contradictions in order to engage with a real social economy and to bring to this economy a transgressive and transformative language by which an ideal reflection on the possibility of the future can be constructed.

Speaking Through Silence

FEMALE VOICE IN THE PHOTOGRAPHY OF NINA RAGINSKY, CLARA GUTSCHE AND LYNNE COHEN

CAROL COREY PHILLIPS

Hang on to the ability to observe and to judge.
If dissent must be silent, dissent nonetheless.

ELIZABETH JANEWAY
Powers of the Weak

Nina Raginsky, Clara Gutsche and Lynne Cohen have made major contributions to Canadian photography over the past twenty years. Raginsky's mid-1970s *Portraits*, Gutsche's late-1970s *Inner Landscapes*, and Cohen's continuing exploration of interiors (last seen at the National Gallery of Canada in the 1985 exhibit *Environments Here and Now* and recently published in the book *Occupied Territory*)[1] all provide significant points of reference for reassessing the photography of women working on the borders of the social-documentary tradition. While each photographer has retained certain features of the documentary mode — the "straight" photographic trace of physical reality and the naming of the social territory that appears in the image — their photographs also may be said to contain an "unspoken text" beyond, or alternative to, the closed, literal meanings conveyed by their titles.

Each of these photographers has employed the documentary procedure of direct, physical confrontation with the social field. But their photographs also make ironic references to other photographic practices, such as the family album, advertising and surveillance systems. These latter practices, in popular or institutional use, normally support a firmly entrenched symbol system of socially "correct" human models, in the same sense that mainstream cinema has been described as a mechanism for the "production of social subjects."[2] The irony employed by Raginsky, Gutsche and Cohen is destabilizing. As Teresa de Lauretis explains, "The woman cannot transform the codes; she can only transgress them, make trouble, provoke, pervert, turn the representation into a trap...."[3]

Nina Raginsky belongs to the first group of Canadian photographers whose works were published by the National Film Board (NFB) Still Photography Division in the late 1960s.[4] It is useful to review the Canadian documentary tradition and its influences on her vision.

It has long been recognized that the documentary mode, as institutionalized by John Grierson, submitted photographic images to the domination of language codes. Grierson instituted the use of the "voice of authority" in voice-overs at the NFB; and he never denied that this didactic device in war films imposed a "conscious ordering of perception."[5] Imposition of a narrative discourse continued in the NFB Still Photography Division's "photostories" of the 1950s, when meanings in still photographs were controlled by the written texts of NFB editors. Martha Langford identifies the narrative closure of NFB photostories:

NFB photostories [reflected] a point of intersection between the nicest common sentiments and sanctified legislative response... [and] as government sponsored publications... [they ignored] poverty, unemployment, inequality and general unpleasantness....[6]

It is clear that in the 1950s and early 1960s documentary images were made to serve an affirmative government discourse and that to a large extent the Griersonian "voice of authority" denied the voice of the individual who had created the image. The Still Photography Division practice during the 1960s, including the production of the Centennial books *Stones of History* and *Canada/A year of the land*,[7] might be described as "a kind of visual exercise in nation-building."[8]

In her 1968 book, *Call them Canadians*,[9] Lorraine Monk, then head of the Still Photography Division, began to subdue the affirmative voice of the Griersonian tradition: Monk commissioned poetry by Miriam Waddington to serve as a literary accompaniment to a series of documentary portraits of Canadians. While Monk's selection and layout of images resulted in a human-family narrative, a sort of Canadian "family album," Waddington's poetic text was a subversive reading of the difficult social conditions appearing in several of the images (notably Raginsky's portraits of children).

The combination of poetic text and photographic image in *Call them Canadians* revealed a growing recognition of social inequities by Canadian documentary photographers. The first-person female voice of Waddington — a dissenting vision of the status quo — replaced the third-person affirmative voice of government:[10]

Tom Thomson's savage brush once drew
the west wind braver than he knew,
but who to wilderness of slum
will now with sweeping colors come?[11]

Within the photographs of Raginsky, Gutsche and Cohen, we sense a distinctly female voice, like Miriam Waddington's, silently questioning the status quo. Unspoken meaning emerges from their photographic reconstructions — meaning that remains separate from, even contradictory to, the social environments identified in the photographs' titles.

Raginsky's 1972-1976 *Portraits* series (photographs of ordinary people in Vancouver and Victoria) bears some resemblance to the communal vision of *Call them Canadians*: the presentation of recognizable social subjects — children, workers, military types and the elderly. But Raginsky refrains from any record of family groups: she most often documents a lone human figure on the street or in a work environment. Not only does the viewer respond to a collective memory of "traditional models of English Canadian society,"[12] but also to the familiar, family-album language used in her titles. However, as with NFB photostory texts, family-album constructions can produce a narrative closure, which excludes portions of family experience. A *Photo Communique* editor describes this phenomenon:

Not everything is there. For example, family albums seldom show pain or hardship, they tend to be selective, to express a wish for a family without mishap. They are a sort of homage to well-being, as much as they are a record.[13]

Raginsky's photographs of ordinary people contain an excess of information, which seems to destabilize the voice of "well-being" found in her cheerful family-album titles. This surplus of meaning, often presented in the relationship of the human figure to its environment, delivers a sense of ambiguity that has long been associated with Raginsky's portraits.

Another subtle disturbance of the documentary information in Raginsky's photographs is her application of hand colouring. The hand-tinted aesthetic of Victorian portraiture, as Penny Cousineau has noted, returns the portrait to its "origins as a cult object,"[14] which held the image of a lost loved one. Raginsky's use of this device dislocates its mid-1970s (or factual) time frame, removing it to the realm of memory-spectacle, remembrance of a time now lost. Beneath this construction of a memory-spectacle is an undeniable pathos — a witness to people who cling to outdated social customs as if removed from contemporary experience.

Raginsky's intense scrutiny of bodily gestures and facial mannerisms makes allusions to dated cultural values; and this produces a profound record of "human types whose common denominator is an evident innocence."[15] The conventional frontal pose reveals both the subjects' complicity with the camera ritual and their willingness to be regarded as belonging to a distinct, symbolic order of safe and dutiful citizens, whose dress codes register their place in this order. The photographer's consistent physical distance from her subjects makes it clear she is registering a personal and philosophical distance:[16] Raginsky is on the borderline of her constructed community.

The majority of Raginsky's subjects are captured in uniforms of the work force or the military base; but the significance of "uniform" also is strong in her images of children and the elderly. In Raginsky's studies of children in *Call them Canadians*, there is an arresting quality in the depth of emotion, in the spontaneous, unposed gestures of the subjects. Their clothing is not pertinent to the experience in which they were captured. In contrast, the subjects in *Garry Code at the Boy Scout Jamboree, Sooke, B.C.* (1974) and *Maria Fonsecca in Front of Her Father's Bakery, Vancouver* (1976) are presented as visual emblems of the social positions they inhabit. The emotions of these children are withheld, their body postures are rigid, and their uniforms dominate any expression of the unique child within each of them.

Raginsky renders a vision of children locked within an unnamed class structure. Similarly, her record of adults enclosed in work environments gives a sense of isolation and restricted experience within rigidly fixed cultural scripts. The subjects' identities seem to have been determined by stifling work environments. This provides an alternative, silent narrative —at odds with the light-hearted titles.

The viewer can sense a "multitude of meanings as against single, fixed meanings"[17] in Raginsky's titles, as if her authentic voice resides within her photographic vision. The titles speak with the voice of myth — the selective memory of a Canadian community in which "poverty, unemployment, inequality and general unpleasantness" are conveniently erased.

Julia Kristeva has defined the experience of women as "that which is unspoken, that which is left out of namings and ideologies."[18] Similarly, Susan Gubar has written of female creativity as if it were the silence of a "blank page," an absent discourse which ruptures the "final word" of written histories.[19]

This concept of an unspoken text is most apparent in Raginsky's portraits of the elderly. The family-album titles often narrate the anticipation of a social ritual, for example *The Kirkpatrick Sisters at the Empress Hotel* (1975) or *Clarence Adamson on His Way to Lunch, Victoria* (1975). These images recall the snapshot's function to "record and reinforce social rituals."[20] And yet the actual ritual does not appear in Raginsky's photographs. Instead, the exterior environments in these portraits of the elderly suggest anonymous urban space, in which the subjects might be isolated from active social participation — merely playing the myth of British matrons and retired gentlemen about to take tea at the Empress. The viewer sees women living within the confines of a memory-scenario, especially in the images of the Kirkpatrick sisters and *Mrs. Morton Going for a Walk in Victoria* (1974), in which their costumes typify the uniform of proper ladies. We respond to Raginsky's meticulous hand-tinting of gloves, hat, coat and scarf, to identical gestures of purses held securely. But this is not mere recognition of characters lodged in our own social memory; it is more deeply felt: it is acknowledgement of their open innocence and vulnerability. They are being type-cast; and the poetic relationship between the fallen leaves in the photographs and the aging process in these women is stunning. The heretical voice of Margaret Atwood could be the authentic voice of Raginsky as the photographer records the presence of *Mrs. Morton Going for a Walk*. "What is my mother's secret?" wrote Atwood:

For of course she must have one. No one can have a life so apparently cheerful, so seemingly lacking in avalanches and swamps, without also having a secret. By *secret* I mean the price she had to pay. What was the trade-off, what did she sign over to the Devil, for this limpid tranquility?[21]

As Frank Davey concludes in an analysis of Atwood's prose, the "price... is innocence, not knowing."[22] Similarly, in Raginsky's vision we sense that the price of her people's cheerful acceptance of a confined social space is an innocence that refuses to question, an innocence that refuses to be fully aware of the real limits within which they exist. We read a "limpid tranquility" in Mrs. Morton's facial expression, while the arching tree branches seem to trap her within a tightly-meshed pattern — as if the deserted park, its trees and its leaf-strewn path are metaphors of Mrs. Morton's confined life.

While Raginsky's women fulfil the anachronistic role of the "lady," her male subjects predominantly play the role of the clown. Robert Fothergill has identified many clown figures in Canadian films and asks, "Does [this]... blight on male characters... reflect a sense of limitation and inadequacy experienced half-consciously by Canadians in their real lives?"[23] *Clarence Adamson on His Way to Lunch, Victoria* (1975) shows a figure standing in front of a massive chain-link fence, territory from which the subject is excluded. There are signs of a marginal existence in his worn, dated clothing: a tight sweater, baggy pants and long coat-sleeves. Despite the title explaining that Adamson is "on his way to lunch," and despite his cheerful grin, the viewer can sense the subject's isolation from active social participation, his acceptance of self as a humorous figure drifting through public territory.

Raginsky has constructed a communal vision in this series, placing her subjects within a time-distanced scenario of a collective social memory. Yet the "limpid tranquility" that her subjects reflect is undermined continuously by the muted documentary record. The family-album titles deliver a happy account of the subjects' immersion in conventional social roles and rituals; but Raginsky's own stance vis-à-vis her subjects' confinement is a distanced one, as if her own experience has been severed from traditional social order. One senses the photographer's loss of cultural identification with her subjects, which recalls Gaile McGregor's analysis of the photographic references in Canadian literature as visual markers of a past the author has long outgrown, evoking a "guilt for neglect, for forgetfulness, maybe simply for growing up and away..."[24]

The Raginsky portraits exemplify a vision prevalent in Canadian documentary photography in the early- to mid-1970s. During that period the NFB Still Photography Division exhibited the work of several photographers who recorded distinct communities culturally removed from contemporary experience. (Other projects included Orest Semchishen's Byzantine churches and Gabor Szilasi's rural Quebec.[25])

Visions of a "fixed" society, enduring as a historical relic, also have been predominant in Canadian film. Piers Handling has offered a useful analysis of the effects of the realist heritage:

> While the realist heritage allows work to be rooted in an identifiable social context, it also has its disadvantages. In its faithful adherence to reality... it depicts social and political relationships as they are, not as they can be, and there is often something immutable about that reality.... Reality seems fixed within patterns that are beyond the power of the individual to influence.[26]

These documentary visions produced an "immutable" reality; but the photographer's role remained that of an observer — as if his or her own life, as social subject, were not implicated within the culture being photographed.

In Clara Gutsche's *Inner Landscapes* series, the realist heritage is extended to personal confrontation with consumer culture: the photographer, as social subject, enunciates a direct involvement within the culture she witnesses. This replaces the former practice, which left the viewer with the record of an immutable reality. Gutsche proceeds to engage the viewer's own subjecthood in a deliberate questioning of the image of woman in mainstream advertising.

Gutsche's *Inner Landscapes* is, in part, a documentary record of shop windows in Montréal during the period 1976-1978. Her titles name each store's owner, the exact address, and the year in which the negative was made. These data suggest a traditional documentary mapping process, specific to time and place; but through the photographer's repetition of signs of woman-as-object, the series becomes a personal mapping process as well.[27] We sense Gutsche's attraction to and repulsion by "the production of 'woman' as commodity."[28]

Surrounding each image with a wide black border, Gutsche transforms the documentary record into an imaginary journey past a series of sealed glass enclosures. The black frame, together with the vertical bars of window panels, conveys the sense of a fully sealed trap, often featuring the fragmented image of woman. As de Lauretis has written, "Radical difference cannot perhaps be represented except as an experiencing of borders."[29] Highly detailed contact prints heighten the sense of entrapment: knife-like edges of backdrop material and dark shadow areas distort the dimensions of the window space.

Gutsche also deflates the intended messages of advertising. In *Bain de Soleil, C. Vakis Pharmacy, 5001 Park Ave., Montréal* (PLATE 26), Gutsche destabilizes the meaning of *bain de soleil* by framing the model in such a way that she appears trapped behind bars. Several windows display dismembered mannequins, headless torsos and rows of female mannequin heads, all suggesting an unspoken text — an undercurrent of violence beneath advertising's reduction of woman to object. In *Mme Courval, Corsetière, 4491 St. Lawrence Blvd., Montréal* (1976), upper-body forms and legless torsos appear caught in a web of vines and underwater fern, suggesting the remnants of drowned women. In a statement accompanying the NFB exhibit *Windows*, Gutsche defined this work as a coming to terms "not only with the darker side of society, but with the darker side of myself."[30]

Gutsche disrupts other advertising messages by including in her photographs a view of the environment outside the shop window, reflected off the surface of the glass panel. Since the reflection reveals Gutsche's own location, outside the window enclosure, the viewer senses that the photographer is resisting "confinement in... symbolic space."[31] In *Latella Pharmacie, 6807 St. Lawrence Blvd., Montréal*, a reflection makes the image of celebrity Catherine Deneuve appear to be riding on the roof of a parked car. This destabilizes the conventional image of the movie-star woman as an object of male desire. By distorting an icon of consumer culture, Gutsche affirms her own subjecthood, refusing to accept the authority this image demands. As Richard Bolton has written (about advertising), "Our specific inner lives, denied a language, cease to exist."[32] By offering a reconstruction of consumer culture's representations, by altering intended meanings, Gutsche enunciates a silent voice of dissent.

Among Gutsche's images expressing an identity in opposition to the status quo, the strongest is found in her own intrusive self-portrait as a reflection in the window of *Kimon Caragianis, Architecte, 4113 St. Lawrence Blvd., Montréal* (PLATE 27). Vertical barriers, seen throughout the series, reappear; but in each glass panel a large "X" is marked, and the photographer can be seen in reflection within the central panel. This document serves to underline the photographer's refusal to enter symbolic territory in all the other window enclosures, her silent refusal to obey advertising's call to transform oneself into object. As de Lauretis has observed, "[O]nly by knowingly enacting and re-presenting [the signs of "woman" we confront in our daily experience] does a woman today become a subject."[33] Through Gutsche's reenactment of the experience of female subject in daily confrontation with iconic representations of woman, the viewer is urged to re-see advertising's images in the urban landscape and to question the "pleasure [that] comes from identification with objectification."[34]

The suggestion that "radical difference cannot be represented except as an experiencing of borders" might also be brought to a reading of Lynne Cohen's series of public interiors. During the mid-1970s Cohen moved from the documentation of private living spaces to a long investigation of public meeting halls and business offices. In the 1980s Cohen has been intruding into institutional space, suggesting the experience of an interloper crossing borders into structures of power.

By the term "interloper" I refer to the photographer physically present within the territorial boundaries of institutions, as if in the role of uninvited observer. It is as though Cohen were gathering hidden information. This recalls Walter Benjamin's remark that, "With Atget, photographs become standard evidence for political occurrences, and acquire a hidden political significance."[35] The evidence Cohen presents is not the result of her manipulation of the rooms' physical contents. Rather, as Cousineau has written, "Cohen allows the spaces she photographs to speak for themselves."[36]

In the *Environments Here and Now* exhibit at the National Gallery of Canada in 1985, Cohen used documentary titles identifying each institution's name, its city and country of origin, and the date of each print. This technique confirmed a "contact with the real,"[37] bringing the viewer into proximity with questionable social forces. Cohen abandoned such titles in the more recent monograph, *Occupied Territory*. A certain quality of disobedience, present in the *Environments* exhibit, is now diminished. The former appropriation of the actual names of institutions is replaced by the more neutral description of each room's function. Perhaps even more significant is that the national origin of each site no longer is given; Cohen now suggests that a single ideology occupies the territory of each interior she photographs.

Cohen's photography demonstrates a mastery of printing techniques, an ability to render the most minute detail. Such precise scrutiny, brought to the investigation of institutional space, suggests a parallel with the surveillance practices used in prisons, mental hospitals and department stores. A similarity to the aerial reconnaissance photograph also can be seen: Cohen's deletion of the human figure is similar to reconnaissance imagery in that it records only the structural environment, ignoring any human inhabitants.

Cohen's references to surveillance create what Julia Kristeva identified as a "permanent alternation" in oppositional cultural practices, "a double discourse that asserts and then questions power."[38] Cohen achieves this double discourse by documenting surveillance devices in use at several institutions: one-way windows, mirrors, dangling microphones, video and slide screens. Cohen's record contains evidence of a massive surveillance system throughout North American social territory — and evidence of her own counter-surveillance upon the power structure.

As Mark Poster has observed, "Implicit in surveillance systems is the criterion of the norm."[39] While Cohen's 1970s work drew attention to the rigid and often geometric patterns confining human movement, the 1980s documents bear witness to a growing system of mind control: training centres, psychology labs and security organizations are exposed as centres for the production of "normalized" social subjects. Police training schools, fitness facilities and therapy rooms all employ instruments for the measurement of human behaviour, implying a standard that Michel Foucault described as "the universal reign of the normative."[40] This vision of a rigid enforcement of normality also contains an unspoken text; and Cohen impresses upon the viewer an urgency to reexamine and reevaluate the seemingly benign, or "neutral," presence of surveillance techniques. The viewer senses a silent plea to join in a reconnaissance (or a new awareness) of the implementation of universal standardized normality.

Jean-François Lyotard has stated that recognizable images are often employed in order to "preserve various consciousnesses from doubt."[41] Cohen constructs a recognizable social structure, but this structure raises viewers' doubts about arbitrary standards of normality. While Raginsky's work suggests the recollection of loved ones lodged in our social memory, Cohen's photographs imply the loss of subjects in the here-and-now, perhaps also implying that the artist-as-social-subject occupies an increasingly threatened position.

Cohen's vision has been compared to the perverse one present in Diane Arbus's record of social victims. But there is a huge difference between the two at the level of viewer identification. As Susan Sontag writes, "Arbus's work does not invite viewers to identify with the pariahs and miserable-looking people she photographed."[42] Conversely, Cohen's images encourage viewers to place themselves within the "official realities"[43] of the public domain, even though she undermines their conventional meanings and our acceptance of their necessity.

A broad sampling of Cohen's work reveals an unspoken progression relating to the artist's physical intrusion into successively diminishing enclosures. The photographer's silent narrative expresses an "identity in negation"[44] to programs of human normalization. (This is similar to Gutsche's journey past still-life enclosures, which seemed to demand the photographer's entry into symbolic territory.) Cohen's progression begins with a distanced view of enormous spaces in meeting-halls and gymnasiums, such as *Party Room* (1975) and *Skating Rink* (1975). Compare these immense spaces to the claustrophobic entrapment seen in her 1983 therapy cubicles, such as *Therapy Room* and *Observation Room* (PLATE 28). Now Cohen's physical location, nearing the institution's very centre of absolute control, implies her own historical experience as social subject, under the domination of the "universal reign of the normative."

Implicit in Cohen's vision is a hidden victim, a subject judged deviant and under surveillance, a subject removed from the institution's representation of itself. There also is a strong premonition of eventual incarceration: stairwells, hallways, partially-opened doors — and the frequent appearance of a closed door that suggests a "final room" from which there is no exit. Jacqueline Fry has compared Cohen's rendering of the dread of impending incarceration to the "dead point" of Jean Baudrillard's *Les Stratégies fatales* and George Orwell's Room 101 in *1984*.[45] Cohen's silent text recalls Julia Kristeva's definition of women's practice as one that addresses "that which is not represented, that which is unspoken, that which is left out of namings and ideologies."[46]

Not only does Cohen illustrate the dread of an eventual closing-off of individual human autonomy; attention to the presence of clocks in institutions also delivers a dread of "time running out" toward an unspeakable, unthinkable conclusion. There is the suggestion of an "endgame" in images such as *Police School* or *Observation Room* (1983), in which the clock marks the precise moment of the photographer's experience on the borderline of absolute control. Yet we might also grasp this mark of time as a moment withheld from the room's ongoing function — a moment of revelation, seized from this functional world, questioning the inexorable permanence of such rooms. The viewer recognizes what has been re-presented for scrutiny: a silent warning, beyond language. "It [photography] is a prophecy in reverse: like Cassandra, but eyes fixed upon the past...."[47] writes Roland Barthes of the photograph's relentless witness to what has been. In this Cassandra prophecy, the near past remains our historical present and insinuates its future, its power and its legitimacy to define the limits of human autonomy.

Another frequent element in Cohen's recent work is the blackboard, often devoid of any intelligible information, sometimes bearing evidence of erasure. Where handwriting or hand-drawn diagrams do appear, the messages seem to have been written in haste, the diagrams alluding to symbolic markings depicting animal targets in prehistoric caves. Perhaps this parallel to cave paintings is most applicable if one considers Cohen's frequent recording of the human-figure-as-target in her documents of medical and security institutions. Now the human animal is the target, human difference the enemy.

Emergency Measures Auditorium (PLATE 29) is an image representative of Cohen's entire body of work. The stage-set construction, the depth of space, the rigid organization of objects, and the symmetry and consistency (which Kenneth Clark defined as qualities that act as "enemies of movement"[48]) all recall Cohen's meeting-halls of the 1970s. Cohen positions her camera within the borders of the large floor-map of Ontario, making herself a social subject under the all-seeing "eye" of surveillance devices. But in her direct framing of the two blackened windows and the clock occupying centre stage, we sense the photographer's critical gaze upon a recognizable construction of stability: order and control over social territory. Modern society, as Terry Eagleton writes, is " 'logocentric,' believing that its discourses can yield immediate access to the full truth and presence of things."⁴⁹ But Cohen's documents insist that modern society in fact obscures the truth — that this "age of information" in which we live involves the withholding of information by those in power.

"What I can name cannot really prick me. The incapacity to name is a good symptom of disturbance," wrote Barthes.⁵⁰ In Cohen's direct stare at a clock marking time in an image of conspicuous power we sense an unnamable disturbance, a deep foreboding. Cohen allows the room to "speak" in the *Emergency Measures Auditorium* image; but the room's appearance issues an altered meaning that transgresses the implied authority of its name.

Documentary photography has always carried with it the literal identification of social territory. But in the social records of these women photographers we begin to see the power to visualize that which is not named — that which is "left out of namings and ideologies." The capacity of the still photograph to exceed literal meanings has given women a silent, visual language with which to express personal visions of the social world.

1. *Occupied Territory*, ed. William A. Ewing (New York: Aperture Foundation, 1987) All photograph titles cited in reference to Lynne Cohen are published in the catalogue *Environments here and now: Three Contemporary Photographers, Lynne Cohen, Robert del Tredici, Karen Smiley* (Ottawa: National Gallery of Canada, 1985). Nina Raginsky's photographs may be seen in *artscanada* No. 192-195 (December 1974), pp. 34-36, and in *The Banff Purchase*, The Banff Centre (Toronto: John Wiley & Sons, 1979). Clara Gutsche's *Inner Landscapes* images, first seen in an exhibit at the Yajima/Galerie, Montréal, in January 1980, became a travelling exhibit, *Windows* (National Film Board Still Photography Division, 1980) and are retained in the collection of the Canadian Museum of Contemporary Photography, Ottawa.
2. Teresa de Lauretis, *Alice Doesn't: Feminism, Semiotics, Cinema* (Bloomington: Indiana University Press, 1984), p. 84.
3. Ibid., p. 35.
4. See Penny Cousineau's introduction to *The Banff Purchase*.
5. Seth Feldman, "The Silent Subject in English Canadian Film," in *Take Two: A Tribute to Film in Canada*, ed. Seth Feldman (Richmond Hill, Ontario: Irwin Publishing, 1984), p. 51.
6. See introduction by Martha Langford in *Contemporary Canadian Photography from the Collection of the National Film Board*, National Film Board of Canada (Edmonton: Hurtig Publishers, 1984), p. 9.

7. National Film Board of Canada, *Stones of History: Canada's Houses of Parliament* (Ottawa: National Film Board of Canada, 1967); *Canada/A year of the land* (Toronto: Copp Clark Pitman, 1967).

8. Geoffrey James, "Responding to Photographs: A Canadian Portfolio," *artscanada* No. 192-195 (December 1974), pp. 1-7.

9. National Film Board of Canada, *Call them Canadians* (Ottawa: Queen's Printer, 1968).

10. Kay Armatage, "About to Speak: The Woman's Voice in Patricia Gruben's *Sifted Evidence*," in *Take Two*, p. 301.

11. Poetry by Miriam Waddington, in *Call them Canadians*, p. 179.

12. Cousineau, *The Banff Purchase*.

13. "The Family Album," *Photo Communique*, 5,4 (Winter 1983-84), p. 20.

14. Cousineau, *The Banff Purchase*.

15. Ann Thomas, "Vahé Guzelimian, Stephen Livick, Scott MacEachern, Nina Raginsky," *artscanada*, No. 218-219 (February-March 1978), p. 68.

16. Cousineau, *The Banff Purchase*.

17. Annette Kuhn, *Women's Pictures, Feminism and Cinema* (London: Routledge & Kegan Paul, 1982), p. 11.

18. Julia Kristeva, quoted in de Lauretis, *Alice Doesn't*, p. 95.

19. See Susan Gubar, "'The Blank Page' and the Issues of Female Creativity," in *Writing and Sexual Difference*, ed. Elizabeth Abel (Chicago: University of Chicago Press, 1982), pp. 73-93.

20. James, p. 7.

21. Margaret Atwood, "Unearthing Suite" in *Bluebeard's Egg* (Toronto: McClelland and Stewart, 1983), p. 276.

22. Frank Davey, *Margaret Atwood: A Feminist Poetics* (Vancouver: Talonbooks, 1984), p. 152.

23. Robert Fothergill, "Coward, Bully or Clown: The Dream-Life of a Younger Brother," in *Canadian Film Reader*, ed. Seth Feldman and Joyce Nelson (Toronto: Peter Martin Associates, 1977), p. 242.

24. Gaile McGregor, *The Wacousta Syndrome: Explorations in the Canadian Landscape* (Toronto: University of Toronto Press, 1985), p. 345.

25. For Semchishen, see *The Banff Purchase*. For Szilasi, see *artscanada*, December 1974.

26. Piers Handling, "A Canadian Cronenberg," in *Take Two*, p. 82.

27. See Katherine Tweedie's introduction to the exhibition catalogue *Clara Gutsche: Inner Landscapes* (Montréal: Yajima/Galerie, 1980).

28. Sandy Flitterman and Judith Barry, cited by E. Ann Kaplan in *Women and Film: Both Sides of the Camera* (New York: Methuen, 1983), p. 33.

29. De Lauretis, p. 99.

30. *Windows*, National Film Board Still Photography Division, 1980.

31. De Lauretis, p. 139.

32. Richard Bolton, "territories of... advertising!" *Photo Communique* 9,1 (Spring 1987), p. 2.

33. De Lauretis, p. 186.

34. E. Ann Kaplan, p. 33.

35. Walter Benjamin, "The Work of Art in the Age of Mechanical Reproduction," in *Illuminations*, ed. Hannah Arendt, trans. Harry Zohn (Bungay, Suffolk: Richard Clay [The Chaucer Press], Fontana/Collins, 1973), p. 228.

36. Penny Cousineau, "Lynne Cohen: International Centre of Photography, March 22 – April 16," *artscanada* No. 222-223 (October-November 1978), p. 68.

37. Philip Monk, "Axes of difference," *Vanguard* 13,4 (May 1984), p. 11.

38. See Jessica Bradley and Diana Nemiroff, "Songs of Experience," in the exhibition catalogue *Songs of Experience* (Ottawa: National Gallery of Canada, 1986), p. 31.

39. Mark Poster, *Foucault, Marxism and History: Mode of Production versus Mode of Information* (Cambridge: Polity Press, 1984), p. 114.

40. Michel Foucault, cited by Mark Poster in *Foucault, Marxism and History*, p. 104.

41. Jean-François Lyotard, *The Postmodern Condition: A Report on Knowledge*, trans. Geoff Bennington and Brian Massumi (Minneapolis: University of Minnesota Press, 1984), p. 74.

42. Susan Sontag, *On Photography* (New York: Farrar, Straus and Giroux, 1977), p. 32.

43. Ibid., p. 55.

44. Monk, "Axes of difference," p. 14.

45. Jacqueline Fry, "Lynne Cohen: Un théâtre d'objets de plus en plus inquisiteurs," *Parachute 33*, December-January-February 1983-84, p. 11.

46. Julia Kristeva, cited by de Lauretis, *Alice Doesn't*, p. 95.

47. Roland Barthes, *Camera Lucida: Reflections on Photography*, trans. Richard Howard (New York: Hill and Wang, 1981), p. 87.

48. Kenneth Clark, *Civilisation: A Personal View* (London: British Broadcasting Corporation and John Murray, 1969), p. 293.

49. Terry Eagleton, *Literary Theory* (Minneapolis: University of Minnesota Press, 1983), p. 189.

50. Barthes, *Camera Lucida*, p. 51.

Ruptures in the Landscape of the Photograph

MONIKA GAGNON

[Imagine] the photograph in the form of a paradox — that which makes of an inert object a language and which transforms the unculture of a "mechanical" art into the most social of institutions.

ROLAND BARTHES

In 1974, Judy Dater photographed Imogen Cunningham, then ninety-one years old. In the photograph, Cunningham angles her own camera toward her subject Twinka, a demure nude model who stands beside a large tree.[1] Sixty years earlier a younger Cunningham had framed husband Roy Partridge in her twin-lens reflex camera in a similarly idyllic setting. Cunningham's bold attempts to invert the conventions of the female nude, figured in nature, are evident in a number of photographs featuring her husband's youthful, naked body gracefully posed amid the wild landscape that surrounded their home town of Seattle.[2]

On the other side of the Atlantic, sixty years before Cunningham photographed Roy Partridge, the acceptability of the photographic nude as an aesthetic form was debated by the Société Française de la Photographie, a discussion sparked by assertions that "the photographic nude, almost by definition, could not accede to the aesthetic."[3] The decorous refinements of the painter, which transformed the body from naked to nude, was a metamorphosis to which the camera could not aspire. The acute lack of mediation between model and photographic image was perceived as denuding the idealized figure of high art — the languorous, flawless nude of painting and sculpture was degraded by a problem of unsightly hairs, perhaps, or even distasteful "dirty feet."[4]

The scandal produced at the salon of 1865 by Édouard Manet's portrait of a nude prostitute in *Olympia*, however, confirms how the improprieties of the photographic nude that the Société had debated could not ontologically be posed as a problem inherent to any specific medium. As Abigail Solomon-Godeau underlines, the defiant posture and unflinching look of Manet's *Olympia* had an illicit, if then unspoken, counterpart in the pornographic photograph.[5] The extent to which the prostitute's image was already in circulation photographically throughout Second Empire France was, in part, why her portrayal in art historical traditions of painting (such as Titian's *Venus of Urbino*) proved to be so notorious. Although, socially, the courtesan was a suitable nude model for the artist, the prostitute was implicitly and morally out of bounds; as such, she threatened to corrupt the sanctified space of painting. *Olympia*'s reception underscored the discursive operations underlying representations of the woman's body, the constraining devices that not only provided representations but also constructed knowledge, making woman both knowable and manageable.

While *Olympia* made clear the tenuousness of the painted nude's inviolability, the photographic nude already was the subject of multiple discourses all vying for its interpretation: fine art (as *académies*), ethnography, medicine, erotica and pornography. Unlike painting, these categories were porous and the definitions shifty. The availability of nude studies was regulated by the École des Beaux-Arts to ensure their appropriate use by artists only, thereby acknowledging the potential for their misinterpretation. Pseudo-medical and pseudo-ethnographic treatises were coveted as pretexts for private delectation. As Solomon-Godeau writes, "The barriers between what is deemed licit and illicit, acceptably seductive or wantonly salacious, aesthetic or prurient, are never solid because contingent, never steadfast because they traffic with each other — are indeed dependent upon each other."[6]

Photography would later undertake the double movement away from the realm of corporeal, naked bodies to affirm the attributes of the *nude* as laid down by painting — with the partial sublimation of the erotic and through fetishization. The diverse manifestations of a "replete flawlessness" of the body as developed through photography — its supine positioning, the careful display of (manicured) genitals, the reassurance of stereotypes — all function to postpone the recognition of the reality of the woman's body, of her difference. The overdetermination of the woman's image allays the fear of difference in a way that can be likened to the movement of disavowal that is

[129]

characteristic of the fetishistic relation. Fantasy, in this instance, works to reassure the masculine subject, providing him with the illusion of woman as whole.[7] As Octave Mannoni has remarked, the "I know very well, *but...*" was considered by Freud to be exemplary of the separation of knowledge and belief. This "willing suspension of disbelief" is similarly accomplished in photographic representation itself, where the viewer knows that the photograph is only a *representation* of absence but, *nevertheless*, continues to believe in its reality.[8] Both the fetish and the representation stand in for precisely that which is (perceived to be) absent.

The poised torso in Geneviève Cadieux's *Nature morte aux arbres et au ballon* (PLATE 30) emerges from the later tradition of photographic nudes that duplicate the sublimated eroticism of classical painting. The nude model in Michael Snow's *Repeat Offender* (1986) and the kitsch illustrations from 1950s pulp-novel covers in Nina Levitt's *Conspiracy of Silence* (PLATE 31) are immediately recognizable as drawn from the visual stockpile of pornographic and illustrative images in popular culture. The Brazilian Indian women's painted faces and bodies in Jamelie Hassan's *vitrine 448* (PLATE 32), the Japanese women exercising and the dozens of confiscated cars parked in Vancouver's Hastings Park in Roy Arden's *Abjection* (PLATE 33) are identifiable as anthropological and historical documentation.

These works are linked by their interest in the different uses and histories of the photograph and, specifically, the discursive frames that culturally construct, explain and constrain the body — art, pornography, illustration, anthropology and documentary. But these photographs are also differentiated by the divergent and distinctive passages they are forced to undergo, from image *out there* (dispersed within Western culture), to image *in here* (for now, in art). Have we seen these images before? Something like them? The "'pre-photographic' stage in the photographic production of meaning" that Victor Burgin describes[9] effectively characterizes the dimension these artists' works not only acknowledge, but on which they ultimately pivot: that it doesn't matter if we've seen *these* photographs before, just that we know where they're coming from.

The many critical operations at work here — juxtaposition, seriality, cropping and other mediating strategies — are also pervaded by a simultaneous ambivalence, a detectable nostalgia for the photograph itself. Cadieux's poetic juxtaposition of art photographs reflects on their proper history, while Arden's minimal cropping and reframing gestures remain within a formalist aesthetic; Levitt revives a 1920s technique of photogramming, and Hassan herself wields the camera. Snow's choice of subject matter conjures up the intimacy of masturbation, stimulated and inspired by the image; here it is used up, passed on.

The title of Michael Snow's work, *Repeat Offender*, cleverly alludes to his tactics: the use of an eight-page nude-photo spread from *Penthouse*, itself entitled *Repeat Offender*.[10] Coyly acknowledging the camera as she pinches her nipple or leans back into masturbatory *jouissance*, eighteen-year-old Cami O'Connor unwittingly found her way into the pages of a "serious" photographic magazine. Selected from the easily available repertoire of soft porn, the images employ conventional poses, lighting, props and backdrops. Overlaid are the aesthetic codes of appropriation: the once colour images are reproduced in black and white, along with the accompanying captions, exactly reversed; the pages are gently turned back, producing reflective glimmers of light on their surfaces as if one were reading the magazine; traces of dust and dirt speckle the prints.

In spite of the evident handling of the images, the preordained codes of sexual titillation remain virtually uneffaced. Merely through recontextualization, *Repeat Offender* elicits a spiral of questions and problems: Can the stamp of the artist, the assurance of "artistic merit," circumvent the problems raised by the use of soft-core pornography?[11] How do we respond (indeed, how do we respond differently as women and men?) to nudes in the art magazine, in the pornographic magazine, or in the shameless hybrid, the technical photo magazine, such as *Photo* or *Zoom*? What differentiates *Penthouse*'s *Repeat Offender* from Snow's (*Photo Communique*'s) *Repeat Offender*?

The divisive tenets within feminism over the question of pornography ultimately recall radical differences in understanding representation itself. Like the debates within the Société Française de la Photographie, they reveal how the technologies of photography elicit a simplification equating reality with its image. The logical extension of this simplification asserts that pornographic images of women themselves produce social and physical violence against women, profoundly disavowing the complex and circuitous psychic,

[1 3 1]

social, economic and historical factors that make actual and symbolic violence possible.

Berkeley Kaite suggests that a kind of transgression is produced by the descriptive texts accompanying the nude photospread, a transgression that disputes any simple relation of subjugation and domination between male viewer and displayed female model. The model's speech (this voice as a caption that guides, affirms, supports the viewing of the image, the caption that almost no photograph will be without), Kaite says, "challenge[s] the privileged masculine position within sexual discourse by imposing sexual demands... [creating] instabilities around male sexual identity, performance and 'equipment'...."[12] In one sense, "Cami" is not a real woman, but a repository of programmatic appearances (the bedroom set, soft lighting, various sexual poses and clothing accoutrements) anchored by the simulation of an identity — a name, body and voice endowed with a threatening history. Her inviting postures and glances to the camera (the looks that frame the sequence), the anchoring of her image to the caption's citation of her name, likes and dislikes, produce a significant instability around her status as mere image, an agitation between reality and fantasy.

Both the conventions of pornographic imagery and the discursive structures of art photography are implicated in Snow's *Repeat Offender*, in an emphasis converging on the voiceless, glossy surface of the woman's nude body. Although the reversal of pages in Snow's work produces a minimal effect on the images, the legibility of the accompanying descriptive texts is dramatically reduced (if not rendered completely unreadable on some pages). The ushering of these pornographic nudes from *Penthouse* to *Photo Communique* is thereby marked not only by a reproduction from colour to black-and-white with evident traces of the artist's appropriating gestures, but also by the effacement of the nude model's pseudo-speech, an erasure of her demands. With a lack of decorum for the "serious" photographic magazine, *Repeat Offender* frames Cami's image within the structures of containment and idealization inherited from classical painting. Her absent voice bespeaks a fundamental distinction between the pornographic and the artistic nude; and the tension between real and fantastic, so essential to *Penthouse*, disintegrates under the strain of "artistic" nude photography's requirements: the objectifying, formalist reduction of the body to a virtual landscape, an aesthetic that would only barely withstand Cami's purring voice.

On the landscaped terrain of the Musée d'art contemporain de Montréal, a large Mediacom advertising lightbox encases a black-and-white photograph of a female nude and a second image of a dark sky covered with clouds. [13] Framed discursively within an art context — and quite literally by an advertising format — Geneviève Cadieux's *Nature morte aux arbres et au ballon* (1987) induces a layering of relations that are seemingly antagonistic: black-and-white "artistic" photographs are framed in an outdoor advertising lightbox; the controlled viewing environment of the "art" photograph is accorded an expanded visibility beyond the museum grounds; the advertising space promotes no product.

The photograph of sky and clouds induces a sense of reverie, while its location within the actual landscape alludes to the cultural investment placed in representations of nature. The woman's taut, elongated back is turned to the camera as she poises a large ball above her head and faces an expansive, sparsely clouded sky. (This was one of the less revealing nudes from a 1940s book entitled *Perfect Womanhood*, which originally carried a flyer stipulating its use "by art students only"!) *Nature morte aux arbres et au ballon*'s title draws the actual trees (and by extension, the natural environment) together with the woman's poised ball in the photograph, implicating both as part of a "still life," but simultaneously (and with perturbing appropriateness in this case), also as "dead nature." The relationship between photographic representation and death is evoked in the sense that the photograph "suppresses from its own appearance the primary marks of 'livingness,' and nevertheless conserves the convincing print of the object: a past presence." [14] The living trees and surrounding landscape are textually immobilized by the captioning operations of the title — *Nature morte* — but they continue to stir against the quietude of the sky, the ball, the body in the images. The model's own stillness inaugurates her transition from abject (naked) body to flawless illusion, from "life as inferior and feminine" to "art on the side of death and masculinity." [15]

The model's classical sculptural pose (a female Atlas, perhaps, as has been pointed out to me), conforms to the traditional syntax of the nude, while its placement recalls the repetitive currency of the woman's image in mass media's marketing of commodities. Cadieux's coupling of images suggests the complex cultural history that repeatedly figures the woman not only as an object promoting consumption, but also as an object to be consumed. Evoked as well is the figuration of the woman as nature: as natural landscape, as cultural receptacle for the representation of nature itself. Such "landscaping" is perceptible in Beaumont Newhall's *The History of Photography*, where Edward Weston's *Cloud, Mexico* (1926) is reproduced above the elongated, isolated torso of *Nude* (1925) in a remarkable congruity of forms and tones.[16] This is echoed in a photograph by Brassaï, where female bodies become curved mountains and cloud-filled skies, indistinct and interchangeable, depending on which way the image is viewed.[17]

The haunting effect created by reversed coloured photographs literally figures the subjects of Nina Levitt's *Conspiracy of Silence* (1987) as negative — an apposite metaphor for the homosexual's position within heterosexual culture and for cultural definitions of the woman's position vis-à-vis man. Verging on a parodic characterization of homophobic excess, *Conspiracy* underlines the predominant socio-cultural containing devices for female homosexuality in spite of the male's explicit exclusion (the frequency of the lesbian couple within pornography exemplifies the eroticization and mastery of feminine transgression as a spectacle presented for the masculine gaze).

In the recognizable melodramatic style of pulp novels, three of *Conspiracy*'s five enlarged book covers illustrate scenes after lovemaking. In *The Shadowy Sex*, a woman clutches herself beneath bedsheets while another, seated on the opposite side of the bed, adjusts her hair. Women dressed in lingerie smoke cigarettes while lounging about the bedroom, vices operating like cinematic codes of cheap or illicit sex (a brief afternoon encounter in a motel room?). In *We Walk Alone*, a woman donning a long backless dress embraces herself as she walks through a fiery orange smoke-filled landscape.

Texts abound on all the covers producing a disjunctive but coherent narrative across the five panels. The captions recount the perceived depravity of the books' contents with sensational defiance: "Desire and Torment," "a haunting and shocking story," "the love that can never be told." The spectre-like traces of photogrammed panties and camisoles produce a partial obscuring of the more copious texts on the two back covers. These photogrammed undergarments, functional rather than titillating selections, quietly

[1 3 4]

refuse the erotic allure attributed to these signs of feminine sexuality. Phantom-like, they disturb the skewed coherence of the insistent texts, splintering them into veiled (also illegible) fragments: "visiting motels with," "to the twisted de-," "become an incorrigible lesbian." The captions delineate the intolerance of the operative central term, "normal" heterosexuality, as the lesbian's transgressive sexuality is exigently cast beyond the realm of sanctified behaviour. She is represented as succumbing to animalistic impulses and is thus situated outside of "human" sexuality ("the savage novel of a lesbian on the loose!" or "a young girl's hunger for love made her *prey* [emphasis added] to tormented and forbidden passion"). But she is simultaneously belittled and explained by her "fear to love men" and thereby potentially reformable and recuperable as sexual object for male pleasure.

Conspiracy of Silence considers how power is written across the body of the lesbian by (an out of frame but omnipresent) masculinity and how such representations operate to naturalize male dominance within culture. Roy Arden's *Abjection* (1985) and Jamelie Hassan's *vitrine 448* (1987-1988) underline analogous operations of power across the image, exploring the construction and subjection of a different other in anthropological and historical photography. Arden's austere, melancholic series of appropriated archival photographs depicts British Columbia's internment of Japanese Canadians and the confiscation of their property during World War II; while *vitrine 448* creates a galaxy of relations revolving around Hassan's research of Claude Lévi-Strauss's fieldwork on Brazilian Indians during the 1930s. Both query the presumptions guiding objective photographic documentation, undermining in different ways the basic premises of alleged neutrality upheld by these representations.

While the concern for different histories is implicit in all the works engaged here — enacted by the very gesture of recirculating images from the past — *Abjection*'s explicit subject matter is a specific regional history: in February 1942, Canadian Prime Minister MacKenzie King, perceiving a threat to Canadian security, issued an order forbidding Japanese-Canadians and all persons of Japanese racial origin residing on the Pacific coast to possess automobiles. The confiscation of their property (also including cameras, radios, fishing boats and land) had been preceded in late 1941 by the registration of 23,428 British Columbian residents of Japanese descent, which anticipated their eventual internment in camps for the duration of the Second World War.

Abjection comprises ten photographs culled from the archives of Vancouver's public library. Each is coupled with an equal-sized panel of exposed photographic paper placed above each image. Exhibited as an ordered series, two flanking diptychs portray interned women performing group calisthenics. The eight remaining images centre on the surrender of automobiles by men in a large stadium surrounded by carousels and roller coasters, then "Happyland" in Vancouver's Hastings Park.

Like *Nature morte*, a nostalgia for the ideal photographic image pervades *Abjection*. The tonal clarity of the black-and-white fine silver print and the formal aspects of composition are persistently upheld, in clear contrast with the foregrounded disintegration of images in *Repeat Offender* or with the shared importance of photograph, format and text in *vitrine 448*. The absence of captioning seems to further underline the integrity of the image *in and of itself*. Thus, the allegorical potential of the series also seems restricted to a photographic reference to each photograph's pairing with the blackened photographic paper and the latter's allusion to the inevitable passage through time and history.

In a literal sense, it is very difficult to detect any sign of abjection within or across these photographs, except in the juxtaposition of sequestered women and cars, an implicit equation of women and property. There are photographs of women doing exercises; of the orderly parking arrangement and systematic classification of the vehicles within the stadium; and of notably well-dressed men walking in solitude from the park, with the Happyland playrides looming (not without irony) in the background.

The slight variations amongst the images belie any attempt to provide a "representative" photographic history or an enlarged thematic cross section of the Japanese internment.[18] As Ian Wallace has suggested, the abstract and representational components of the diptych give the work a "relentless declarative formality or formalism that overcomes the specificity of the images and their subject" (although I would take exception with his prefacing comment that this effect occurs only on "first viewing").[19] Wallace concludes that *Abjection* "convey[s] a multiple reading that moves from the literal to the indexical to the allegorical; one that shifts from its historical, social subject to the artistic (as in the formal organization of the photographic materials), to the expressive."[20] While acknowledging that these images do in fact retain a fragmentary reference to a particular moment in time, I would maintain that the *shift* between levels of meaning is less significant than the *tension* retained between the work's overt formalism and the partial history to which the photographs make reference. As Jean-Luc Godard might ask, why have *these* images been brought to light (by *The Province* newspaper, its anonymous photographer, and through Arden's re-circulation)? Consequently, what images have not made an appearance?[21] How do these images speak to a specific history of xenophobic government practices, a policy of incarceration and seizure of private property, indeed, of racially motivated abjection?

Abjection seems to suggest that any photographic reference can only purport to address a particular history in an oblique and inadequate way. The incongruity between *Abjection*'s title and the relatively innocuous images testifies to the capacity of photographic representation to effectively mask a troubled and ugly history. Not (an image of) incarceration, but healthy women doing exercises. Not (a document on the) confiscation of property, but orderly ticketing of cars in an amusement park. Manifestations of racism? But what balanced compositions they can have!

The blackened photographic paper further hints at photographs that did not happen, unspeakable images, impossible representations (as Barthes might propose, a little parlour game: what would a truly sexist or racist image be?). Insofar as this expulsion is unspeakable, Arden locates the abject racial other of his work, the Japanese, in a position analogous to one described by Julia Kristeva, as "...a burden both repellant and repelled, a deep well of memory that is unapproachable and intimate: the abject."[22] Following Kristeva, Burgin describes how, symbolically, women are "perpetually at the boundary, the borderline, the edge, the 'outer limit' — that place where order shades into chaos, light into darkness."[23] The racial other, too, symbolically occupies this space: "The abject is the means by which the subject is first impelled towards the possibility of constituting itself as such — in an act of revulsion, of expulsion of *that which can no longer be contained* [emphasis added]."[24] Thus again (unremarkably), a problem of boundaries, of territory, of assuring the dominance of an already determined term; in the name of *Canadian* national security, but more importantly, in the name of a white Canada.

Admittedly, a dangerous elision is made here between the specificity of sexual difference and racial difference and, within each, many more differences. Yet, there remain revealing similarities, a homogeneity in the conceptual subordination of one term in the binary relation, of the "outside" in opposition to the "inside," nature to culture, woman to man, non-white to white. The oriental and the woman as discursive categories are aligned in their alterity in Western representation, submissive and exotic certainly, but also evil handmaidens to subversion, chaos, disorder; in need of "correction," discipline and governing.

Abjection's attention to form conspires to camouflage the discipline and correction founded on racist paranoia; but in its excess it underlines the provocation to search beyond the surface of the developed photographs. The integrity of the anthropological photograph as a document of the real is challenged toward similar ends in Jamelie Hassan's *vitrine 448*, where Lévi-Strauss's ostensibly "objective" field research becomes entangled with subjective, disruptive narratives and ambiguous, double-exposed family and tourist snapshots.

Vitrine 448's format replicates Lévi-Strauss's system of classification in the anthropological archives of the Musée de l'homme in Paris. Vertical and horizontal lines sub-divide large filecards into three distinct sections, each holding specific information: geographical specifications, numerical classification, photographic documentation and additional descriptive notes. Across eighteen panels Hassan alternates direct appropriations of Lévi-Strauss's 1938 field research on the Nambikwara and Bororo Indians (specifically those filecards illustrating the unusual decorative "body" painting of the Caduveo) with a narrative reconstruction of her visits to and research in Paris.

Hassan's selection of Lévi-Strauss's filecards focusses on passages from his *Tristes Tropiques*, in which he described the relatively simple patterns and motifs of the Caduveo facial paintings: "elles font appel à des motifs relativement simples, tels que spirales, esses, croix, macles, grecques et volutes."[25] Seven frontal, head-and-shoulder photographs of women and girls accompany his texts. In the painted faces of the Caduveo he analyses patterns that can be found on the necks of pottery vases — a seemingly unremarkable elision that resounds in a later panel. The subjective travelogue style of texts on Hassan's panels describes her arrival in Paris and the beginnings of her research on Lévi-Strauss, while her first three photographs portray the Eiffel Tower and the Musée's exterior. The remaining images, all accidental double exposures, encompass both Paris and a family gathering at her home in London: a young boy playing in a garden with a water hose is superimposed by the Eiffel Tower; another boy is superimposed by the façade of the Musée; the smiling faces of two young girls are doubled eerily within the doorframe of the Musée, its name boldly identified above the entrance.

The effect of the superimpositions subtly collapses the separation between the narratives of Lévi-Strauss and those of Hassan, a parallel that is formally reinforced by the strict alternation of their respective panels. Nothwithstanding the feigned, precise organization of materials in *vitrine* (the standardized format, the obsessive attention to detailed classification, the clandestine nature of the numbering), Hassan's juxtaposition of panels subverts the authority of Lévi-Strauss's discourse, to speculate instead on the construction of his object of research: the Brazilian Indian. Three initially disparate subjects are slowly drawn into a disturbing communion: the Caduveo girls' and women's painted faces and bodies are highlighted as sites of a literal, permanent cultural inscription; their subjection as the object of Lévi-Strauss's research doubly articulates this cultural writing on their bodies; and Lévi-Strauss and the Caduveo both become objects of *vitrine*'s own reflection. The implication of the two narratives is further heightened by the direction that Hassan's texts begin to take. She develops a preoccupation with a collection of artifacts from Lévi-Strauss's field trip in Brazil in 1938: "the image of *vitrine 448* began to occupy my thoughts," she writes. "In Canada I realized that unconsciously I had carried back an almost photographic memory of *vitrine 448*."

Vitrine's final two panels reveal the object of Hassan's obsession: display window 448 at the Musée. The museum's official documentation describes it simply as "vitrine 448." Hassan's photograph admittedly has been taken illicitly: her accompanying text discloses that "a letter of introduction allowed me access to the archives, though not the right to photograph," while an earlier panel describes how Hassan was "told to leave the museum for attempting to photograph." Doubling this photograph is a shadowy silhouette that is hauntingly reminiscent of Lévi-Strauss's own documentation of girls and women, faces and bodies understood and analysed as mere surfaces for ornamental painting, not unlike the pottery vases contained within this glass tomb, numbered 448.

While Hassan and her camera were banished from the museum, Lévi-Strauss's access to his subjects was undoubtedly presumed by anthropological right — the photographs of Caduveo girls and women operating simply as illustrations of the facial and body tattoos. The seeming neutrality of this photographic activity is undermined, however, with the denial of photographic access to Hassan, which illustrates quite pointedly the way in which power is invested in the photograph. In an ironic regulation, the very institution that upholds the truth value of the neutral representation also controls and prohibits the production and dissemination of representations deemed inappropriate. The "amateur" is banned from photographing display case 448, but may acquire its official documentation on request.

This policing of representations, a ritualistic performance of power that here is implicitly (if unconsciously) played out, further suggests how the terms of the "reality effect" produced by documentary are dependent upon authentication through particular codes — an integrity that the institution (in this case the Musée) both constructs and protects. In this hierarchy of photographic products, the amateur's snapshot is devalued and removed, while the sanctified documentation of the Musée's collection by an official photographer reinforces the professional conduct and objectivity of the anthropologist. In this sense, neutrality and the representation of the "real" are not only authored (authenticated by professional codes of conduct), but are also founded on and guaranteed by this authority and the institutions that produce and uphold it.

As Arden's *Abjection* suggests, the veneer of objectivity may effectively mask, indeed override, the presence of troublesome histories. Anthropology effectively retreats into a fiction of the real, to absolve itself from "implication in historical situations and real, political contradictions,"[26] from "informing colonialist practice in every aspect from religious indoctrination to labour laws and the granting of basic political rights."[27] Johannes Fabian has characterized the idealized role of Lévi-Strauss's ethnographer as that of the medium, through whom anthropological data simply flow;[28] and it is against this alleged neutrality that Hassan's subjective descriptions and photographs may be understood as extolling themselves. An entangled imaginary space is produced by *vitrine*, where windows, frames and display cases exhibit children, painted women and artifacts. A virtual vertigo of images and texts is created as Lévi-Strauss's imposing trace becomes invasive: it structures Hassan's own data, preoccupies her thoughts and permeates her family photographs. In turn, Hassan's panels force the subjectivity of Lévi-Strauss's own work to become apparent, as his so-called neutral observations become equally pervaded by his trace. Being framed by the Musée de l'homme — hunted down, "discovered," classified, numbered, photographed, encased by Lévi-Strauss — becomes a threatening fantasy, a hallucination that resonates within every picture and every text.

Hassan's *vitrine 448*, as well as *Abjection*, *Conspiracy of Silence*, *Nature morte* and *Repeat Offender*, interrupt the submerged patterns of meaning that usher readings toward their assigned, virtually programmatic effects: documentation, illustration, aestheticization and titillation. The ensuing redirections evoke a space beyond the photograph, foregrounding the complex web of relations that underpin a reading of the image. The naturalization of certain social relations and their representational conventions are ruptured by destabilizing effects that transform the photograph from site of certainty to site of collusion. A layering of oblique affinities across these five works highlights structural parallels in the position of the photographer: photographer is to nude model as anthropologist is to native, documentary photographer to social outcast; in all instances, the act of subjugation is necessarily masked as purely aesthetic or objectively scientific and true.

When Cunningham attempted to invert the conventions of the female nude in photography, the heavy traffic surrounding the body of the woman blocked her attempts to photograph the object of her desire. "The awkwardness of this transposition," writes Solomon-Godeau, "its lack of persuasiveness, is not fundamentally to do with any aesthetic deficiency on Cunningham's part. The problem, rather, is to do with the non-reversibility of the convention that associates the body and image of the woman with nature."[29]

The landscaped nude typifies the idealized docility of the

woman. The photograph can effortlessly, aesthetically, erase history with cool frames, "objectively" camouflage violent gestures of mastery. In the pornographer's contorted, oiled and trimmed model a disturbing echo of history resounds; and ritualized inspection, not unchallenged, moves with silence into Art. Resounds again, as culture transforms into "nature," that which becomes this history.

The author thanks Mark Lewis for his critical readings and comments.

1. See Judy Dater's photograph *Imogen (Cunningham) and Twinka at Yosemite* (1974) in Jorge Lewinski, *The Naked and the Nude: A History of the Nude in Photographs, 1839 to the Present* (New York: Harmony Books, 1987), p. 160.

2. Imogen Cunningham's photograph *Roi on the Dipsea Trail 3* (1918) has been published in Lewinski, p. 204. Her photograph *Roi on the Dipsea Trail 4* has been published in Peter Weiermair, *The Hidden Image: Photographs of the Male Nude in the Nineteenth and Twentieth Centuries*, trans. Claus Nielander (Cambridge and London: The MIT Press, 1988), p. 76.

3. Abigail Solomon-Godeau, "The Legs of the Countess," *October*, 39 (Winter 1986), p. 98. This essay and Solomon-Godeau's *Sexual Difference: Both Sides of the Camera* (see note 25, below) have been important for the framework of my discussions here.

4. Solomon-Godeau, "Legs of the Countess," p. 98.

5. Ibid., p. 98. Also see Timothy J. Clark, "Preliminaries to a Possible Treatment of 'Olympia' in 1865," *Screen*, 21 (Spring 1980), pp. 18-41, and Peter Wollen's response, "Manet: Modernism and Avant-Garde," *Screen*, 21 (Summer 1980), pp. 15-25.

6. Solomon-Godeau, "Legs of the Countess," p. 104.

7. According to Freud, the woman's lack (or as some feminists have recast this formula, her lack of lack) raises the possibility of a radical sexual difference and consequently, for the male at least, the anxiety of (symbolic) castration. The complexities of this relation have been extensively discussed within feminist theory. See Jacqueline Rose, *Sexuality in the Field of Vision* (London: Verso, 1986), and Mary Kelly, *Post-Partum Document* (London: Routledge and Kegan Paul, 1983). Specifically in Sigmund Freud, see "Some Psychical Consequences of the Anatomical Distinction between the Sexes," in Sigmund Freud, *On Sexuality*, trans. Angela Richards (Harmondsworth: Penguin Books, 1977), pp. 323-343.

8. See Christian Metz, "Photography and Fetish," *October*, 34 (Fall 1985), p. 88.

9. Victor Burgin, "Photographic Practice and Art Theory," in *Thinking Photography*, ed. Victor Burgin (London: Macmillan Press, 1982), p. 47.

10. *Photo Communique*, 8,3 (Fall 1986): 22-29.

11. See "Exchange," *Photo Communique*, 8,4 (Winter 1986-1987), p. 2.

12. Berkeley Kaite, "The Pornographic Body Double: Transgression Is the Law," in *Body Invaders: Panic Sex in America*, eds. Arthur and Marilouise Kroker (Montréal: New World Perspectives, 1987), pp. 150, 152.

13. In the group exhibition *Elementa Naturae*, curated by Michiko Yajima for the Musée d'art contemporain de Montréal, 1987.

14. Metz, p. 85. Metz also proposes that "photography is linked with death in many *different ways*" (ibid., p. 84), of which the quote demonstrates but one relation.

15. Andreas Huyssen, "Mass Culture as Woman," in *After the Great Divide: Modernism, Mass Culture, Postmodernism* (Bloomington and Indianapolis: Indiana University Press, 1986), p. 54.

16. Beaumont Newhall, *The History of Photography*, 4th ed. (New York: The Museum of Modern Art, 1964), p. 125.

17. Brassaï's photograph was published in André Breton, "La beauté sera convulsive," *Minotaure* (December 1934). It also was published to illustrate an essay by Mary Ann Caws, "Ladies Shot and Painted: Female Embodiment in Surrealist Art," in *The Female Body in Western Culture: Contemporary Perspectives*, ed. Susan Rubin Suleiman (Cambridge and London: Harvard University Press, 1985), p. 277.

18. Of the dozens of available photographs surrounding the Japanese internment, including those showing postings of internment notices; makeshift dormitories in city-owned stables, cafeterias, and government offices etc., Arden limited his selection to photographs of women exercising in holding camps and of the confiscation of vehicles at Hastings Park.

19. Ian Wallace, "Image and Alter Image II: Roy Arden," *Vanguard*, 16, 1 (February-March, 1987), p. 26.

20. Ibid.

21. Jean-Luc Godard's question occurs in his and Anne-Marie Miéville's video *Tour/détour/France/deux/enfants* (1978). A similar interrogation of the photograph occurs in Godard's earlier *Letter to Jane* (1969).

22. Julia Kristeva, *Powers of Horror: An Essay on Abjection*, trans. Leon S. Roudiez (New York: Columbia University Press, 1982), p. 6.

23. Victor Burgin, "Geometry and Abjection," in *Public*, 1 (Winter 1988), p. 25.

24. Ibid., pp. 24-25.

25. All excerpts from Levi-Strauss's *Tristes Tropiques* and Hassan's own texts are quoted from *vitrine 448*.

26. Johannes Fabian, *Time and the Other: How Anthropology Makes Its Object* (New York: Columbia University Press, 1983), p. 67.

27. Ibid., p. 63.

28. Ibid., p. 66.

29. Abigail Solomon-Godeau, in the exhibition catalogue for *Sexual Difference: Both Sides of the Camera* (New York: Miriam and Ira D. Wallach Art Gallery, 1988), p. 2.

[143]

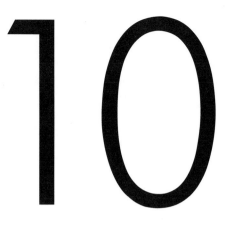

At the Epicentre

GAIL FISHER-TAYLOR

The women's movement changed my life in many ways, not the least being my approach to criticism.... There is a new freedom to say how I feel, and to respond to all art on a far more personal level. I'm more willing to be confessional, vulnerable, autobiographical, even embarrassing, if that seems called for.[1]

LUCY LIPPARD
From the Center: Feminist Essays on Women's Art

Not long ago I began to excavate my psyche for memories of childhood experiences I suspected were at the epicentre of a lifelong earthquake of feeling. What I have unearthed is a complex of psychic constructions which protected and isolated me from terrifying memories of my childhood. Recalling certain events and connecting them to the rest of my life, I've been fascinated by how my psyche has created intricate structures to prevent those traumas from overwhelming me. I now see that my interest in all kinds of external formations and transformations around experience and feeling has been an extension of an important internal process.

What strange fruit can be produced by an intellectual construct that disguises the truth and how easily it can confuse even its highly gifted creator....[2]

Photographs, of course, are also constructions. Victor Burgin describes how,

in the very moment of their being perceived, objects are *placed* within an intelligible system of relationships.... They take their position...within an *ideology*. By ideology we mean, in its broadest sense, a complex of propositions about the natural and social world which would be generally accepted in a given society as describing the actual, indeed necessary, nature of the world and its events. An ideology is the sum of taken-for-granted realities of everyday life; the pre-given determinations of individual consciousness; the common frame of reference for the projection of individual actions. Ideology takes an infinite variety of forms; what is essential about it is that it is contingent and that *within it the fact of its contingency is suppressed.*[3]

In other words, we usually are not aware of how our perceptions are affected by the particular environment of ideas in which we live. This is how a photograph is so often mistaken for factual reality rather than understood as an interpretation or representation determined by, among other factors, the photographer's extractions of subject matter out of time and space, the posing of subjects and the placement of objects in relation to one another through camera angle and optics — all of which are unconsciously (and possibly, to an extent, consciously) affected by the photographer's personal ideology, which in turn is interactive with the ideology of his or her culture. Photography is a visual language; and when language comes into play, so of course does ideology, which restricts meaning. In the words of Rozsika Parker and Griselda Pollock, "Language embodies symbolically the laws, relations and divisions of a particular culture.... It also controls what can be said, or even thought, and by whom."[4] In cultures where a photograph has never before been seen, anyone who is presented with a photo of himself or herself will not know what it is nor how to comprehend it without instruction.

■

Because psychic structure must always be passed from generation to generation through the narrow funnel of childhood, a society's child-rearing practices are not just one item in a list of cultural traits. They are the very condition for the transmission and development of all other cultural elements....Specific childhood experiences must occur to sustain specific cultural traits, and once these experiences no longer occur the trait disappears.[5]

LLOYD DEMAUSE

While psychoanalysts, psychologists and psychiatrists have long acknowledged the connection between early childhood experience and individual emotional health, it is much more recent that psychohistorians like Lloyd deMause have begun to look at the cultural ramifications of what happens in childhood. Child rearing is an ideological practice, one which, according to deMause, is the primary determinant in culture and history. If he is correct, then child-rearing practices must ultimately have a significant impact on visual representation.

A very direct example of this is presented in a recent article by photographer and historian Barbara Norfleet, in which she discusses family photographs made in two generations with very different child-rearing practices. She compares similar photographs, one from the Paul Gittings Studio from 1930 and the other from the Lucien Brown Studio from the 1950s, and quotes child-rearing manuals from the two eras.[6]

In the 1920s and 1930s, John B. Watson's *Psychological Care of Infant and Child* was the most popular child-rearing guide. This was Watson's advice to the mother:

Treat them as though they were young adults... Never hug and kiss them, never let them sit in your lap. If you must, kiss them once on the forehead when they say good night. Shake hands with them in the morning.[7]

Benjamin Spock counselled mothers quite differently a generation later:

For his spirit to grow normally he needs someone to dote on him, to think he's the most wonderful baby in the world, to make noises and baby talk at him, to hug and smile at him, to keep him company during wakeful periods.[8]

Norfleet finds stiffness and reserve in the 1930s family photographs from the Gittings Studio and connects this to the child-rearing approaches of "experts" like Paul B. Watson. She contrasts this with the intimacy in the 1950s Lucien Brown Studio photos, which seem to be influenced by a generation of baby-raising according to Benjamin Spock. Norfleet's interest is not only in how "a society's attitudes and images reflect and influence each other," but also how "child rearing practices of two generations are reflected in photographs of their times."[9]

My own interpretation is slightly different, since I question that actual child-rearing practice behind closed doors and in the privacy of the home is the same as the *image* of child rearing presented to the camera and the photographer. In their own eras Watson and Spock presented what came to be accepted as *ideals* of child rearing; and the camera recorded the *representation* of what people wanted to be, not necessarily what they were.

Psychoanalyst Alice Miller, writing in more recent times, suggests an image of contemporary parent/child relations that does not appear in homey picture frames hung on living room walls or propped on desks or mantelpieces: "The former practice of physically maiming, exploiting, and abusing children seems to have been gradually replaced in modern times by a form of mental cruelty that is masked by the honorific term *child-rearing*."[10] Miller explains how important it is for children's "emotions, sensations and their expression from the first day onward" to be "regarded and respected," but that

parents who did not experience this climate as children are themselves…deprived; throughout their lives they are looking for what their own parents could not give them at the correct time — the presence of a person who is completely aware of them and takes them seriously, who admires and follows them.[11]

Miller talks about adults projecting unresolved childhood experience onto their own children. DeMause asks "how each generation of parents and children creates those issues which are later acted out in the arena of public life."[12] Another question to ask is how these issues emanating out of childhood interact with ideology and, more particularly, with art making and art viewing.

As viewers or as image makers, we are enmeshed in an enveloping web of interactive personal and cultural experience. It imposes on us and determines who we are, what we know and what we see, affecting all interpretation.

■

The man's power is active, progressive and defensive. He is eminently the doer, the creator, the discoverer. His intellect is for invention and speculation. But the woman's intellect is not for invention or creation but sweet ordering, arrangement and decision. Her great function is praise.[13]

JOHN RUSKIN

No matter how we respond to Ruskin's 1905 statement, our reactions are influenced by over eighty years of evolving and changing ideology and informed by twenty-five years of recent feminist analysis. Ruskin's patriarchal attitudes are still very much with us; yet if someone were to make such a statement today, we would think of him or her as an eccentric, someone not in sync with the ideas (or ideology) of the times. In some ways it is easier to identify and dissect (deconstruct) an ideology if we are disengaged from it either by time or by place; our identification is by difference. But even then there is the possibility that someone else will be able to point out how the limitations of our own ideology have restricted our analysis of another time or place. The problem becomes even more difficult if we are trying to analyse something within our own culture.

Why do we try? The answer probably goes back to a process that begins at conception: to strive for some kind of equilibrium.

■

[1 4 8]

I have before me slides, reviews and recollections of the work of two women: Suzy Lake and Susan McEachern. I sat with each of them individually, discussing their work. My responses to and ideas about their imagery have been enhanced by what each had to say.

I have chosen to discuss the artwork produced by these particular women for a number of reasons: each has consciously constructed imagery around issues that extend from the personal to a broader feminist and social context; yet the rationality of the work does not supersede the more expressive, intuitive elements. Instead there is a tension and an edge between the rational and the intuitive, one that in my opinion prevents the work from becoming didactic and boring. Although some of the issues and concerns in Lake's and McEachern's imagery are the same or similar, the appearance of the work of each is radically different and (to paraphrase Victor Burgin) stimulates, awakens and reactivates aspects of my own "dormant knowledge" that merit examination. [14]

Lake and McEachern occupy a similar social stratum and function within a particular subculture. They are white, middle-class women who have been recognized by the established systems (galleries, magazines, arts councils) as artists. Both have received education in the arts and are aware of historical and contemporary art production, criticism and theory. Each acknowledges the influence of the women's movement on her life. I think it is accurate to say that their relationships with the dominant ideology, including its power structures, involve many questions. They are both challenging in some way what Parker and Pollock call the underlying values, assumptions, silences, prejudices. [15]

Suzy Lake's large photographic works, produced since the early 1970s, have been variations on a theme: control and lack of control, power and powerlessness, voice and voicelessness. In *Transformation Series* she used herself as a photographic subject, giving up her identity to others; in *Choreographed Puppets* she forced herself into submission to those who pulled on marionette strings attached to her limbs; and in *Authority is an attribute...* she has symbolically represented herself as a delicate vase of flowers tenuously positioned beneath the impending crash of a heavy sledgehammer. Why does she do these things?

Lake's work consistently has had an interesting effect on me. I go to the gallery, see her installation of photographs, and react with a certain reserve and perhaps some puzzlement. Then months later I catch myself thinking about the work, reacting emotionally to the image I carry in my head, recognizing the ominous undertones that initially I didn't want to acknowledge but on a subconscious level stayed with me. The work becomes familiar, and in a sense I possess it through the meaning I have attached to it.

In *Transformation Series* she uses large photographs of herself, gradually and sequentially replacing her own features with those of someone else until there is very little of the original Suzy Lake still there. There are two rows of photographs. In the top row each photo is a step in her metamorphosis into another person. In the bottom row are photographs of the face whose features she is gradually taking on. The features Lake has assumed in each upper photo are scratched out with pencil from the corresponding photo below. Is this a clever game? An annihilation of self? Should I be amused? Or alarmed?

The early 1970s (when Suzy Lake first did this *Transformation Series*) was really an extension of the 1960s, a time of political and social unrest and personal reevaluation. The late sixties and early seventies were the years in which young people were "trying to find themselves" and "searching for their identity." But why was that? When were they lost and where did their identities go? If, according to Alice Miller, there is a common, continuing cycle, a cultural phenomenon, of parents subverting their children's needs, feelings and wills, then of course as adults they/we are significantly affected by that crucial loss in themselves/ourselves. The message that most of us received as children was that any feelings our parents did not like were wrong, must not be expressed and therefore were better not felt.

So the process that Lake symbolically portrays in *Transformation Series*, that of gradually becoming someone other than her original self, is a childhood process that is common to almost all of us. For her metamorphoses, however, Lake has selected people who have been positive influences, perhaps people she wouldn't mind becoming. In a way she turns the childhood process around. But even though these are people she might like to be, she still almost disappears; and the amount of herself that she gives up is extreme. The idea of wanting to be someone other than who we are is a widespread phenomenon, one heavily exploited by advertising and other media. Lake's *Transformation Series* confronts us with the visualization of "losing face" and becoming an idealized other — or, to put it differently, the work compensates for loss with fantasy and hope.

Choreographed Puppets is a body of work that is part of what Lake calls her *ImPosition Series*, in which she set up situations and conditions which are impositions upon herself. Lake's finely tuned sense of staging and theatricality, rooted in performance art and video production, is particularly evident in these images. The groups of still photographs are essentially documents of private performances she set up for the camera. But these still photographs present quite a different effect than they would have as video or live performance. Movement in the photographs is implied, not experienced, leaving the viewer to decipher in her or his imagination what the experience of the performance might have been like — how it might have sounded and felt. And it is up to the viewer to determine the length of time each photograph is viewed; therefore she or he has a certain power over the narrative that also comes with the ability to alter the order of its components.

In *Choreographed Puppets* the stage is a utilitarian wooden structure with white seamless paper covering the rear wall and floor. In front of that whiteness hangs a human marionette: Lake has attached straps to each of her arms and legs, which are pulled and controlled by two faceless, androgynous figures who lie prone on top of the structure. The camera shutter is opened at regular, predetermined intervals, allowing for no artistic intervention by the person activating it. Slow enough to blur movement, the shutter speed accentuates Lake's slightness, making her look ephemeral within the haze of her motions, emphasizing her helplessness and submission to the manipulation of the puppeteers.

If one considers what a marionette actually is, then the extremes of Suzy Lake's symbolic representation become more obvious. A marionette is not alive; it is only a representation of a human being, often a caricature; it has no voice or movement without a puppeteer, who has total control over not only how it moves and speaks but *whether or not* it moves and speaks and the content of what it says. The marionette's voice is not its own but is that of its puppeteer. A toy to be used for amusement, it is not to be taken seriously and often is an object of ridicule and laughter. If anyone talks to a marionette, it is not usually for communication but instead as part of a performance for an audience. And when the performance is over the marionette is put away and deserted.

> The little one's displays of temper as indicated by screaming or crying without cause should be regarded as the first test of your spiritual and pedagogical principles…. [You should proceed] by quickly diverting its attention, by stern words, threatening gestures… [or] by appropriately mild corporal admonitions repeated persistently at brief intervals…. This procedure will be necessary only once or at most twice, and then you will be *master* of the child *forever*. [16]

These words were written in 1858 by Dr. Daniel Gottlieb Moritz Schreber, author of a series of child-rearing books and father of a famous paranoid patient studied by Freud. Though the language is quite dated, the principle that the child should behave according to his or her (or as Schreber says, "its") parents' wishes is still alive and well. The child as marionette is probably more often than not an appropriate metaphor in the 1980s. But this is my interpretation, not necessarily Lake's. It is, however, one of her intentions to create work that can be actively experienced rather than just passively observed. In order for the work to function in this way, the viewer must have prior experience to fuel an emotional response. My contention is that most of us have, in childhood.

While *Choreographed Puppets* can metaphorically represent the position of woman in patriarchal society or the plight of the individual in the face of the modern industrial complex, I find that the work stimulates a more visceral response, one related more to the overwhelming helplessness and dependency of childhood. *Choreographed Puppets* seems to tap at the root of a feeling that originates early in life within the family but is then extended and projected into and onto the world at large.

Are you talking to me? (PLATE 34) is the most recent body of work in the *ImPosition Series*. An installation of eighty-three poster-sized self-portraits were hung so that all mouths were aligned. When Lake began this series she sat in front of the camera and photographed herself talking about things that were "delicate or difficult to handle, to see what that looked like when there was an internal struggle."[17]

In order to reconstruct that experience, Lake photographed it a number of times. To distort some of the images she heated and stretched the negatives before making black-and-white prints. She also bleached out areas of her face in selected prints and then, using traditional oil glazes, carefully rendered those areas in colour. The final part of the process was rephotographing the painted photos in colour.

In *Are you talking to me?* Suzy Lake has constructed a silent monologue, isolating and containing it within the photographic frame, each image a representation of an instant in an emotional continuum. It is like seeing a film with missing frames, and we are left to guess what lies in the spaces between. The other crucial space is the one between us and the work, which operates as a safety zone, enabling us, to an extent, to control our involvement. But in the original installation at the Sable Castelli Gallery in Toronto, the small exhibition space offered only limited relief: Suzy Lake's face was everywhere — expressive, distorted and, in the stretched negatives, contorted. The areas of colour on her face intensify the image, somehow making us more aware of the human being within the representation. Operating like a piece of real flesh in a black-and-white photograph, the colour pulls us closer, sucks us in. But it fades softly into the black and white like an emotional state.

It is difficult to know what is going on here, what has happened, what is being said. Crucial information is missing. As viewers we are on uncertain ground.

Her mouth changes shape, but within the photograph Lake is mute. Her eyes open and close, look at us and then up, like a small child looking at a parent. No matter how hard we try we cannot understand anything other than her vulnerability, distress and anxiety. We cannot hear, and she cannot be heard.

In *Authority is an attribute...* (PLATE 35) Suzy Lake filled the Sable Castelli Gallery with almost life-size photographs of individuals who stood looking intimidatingly at the viewer through

[152]

binoculars. Hand-written text-book definitions and descriptions of authority, power, law and order, social stratification, parent/child relationships, corporate strategy and gamesmanship appeared in the distorted shadow of each subject. Centrally located was a very sensitively rendered watercolour of a fragile-looking vase of flowers with a sledgehammer (drawn in heavier, more graphic oil pastels) being swung at the vase. Flanking each side of the flowers were the only two individuals holding binoculars, rather than looking through them; instead they stared hostilely at the viewer. On the wall opposite the flowers was a slightly bent but larger-scale figure called "The Accuser," who through binoculars scrutinized the flowers and whose shadow text spoke of personal responsibility.

The seeming neutrality of the texts is called into question by the threatening poses of the people who carry the words in their shadows. The way language operates as an authority and as an ideological tool becomes immediately apparent. The words in the images are constructs within a construct, which is similar to the way language operates within ideology.

Like most of Lake's work this installation provokes an uneasiness, a discomfort, an edge of anxiety in the viewer. Clothed in the dress of authority, identities hidden behind binoculars, these figures have the advantage. The viewer is forced into the position of identifying with the extremely vulnerable vase of flowers (which also represents Lake), with the impending doom of the sledgehammer forever suspended in time. We imagine what will happen, but it never does; we are left hanging with our own awful anticipation, once again powerless as young children.

■

Waking up to the cruelty inflicted in childhood comes as a shock to anyone who no longer refuses to see the power imbalance between parents and child.

Only in the intrapsychic world of the individual does the past go on running its unwavering course and keep on being enacted anew in his or her present surroundings. [18]

ALICE MILLER

In most of Suzy Lake's work she is her own victim. Because she is the one who manoeuvres herself into this position, she also is her own victimizer. So she simultaneously is in control and out of control, powerful and powerless. Through this process she encapsulates the psychic struggle we all experience between the child inside ourselves and the parents we internalize.

∎

In the language of patriarchal society women often are equated with children (e.g. "women and children" is a familiar conjunction while "men and children" is not), which both reflects and maintains the actual position of women in society. Traditionally women have not broken out of the powerless position of childhood — except in relation to their own children. In many ways neither have men — except in relation to women and children.

Susan McEachern cites feminist issues, women's experience and women's work as significant influences on her own work.[19] She also draws from a pool of ambivalence: while McEachern respects and enjoys certain traditionally "feminine" occupations centred on home and family, she also feels the entrapment of domestic endeavours. The labour involved is rarely acknowledged, and "women's work" is part of the ideology that renders women powerless in the outside world. In striving to find "how we are located in terms of gender — in family and in history," McEachern includes her own experience. This empowers the work and, I would guess, it also empowers her.

Although McEachern's work is constructed, each individual photograph is not. Instead, the construction of meaning in her work relies upon the accumulation of ideas through the sequencing of photographs, most often in combination with extracted texts.

Photographs of the Preparation of Food (1981) is a body of work without text, a grid of four rows of images that follow the transformation of food from its unaltered state in the top row, to preparation and consumption, respectively, in the next two rows, to dirty dishes in the bottom row. McEachern spent a summer with her camera in the kitchen, visually recording all of the work each meal demanded — in a sense, giving herself the missing recognition for a job well done. But she talked to me about feeling "caught between caring a lot about how this everyday task was done and feeling trapped by what it meant to the division of labour in the home." By pointing her camera at this common, everyday activity and the personal and political implications that surround it, she is also pointing her finger at herself, her questions and her ambivalence.

A critical voice always intercepts her full enjoyment of the activity. The questions remain unanswered, the ambivalence does not go away.

■

The Hope Chest, as a material symbol of women as property and exchange in the kinship structure, collapses practices of patriarchy and capitalism into one. Research by socialist feminists has underlined that, for much of women's history, marriage was the only source of employment. This led, as McEachern's samplers point out, to a "feeling of domination in the home for women" and a "social role... of passivity and domesticity."[20]

WILMA NEEDHAM

The samplers to which Wilma Needham refers are part of a piece by Susan McEachern called *The Hope Chest*, in which she photographed a chest and its intended contents: handicrafts made and gathered by women for use in a future, hoped-for marriage. Accompanying the images is text from William Fielding's *Strange Customs of Courtship and Marriage*, in which he explains that the idea of the hope chest is derived from the original practice of giving a dowry along with the bride in exchange for money (the bride-price). The text offers a perspective from which to view the photographs: it tells the viewer that the romantic light in which these hand-crafted objects have been cast should not be accepted without question. In conversation McEachern talked about the women's handicrafts that hope chests used to contain: "There is a preciousness about this history — yet it represents something I disagree with.... Yes, I celebrate these things, but with a certain amount of resignation and pain. I don't spend my life making doilies, but I don't condemn those who did." One of McEachern's images is of embroidery which, according to Needham, was used by Victorian novelists as a symbol representing the oppression of women. So, in *The Hope Chest*, as in *Photographs of the Preparation of Food*, respect for women's caring labours is accompanied by the contradictory realization of how those same occupations have helped to maintain patriarchal society.

The Family in the Context of Childrearing looks at three contemporary forms of the family: a traditional nuclear family with two parents and their children; a single mother and her child; and a family living in a communal situation. A grid of almost 150 colour photographs shows the everyday activities of child rearing in these three homes — feeding, bathing, dressing, playing, helping with homework, etc. Separated from the photographs are excerpts from sociological, psychological, feminist and popular culture texts, also presented in a grid, along with details of McEachern's own family history.

The photographs seem focussed on the activities of child rearing rather than on the relationships between parents and children. Although there are clues to the nature of these relationships, we cannot hear what is being said and do not know what has and does occur in the crucial spaces between the photographs. In a sense this leaves us in a position similar to the one we occupy when viewing Suzy Lake's *Are you talking to me?* Crucial information is missing, and as viewers we are left on the uncertain ground between what has happened and what is being represented. This is always, in a way, the position of the viewer in relation to documentary photography, where the contingency, as in ideology, is suppressed.[21] In *The Family in the Context of Childrearing* the photographs of familiar activities and situations woo us into the belief we are viewing the "reality" of these people's lives. But of course what we see is only what these people are willing to demonstrate in front of the camera and what the photographer has edited and sequenced for our viewing.

The Family in the Context of Childrearing is not about relationships; instead, the work is a construction which examines the structures of family, child rearing, women's position and domestic occupation. The personal history that McEachern reveals is also about structure: how her grandparents were the first generation in her family to choose marriage partners out of love; how her parents were the first generation to move far from home; how the average number of children has diminished with each new generation. While the texts include a history of changing ideas surrounding family structures, the photographs seem to point more to the overall similarities of the daily routines than to the subtle differences of the three situations in which they are performed.[22]

The structures around child rearing that Susan McEachern is exploring function in the same way as the structures surrounding language: they both determine and are determined by the practice they surround. The structures interact with the practice, and they operate both to facilitate and to trap.

On Living at Home is McEachern's most recent work, and her most complex in terms of the variety of issues she addresses. Once again this work is a combination of text and image; but for the first time the voices of authority (the quoted texts) are graphically integrated into the images, which are either from popular culture (books, magazines and television) or are carefully considered large-format colour photographs of details around McEachern's home. The light, composition and clarity of detail relay to the viewer a sense of comfort, security and caring, which is immediately interrupted by the critical voices of the texts.

On Living at Home, like other bodies of work by Susan McEachern, is in four parts, each addressing aspects of the "ideology of the domestic sphere." Part 1 opens with an illustration extracted from the popular culture of a time past: Mom and the kids watch a blindfolded Dad trying to pin the tail on the donkey (PLATE 36). The accompanying quotation is from Rosalind Coward: "The ideology of the domestic sphere and the love of a good woman allowed people to treat their homes as if the economic world did not exist and as if individuals were not implicated in the injustices of the world." McEachern calls this quote "the starting point for the project."

The rest of Part 1 includes four photographs from McEachern's home and three images extracted from fairy tales. The quotations on the photos are from psychological texts and discuss aspects of agoraphobia, the fear of open or public spaces or, as McEachern calls it, "an extreme form of identification with the domestic location." The illustrations are taken from fairy tales in which the woman is in some way a prisoner: Snow White who, for fear of the Wicked Witch, must stay indoors (though happily playing maidservant to the Seven Dwarfs); Rapunzel, imprisoned in a tower; and Sleeping Beauty, captive to a spell. The correlation between the imprisonment of the fairy-tale women and those in real life who suffer from agoraphobia (a female condition) is striking. So is the symbolism of women as ideological prisoners in their own homes.

Part 2 consists of twelve photographs embedded with text. The first four images — an old sewing machine stitching a floral textile; formal table settings on an embroidered cloth; a chair holding bedding; and stacked bowls — include historical texts about the intricacies of domestic endeavour, comparing the requirements of the job to those of statesmen and ministers. The next four images, which include such things as a basket of sewing and knitting, a blender, and a container full of matched socks, include texts that connect a woman's self-esteem to the cleanliness of her home and show how domestic work is trivialized and invisible, how caring for others can cause a "disintegration of the self" and how the availability of household appliances implies that "menial work is no longer done by people but by machines." The last four images, all of doors and windows, refer in their texts to such issues as how living space controls people's relationships to the outside world, the separation of gender and the distinction between the public and the private. In the text in Part 2 of *On Living at Home* we essentially go from historical claims of how women's work should be respected and elevated, to how it is really trivialized, to how this relates to issues outside the home.

Part 3 is about "media intervention on the domestic front"[23] and includes four images (all of which incorporate some form of media or popular culture) from McEachern's home. These are paired with quotations from a book and with black-and-white images (from television and magazines) about war, violence, poverty, romance and dieting. McEachern's point is clear: the private, domestic space is constantly being invaded by the outside world; the consumption of the public in private leads us to question the meaning of "private."

In the final section of *On Living at Home* McEachern looks at how closely the private is connected to the public. In a photograph of a tangle of electric cords the text points to the political implications of personal consumption: "With 6% of the world's population the U.S. consumes 42% of the planet's resources." (PLATE 37) An image of her garden contains the statement that three-quarters of the world's population are reliant on their own agricultural labour. Inserted beneath the Grumman canoe that rests in McEachern's yard is a text which identifies Grumman as one of forty-five arms manufacturers under investigation for "waste and fraud." This section brings us full circle, back to the earlier quotation from Rosalind Coward. Susan McEachern implicates herself in the "injustices of the world."

In all of her work there is a strong critical voice that won't leave comfort and security alone, a voice that always recognizes the cost, the obligation, the subjugation, the responsibility — always something that is not right within the structures of power and authority. In a completely different form, Susan McEachern's work deals with some of the same issues addressed by Suzy Lake:

power and powerlessness, control and lack of control, personal responsibility — issues of feminism, certainly, but also issues that emanate from having been a powerless child.

∎

Like Lucy Lippard in the quotation that begins this essay, I prefer to present myself as vulnerable. On some level we are all vulnerable, but often there is a construction (defence?) in critical writing that hides that fact: the disguise can take the form of dense language, intellectualism and mystification rather than clarification. Instead, I want the reader to know that within a web of ideology I can *only* be uncertain and, therefore, open to question. Although I have not revealed much about the experiences that prescribe the way I see, one thing should be clear: the contingency of this — and every other — piece of critical writing.

1. Lucy R. Lippard, *From the Center: Feminist Essays on Women's Art* (New York: E.P. Dutton, 1976), p. 2.
2. Alice Miller, *Thou Shalt Not Be Aware: Society's Betrayal of the Child*, trans. Hildegarde and Hunter Hannum (New York: New American Library, 1986), p. 200.
3. Victor Burgin, "Photographic Practice and Art Theory," in *Thinking Photography*, ed. Victor Burgin (London: The Macmillan Press, 1982), pp. 45-46.
4. Rozsika Parker and Griselda Pollock, *Old Mistresses: Women, Art and Ideology* (London: Routledge & Kegan Paul, Pandora Press, 1981), p. 114.
5. Lloyd deMause, *Foundations of Psychohistory* (New York: Creative Roots, 1982), p. 3.
6. Barbara Norfleet, "Studio Photographers and Two Generations of Baby Raising," *Photo Communique*, 10,1 (Spring 1988): 14-23.
7. John Watson, *Psychological Care of Infant and Child* (New York: W.W. Norton, 1928), pp. 81-82, as quoted by Norfleet, p. 21.
8. Benjamin Spock, *Baby and Child Care* (New York: Pocket Books, 1946), pp. 3-4, as quoted by Norfleet, p. 20.
9. Norfleet, p. 15.
10. Alice Miller, *For Your Own Good: Hidden Cruelty in Child-rearing and the Roots of Violence*, 2nd ed., trans. Hildegarde and Hunter Hannum (New York: Farrar, Straus and Giroux, 1984), p. 4.
11. Alice Miller, *Prisoners of Childhood: The Drama of the Gifted Child and the Search for the True Self*, trans. Ruth Ward (New York: Basic Books, 1981), pp. 7-8.
12. DeMause, p. 1.
13. John Ruskin as quoted in Parker and Pollock, p. 9.
14. See Victor Burgin, "Seeing Sense," *Artforum*, 18,6 (February 1980): 64-67.
15. Parker and Pollock, p. 3.
16. Dr. Schreber, as quoted in Miller, *For Your Own Good*, p. 5.

17. Interview with Suzy Lake, April 13, 1988.

18. Miller, *Thou Shalt Not Be Aware*, pp. 198, 201.

19. Interview with Susan McEachern, April 26, 1988. Subsequent quotations from McEachern come from the same interview unless otherwise indicated.

20. Wilma Needham, *Rossiter, McEachern, Fairfield* (St. John's, Newfoundland: Memorial University Art Gallery, 1986), p. 7.

21. Burgin, "Photographic Practice," pp. 45-46.

22. My own interpretation here contradicts that of Susan McEachern, who speaks of the work as emphasizing difference rather than similarity. I think that the differences are more subtle than the similarities of shared race (white), class, ethnic group (Canadian or assimilated Canadian) and child-rearing practices.

23. Susan McEachern, from notes for a lecture on her work.

Photography and Desire
(FOR GAIL FISHER-TAYLOR)

PETER WOLLHEIM

Is the camera inherently sexist? This question and its affirmative answer have been voiced by several sources from within the post-modern feminist movement, as part of a general critique of the objectification of women in contemporary society. The explicit aim of the critique is to take feminism past the point of a demand for women's parity within the established institutions of education, work, religion and the family. It is an attempt to demonstrate instead how and why an essentially patriarchal form of social organization can never accommodate such a demand, since the oppressive nature of patriarchy necessarily positions women as alien, as outsider, or as other. In this reading, the systemic domination of women requires not merely the redress of social injustice but calls instead for a radical redefinition of wo-man (*not man*) as a creature dependent upon the male master for the verbal, intellectual and artistic structures through which she is forced to understand and express herself.

Central to this argument is a close analysis of the power of imagery in the construction of social identity. Images of women fulfilling idealized sex roles are found in every area of cultural production, from the mass media to the more refined enclaves of "high" culture. As Kate Linker writes,

Consider, for example, women's subordination to reproduction, to the family, and to the masculine libidinal economy as advanced through advertising and TV. Or consider the deployment of the fashion model as an idealized image for the male gaze, or for woman's narcissistic identification. Cinema studies have attended to the use of stars and stereotypes and to the function, in narrative, of these passive signs of masculine desire. This constitution of identity such that man is viewer, woman viewed, and the viewing process a mode of domination and control has been applied to the tradition of the female nude; art history has turned, although belatedly, to confront the marginalization of women and the definition of creativity as male.[1]

Other writers have extended the argument to include religious iconography, pornography and even medical illustration as arenas of male social control and power.[2] Photography, as the predominant modern technology for image-making in most of these areas, has come under special scrutiny and attack.

Occupationally speaking, photography is clearly a man's world; the ratio of professional male to female photographers in the United States is approximately six to one.[3] This low number is further distorted by the curatorial process. The major texts on photography, those written by Newhall, Gernsheim, Jeffrey, Pollack and others,[4] typically mention only one female to every ten male photographers. A quick perusal of book lists from photographic specialty publishers suggests that the work of male photographers is often presented in single, biographical volumes, while women are much more likely to be published in surveys of groups or genres. The professional training of photographers is also biassed. Although the membership of the Society for Photographic Education comprises almost equal numbers of men and women, one out of every four men lists institutional affiliations, while only one out of every ten women is similarly identified.[5]

And yet, the argument for an essential, inherent, inevitable bias toward sexism in photography is based less on the question of access to the means of ideological production/reproduction than on the nature of photographic representation per se. To be sure, this more radical thesis draws from the Marxist-structuralist writing of Althusser and from the early Barthes, but it moves beyond the familiar Marxian concepts of alienation and reification to underscore the special problem of women within and across the boundaries of class struggle. In particular it involves a reconsideration of psychoanalysis, despite early feminist attacks on the mental health profession in general and on psychoanalysis in particular. Thus the Freud of "penis envy" and "immature" clitoral orgasms was reread as the key diagnostician of patriarchy as a civilization.[6] This reassessement has its historical precedents in the Frankfurt school's attempts to reconcile Freud with Marx in the Germany of the Weimar period. The turn to Freud seems to accompany a failure of social revolutions as a way of explaining the entrenchment of authoritarianism and the loyalty it commands even amongst those to whose interests it is opposed. Just as Adorno, Horkheimer, Fromm,

Benjamin and Marcuse needed to explain the deeply irrational forces that led workers to embrace Hitlerism, feminists must search for frameworks capable of explaining the leading role of women in defeating so innocuous a document as the Equal Rights Amendment or the continued attachment of women to those mass media images that speak only *about* but never *for* them.

The feminist rapprochement with psychoanalysis comes at a special time also in the history of the profession, when criticisms from within are becoming more prominent. On the one hand, the highly medicalized model of practice adopted in North America makes of psychoanalysis just one more technique in the psychiatrist's armamentarium, along with hypnosis, electroshock, and psychotropics. However, compared with these other therapies, psychoanalysis has had difficulty establishing its claim as a scientific, effective, verifiable method of treatment. On the other hand, psychoanalysis has become increasingly integrated into the standard curriculum of traditional humanistic disciplines, leading to nothing more radical than comparative studies of child-rearing or mating practices.[7] Moreover, psychoanalysis has entered the mainstream of popular culture to such an extent that many patients are already familiar with the "repressed" content they are supposed to discover during treatment. It was a perceived need for both formal rigour and disruptive content that drew analysts and scholars to the work of the French psychoanalyst Jacques Lacan.

The special attractiveness of Lacan's work, despite its difficult, hermetic, often deliberately obscure qualities, lies partly in the attention it has brought to bear on areas of concern previously thought to be only tangentially related: the infant's organization of its perceptual field through vision and language, and the creation of sexual identity. To be sure, mainstream North American analysis has its own theory of identity, worked out in its most elaborate form by Erik Erikson.[8] In Erikson's schema, personality and gender develop through a succession of natural stages, marked in infancy as the progression through oral, anal and phallic levels of development. For Erikson, personality is a matter of seeking "mutuality," or balance, between somatic, narcissistic demands for gratification, and restrictions posed by what social relationships are willing to offer. The central aim of Eriksonian therapy is to strengthen the ego, to enhance self-respect and self-esteem and to foster a positive self-image.

While ego psychology places a high ethical value on social virtues — wisdom, compassion, generosity — it has been criticized as sexist and as a politically naïve addition to the vocabulary of liberal humanism. Lacan also castigated it as revisionist and anti-Freudian. For Lacan the ego is the enemy, the obstacle to more direct access to the unconscious. Specifically, for Lacan the *I* is a term that should perform nothing more than a linguistic function, like the zero in mathematics, which has no meaning except as a place holder, or like those words such as *now* that lose their meaning at the very moment of their utterance. While the Eriksonian ego identity is in a constant process of growth, accommodation and insight, the Lacanian ego can never achieve resolution because it is Imaginary, producing a chain of signifiers chasing other signifiers in a restless attempt to articulate the ineffable, to fill the hole in its own being with an endless series of representations.[9]

Film theorists Laura Mulvey and E. Ann Kaplan, the photography critics Victor Burgin and Abigail Solomon-Godeau and cross-disciplinary writers including Jacqueline Rose have drawn out the implications of Lacan for certain cultural practices. The starting point for all of them is what Lacan called "the mirror stage," which occurs during the first six to eight months of life, when the pre-Oedipal infant experiences itself within the dualism of both subject and object. According to Lacan, the neonate sees in the mirror an image of intactness, wholeness and autonomy and compares this with its own felt dependency and lack of neuro-motor co-ordination. This fall into self-consciousness, and hence into self-estrangement, prepares the child for the subject/object dichotomy it will encounter in language, which is the medium through which it is Oedipalized by means of verbalized prohibitions — "no," "not," "forbidden." As a result of the mirror stage the child begins to see itself through the eyes of the Other, places the Other at the locus of all representations of the self, and channels all its needs through the mediation of the Other.

Following closely upon the visual, or what Lacan calls "specular," nature of the mirror stage is the child's entry into the realm of the symbolic, through the acquisition of language. Yet language is not simply a tool of communication; it positions the child within the social order, as *child, son, daughter,* etc., which is to say within the incest taboo and the genital organization of sexuality.

Thus the Law, given in patriarchy by the Father, comes between the child and the mother. The Father is *the* Other, and the child must renounce its deepest wishes for primordial unity or face a loss of identity. Unable to express its drives without the language of this Other, and simultaneously unable to project itself outside of some symbolic order, the self enters into the insatiable, because impossible, realm of needs that must/cannot be said, the realm of Desire.

The interest of feminists in this sort of argument is obvious. Both when passing through the mirror stage and when entering the symbolic order, the male child can at least identify with the gender of the patriarchal Other and aspire to take His place. Females, on the other hand, are doubly alienated in their self-consciousness, much like blacks colonialized by white exploiters. Passing through the mirror stage, females cannot project themselves into the place from which looking originates — the place, for example, of Jehovah, literally "he who sees all." Women are also barred from identification with the symbolic order but, in Lacanian theory, they become emblems of its taboos. The reason for this is the woman's lack of a penis, the one bodily organ that both signifies sexual identity and, with its visible tumescence, its cycles of excitation and temporary satiation, its pointing outward toward the other, symbolizes Desire.

This cursory and schematized outline of Lacanian thinking is intended as nothing more than an introduction to what might be called the theory of the male gaze. This theory was first introduced by Laura Mulvey in her influential essay "Visual Pleasure and Narrative Cinema."[10] Mulvey sets out to investigate the erotic fascination of the movies and begins as follows:

The paradox of phallocentrism in all its manifestations is that it depends on the image of the castrated woman to give order and meaning to its world.... The function of woman in forming the patriarchal unconscious is twofold: she firstly symbolises the castration threat by her real lack of a penis and secondly thereby raises her child into the symbolic.... Woman's desire is subjugated to her image as bearer of the bleeding wound; she can exist only in relation to castration and cannot transcend it.[11]

Mulvey finds this symbolization to lie at the core of Hollywood's "magic," its ability to encode "the erotic into the language of the dominant patriarchal order" by appealing to the "alienated subject, torn in his imaginary memory by a sense of loss, by the terror of potential lack in fantasy . . . through its formal beauty and its play on his own formative obsessions."[12] As does Lacan, Mulvey sees the "satisfaction and reinforcement of the ego," those "structures of fascination strong enough to allow temporary loss of ego while simultaneously reinforcing it [the ego]," as that which must be overcome.[13]

Citing Freud's *Three Essays on Sexuality* (1905), Mulvey then traces "two contradictory aspects of the pleasurable structures of looking" in the cinema: "The first, scopophilic, arises from pleasure in using another person as an object of sexual stimulation through sight. The second, developed through narcissism and the constitution of the ego, comes from identification with the image seen."[14] But when both are harnessed to Desire, they circle or oscillate around the "traumatic moment of its birth: the castration complex. Hence the look, pleasurable in form, can be threatening in content, and it is woman as representation/image that crystallises this paradox."[15] Moreover, "in a world ordered by sexual imbalance, pleasure in looking has been split between active/male and passive/female." This means that women are placed in an "exhibitionist role . . . [where] they can be said to connote *to-be-looked-at-ness*."[16] Within the cinema, the male movie star takes on the role of the "more perfect, more complete, more powerful ideal ego conceived in the original moment of recognition in front of the mirror," while the female lead is an erotic object for both the male protagonist and the audience.[17]

But Mulvey argues that the female lead is laden with ambivalence: "She also connotes something that the look continually circles around but disavows: her lack of a penis, implying a threat of castration and hence unpleasure." The male flight from the castration complex takes one or both of two routes: voyeurism (the sadistic pleasure of "investigating the woman, demystifying her mystery" and punishing or saving her from her sexual guilt), "or else complete disavowal of castration by the substitution of a fetish object or turning the represented figure itself into a fetish so that it becomes reassuring rather than dangerous." This aestheticization, which Mulvey labels "fetishistic scopophilia," operates by transforming the woman into an object of beauty, the passive recipient of male contemplation.[18]

An extension of Mulvey's thesis was provided by E. Ann Kaplan in *Women and Film* in a chapter titled "Is the Gaze Male?"[19] Kaplan suggests that "if women were simply eroticized and objectified, matters might not be too bad, since objectification... may be an inherent component of both male and female eroticism as constructed in western culture." What disturbs Kaplan about the male gaze is that it "carries with it the power of action and of possession which is lacking in the female gaze. Women receive and return a gaze, but cannot act upon it." Secondly, the gaze "is designed to annihilate the threat that woman... poses," not only because she lacks the penis but also because she does possess a "sinister" genital organ, the vagina. Thus "the camera (unconsciously) fetishizes the female form, rendering it phallus-like so as to mitigate woman's threat."[20]

Abigail Solomon-Godeau has taken up these themes and used them to approach the "structural logic of the fetish" in still photography.[21] Solomon-Godeau historicizes her discussion by referring to the "great male renunciation" of costume, theatricality and other forms of display in the eighteenth century, a suppression which displaced all exhibitionism onto women. Symptomatic of this "division of scopic labor" was a redefinition of *the nude* in art, whereby this term, previously indicating the male nude, changed to mean the naked female. Within the canons of the painted female nude, however, Solomon-Godeau points to the absence of pubic hair as a repression of the vagina, arguing that the "bland and featureless triangle that conventionally connotes sexual difference simultaneously functions to deny it." In photography, however, pubic hair can be eliminated through retouching, a manual interference with the formal purity of the photographic process. But for Solomon-Godeau, the "sign of the fetish" in photography, the location of the "phantom penis" in the nude, is the "idealized, aestheticized body itself... its untroubled perfection, its sinuous lines, its seductive texture, functioning to deny and assuage masculine anxiety." Moreover, photography as a process contains "homologies to fetishism... for photography, before it is anything else, before it *does* anything else, marks the conjunction of a look, an arrest, and an illusion of presence." This fetishism "overarches and exceeds" the ordinary distinctions that are made between the "erotic" and the "pornographic" because "both types of images may point to a similar, if not identical set of subject-object relations which induce or invoke fantasies that are themselves symptoms of an unequal ordering of sexual difference."[22]

Solomon-Godeau places her argument squarely within the context of current debates on pornography. While she personally rejects censorship, it is difficult to see how any number of puritanisms could not take advantage of her analysis to denounce all erotic photographs as obscene. The politics of pornography has made for strange alliances between some feminists and anti-feminist groups associated with The Moral Majority. But the heat of this debate underscores the emotional freight attached by our culture to all the terms associated with sexuality, no matter how academic or technical their contexts. All theories are finally metaphors and derive some of their appeal from their rhetorical elements; but those that employ words such as *fetish*, *castration*, *gaze* and *Desire* merit further scrutiny, perhaps especially on the part of those of us sympathetic to them. Any literate person will object to blanket denunciations of "socialism" for example, because the term covers so general a field as to include Scandinavian social democracy, Russian communism, Czechoslovakian "socialism with a human face," Israeli kibbutzim, and Canadian provincial automobile insurance programs. A word such as *patriarchy* requires similar elucidation. This is not to oppose a phallocentric logos to the feminist eros, but rather to explore the possibility of alternative practices that might address if not transcend the problems diagnosed.

Although all its proponents try to find room for alternatives, the theory of the male gaze rests upon a series of assumptions that push it in a deterministic and narrow-ended direction. The first of these assumptions is that we cannot know reality outside our representations of it. This has been variously expressed in phrases such as "all is text," "all is language," or "all is discourse." This position is argued against both positivism (the idea that there are value-free facts) and biologism (the idea that visual sexual stimulus is naturally more important to men). When applied to photography in general, it has been used by Victor Burgin to undermine naïve beliefs in the photograph as a "purely" visual and unmediated slice of the real world. Paraphrasing Burgin, Kate Linker writes that "Photographs are apprehended *through* language, either through the radicular operations by which we 'make sense' of images, or through more complicated unconscious trajectories that inevitably establish contact."[23] When applied to the nude in particular, it has been used by Abigail Solomon-Godeau to argue that "there is no such thing as an unwritten body. The body is always a function of discourse" and that the nude partakes of the discourse of feminity under patriarchy.

This assumption can be challenged from two perspectives. First, Freud himself distinguished presentation (*Vorstellung*) from re-presentation (*Darstellung*),[24] the urge to frame something in order to call attention to it from the secondary elaborations and codifications that make this discovery communicable. The former may be born of curiosity, play or exploration, drives with profoundly erotic roots for which photography may provide a particularly satisfying outlet. Second, there are non-discursive ways through which we know the body, beginning with the sensations of pleasure and pain. The feminist photographer-writer Jo Spence (PLATE 39) has in fact movingly said and demonstrated that talk of "representations of the body" remains fairly academic in the face of trauma, illness and death or, alternatively, within the experiences of pregnancy and childbirth.[25]

Nevertheless, the primacy of representation remains central to Freud's theory of fetishism. Although Freud recast and restated key hypotheses throughout his career, the nub of his ideas on infantile sexuality was established fairly early, in *Three Essays on the Theory of Sexuality* (1905), *The Sexual Enlightenment of Children* (1907) and in *On the Sexual Theories of Children* (1908). The conceptual problem confronting him was how to account for the metamorphosis of human sexuality from its open-ended "polymorphously perverse" manifestations in infancy to the restricted privileging of genitality in adults. For Freud the child's exploration of "masculinity" and "feminity" begins with erroneous observation: "Children have, to begin with, no idea of the significance of the distinction between the sexes; on the contrary, they start with the assumption that the same genital organ (the male one) is possessed by both sexes..."[26] Their investigation is intensified under the stress of sibling rivalry: "It is aroused under the goad of the self-seeking instincts that dominate him, when — perhaps after the end of his second year — he is confronted with the arrival of a new baby" which prompts him to ask, "Where do babies come from?" Three theories arise to answer this question. The first "consists in *attributing to everyone, including females, the possession of a penis*..."[27] and rationalizing that the girl's is merely underdeveloped. The other two are that birth takes place through the anus (baby = feces), so that even boys can give birth, and that sexual intercourse consists of two adults urinating into or in front of each other. The cornerstone for fetishism in adult life is set down only when boys view the vagina as a "mutilated organ," the signal that the penis can indeed be taken away and the sign that women are really castrated men. Freud interprets male homosexuality as a phenomenon deeply rooted in this fear.[28]

The reason for dwelling on these technical aspects of psychoanalytic theory lies in its cerebralized account of intrapsychic conflict, one which also presumes that girls begin by looking to the other sex for an explanation of themselves. This "mentalist" orientation is clear in Lacan's model of the mirror stage and in his concept of the phallus as the signifier of sexual difference. Postmodernism prides itself on the discovery of difference (or rather of *différence*, the "difference that makes a difference"), of sexual*ties*, of ethnic*ties*, of identi*ties*, of technolog*ies* and of "hybrid" artistic practices, where modernism had only seen the unified, universalized, homogeneous but empty space symbolized and produced by optical perspective. But Lacan's theory of difference, which recognizes that the penis (a bodily organ) is transformed into a phallus (an image or signifier), is particularly dependent on Saussurian linguistics with its dyadic, oppositional analysis of language units (phoneme, morpheme, etc.). Yet despite its adoption by Barthes and others, Saussure's semiological project has always been hampered by this binarism, which has been shown as inadequate in dealing with the brain, the mind or nuanced imagery.[29]

In pragmatic terms this means several things. First, a mentalist outlook leaves no space between *perception* and *conception*, between seeing (or hearing/smelling/touching) and thinking. Aside from being indefensible on the grounds of Gestalt psychology, it does not permit fresh material, from either the unconscious or from art, to disturb existing ideological categories. Second, it places a primacy on the genitals as indicators of gender, whereas breasts or secondary sexual characteristics (vocal timbre, body hair, muscularity) may in fact be much more important to infants and children in recognizing and bonding with their parents. These secondary sexual characteristics also seem to play a much more important role in visual representation, including nude photography. Third, to speak of the phallus as a signifier of sexual difference seems somehow inappropriate in contemporary culture. Skyscrapers and guided missiles notwithstanding, our society knows little of the *phalloi*, *hermae*, lingams and other explicitly sexual statues and architectural ornaments familiar to antiquity. And fourth, a cerebralized conception of the fetish seems to accompany a highly intellectualized praxis of photography. For example, Victor Burgin's work — *Zoo 78*, *Gradiva, Olympia* and *The Bridge*[30] — is, like psychoanalysis itself, fully accessible only to those with the time, training and affluence to familiarize themselves with the required interpretative texts. Presumably the work intends to encourage further reading, but this presumes a great deal. Burgin's portrait of his own reflection in 19 Bergasse, Freud's house, (PLATE 40) is a multi-layered play on the phrase "it's all done with mirrors;" but one wonders to what extent this image furthers social progress.

[171]

Castration is a practice generally thought of as foreign to Western culture; we have no tradition of eunuchs, and even the *castrati* were finally frowned upon by Church authorities. Nevertheless, as we know from black-liberation theorists such as Frantz Fanon,[31] castration is a term that reverberates with threatening significance for oppressed minority populations. Much of the traffic in stereotyping across racial or ethnic lines concerns the organ size and sexual abilities of men who are otherwise perceived as too weak or cowardly to defend their women from organized violence. There is nothing particularly unconscious about all this; it is just not something one normally brings up in polite society. It would seem to be a problem of particular interest to students of human sexuality, but Freud spends only a footnote on it, which is exactly one paragraph more than he devotes to the topic of rape. The folklore of the virulent anti-Semitism that was part of Freud's social environment included the myth that circumcision caused Jewish men to menstruate and that this loss of blood was compensated by the cannibalistic sacrifice of Gentile youths.[32] Freud was personally concerned that psychoanalysis not be dismissed as "a Jewish science";[33] yet from *The Interpretation of Dreams* (1900) to *Moses and Monotheism* (1939) he did circle around the idea that Jewish men — starting with his own father — were less than fully virile when judged by the militarized standards of masculinity of his era.[34] One of Freud's contemporaries in Vienna, Theodor Herzl, went so far as to publicly state: "A half-dozen duels would very much raise the social position of the Jews."[35]

All this is to suggest that the concept of a "castration complex" has to be read with a certain degree of socio-historic sensitivity. Moreover, much of what Freud initially wrote on the sexual theories of children and on the Oedipal and castration complexes is based on fairly suspect clinical material. The major case history of this period in Freud's career is the "Analysis of A Phobia in a Five-Year-Old Boy," (1909) otherwise known as "little Herbert" or "little Hans." It is partly remarkable as one of the three analyses of males that Freud was to perform with little or no direct contact with the analysand, the other two being the case of Schreber ("Psychoanalytic Notes on an Autobiographical Account of a Case of Paranoia," 1910) and a psychobiography of Woodrow Wilson co-authored with Thomas Bullitt (and withheld from publication until 1966). Freud gained access to little Hans by "urging my pupils and my friends to collect observations of the sexual life of children"; and in fact the parents of the boy "were both among my closest adherents."[36]

Such close surveillance of the child was hardly atypical of the late nineteenth century, but here Hans's own father monitored his son's behaviour and reported to Freud in a regular exchange of letters. Leaving the ethical aspects of this procedure aside, the methodological issues raised are considerable. Without going into the fine details of Hans's phobias, it was obviously crucial to Freud that Hans's fear of and aggression toward his father be "innate," that Hans's parents "had agreed that in bringing up their first child they would use no more coercion than might be absolutely necessary for maintaining good behaviour,"[37] and that he was brought up "without being intimidated, and with as much consideration and as little coercion as possible... With him there was no place for such motives as a bad conscience or a fear of punishment...."[38]

The reader need not be detained by the minutiae of Hans's analysis, except to note that almost everything the boy's father reports conveys entirely the opposite impression. As even Freud regrets, Hans's parent was often clumsy and overbearing when interviewing the child, and some of the conversations are nothing less than hostile cross-examinations that lead Hans to complain, "You know everything; I don't know anything" and "O, do let me alone."[39] More to the point, however, is that violence was very much part of Hans's upbringing. Hans indicates that his sister was in fact beaten by their mother, and the father admits that "his mother often threatens to beat him with the carpet-beater."[40] And, "when he was three and a half his mother found him with his hand on his penis. She threatened him in these words: 'If you do that, I shall send for Dr. A. to cut off your widdler.' "[41] Observations such as these suggest that little Hans need not have had an "unconscious" reason for developing a "castration complex." We are, after all, socialized by persons more than by representations.

Psychoanalysis has come under recent attack for repressing the reality of child abuse;[42] and although Freud himself never denied its occurrence,[43] psychoanalysis as a whole has been built on a perspective which favours treating the putative memories of these events as fantasies of infantile wish-fulfilment. In order for any hypothesis to be taken seriously it must have some pragmatic value; and however strongly some analysts deny a necessary link between Freudian theory and clinical practice, it must exist at some level of validity. For Freud's speculations on fetishism, that level is fairly low. Karl Abraham concluded that psychoanalytic therapy was most effective for only the "less pronounced" cases of fetishism;[44] subsequent studies indicate that fetishism is rarely a presenting symptom and that fetishism per se is infrequently treated by psychoanalysts.[45] Recent studies have also focussed attention on trauma and brain disorders as underlying causes of fetishism and on the efficacy of non-analytic methods in treating this condition.[46] It may be objected that this is an overly literal interpretation of fetishism and that psychoanalysis is a hermeneutic rather than empirical science. But even a hermeneutic system must touch bottom somewhere. Laura Mulvey at least offers a reading of films by Hitchcock and Sternberg in support of her thesis.[47] To merely assert, as Solomon-Godeau has done, that the female nude resembles a penis ("its untroubled perfection, its sinuous lines, its seductive texture") is analogous to finding the four-letter words supposedly hidden in advertising photographs.

As to Desire, its popularity as *the* buzz-word for the avant-garde of the eighties has also obscured the philosophical implications of its meaning. Book titles such as *Knowledge as Desire* (epistemology), *The Death of Desire* (psychopathology), *The Age of Desire* (radical psychoanalysis), *Le désir et le pouvoir* (political theory), *Desire in Language* (literary criticism), *Desire and the Sign* (semiotics), *Fictions of Feminine Desire* (literary history), *Subjects of Desire* (philosophy), *Objects of Desire* (industrial design), *Female Desire* (mass media studies) and simply *Desire* (art criticism)[48] attest to the currency of the word itself, which also enjoys increased use in the fields of ethics, theology and meta-theory.[49] In common parlance, desire (*Lust, Wunsch*) is a synonym for need, craving, wishing or some sort of appetite. But as Hegel and Sartre have used it, and as Lacan has agreed, Desire is not reducible to either "organic contingency" (hunger, thirst, sexual arousal) or to the struggle to possess some other material object as such.[50] For Hegel, especially, Desire (*Begierde*) is self-consciousness seeking truth and certitude in another self-consciousness. What Desire desires is to be found desirable by another, to be accepted and comprehended as a Desiring subject.[51] Leaving aside the theological core of Hegel's idealism, one can utilize Desire as a path out of the impasse of the solitary ego, a quest for recognition that takes one into history, communication and the dialectics of human relationships, including that of Master and Slave.[52]

There are several direct implications to these musings. First, one need not resort to the complexities of Lacanian hermeneutics to make the case that nude photography as a cultural practice is embedded within a web of power-driven relationships. It would seem much more straightfoward to argue that the aesthetic idealization of the female body, its encoding as "beautiful," takes place in such a way as to identify beauty with signs of compliance and sexual availability. This encoding generally emphasizes characteristics such as youth, a prepubescent lack of body hair, passivity, languor or repose, anticipation, postures of submission that decrease body height, the absence of signs of involvement with manual labour (including the labour of childbirth) and the model's pleasure in displaying herself for the camera and the viewer. Moreover, and within this encoding, the male gaze is often directed not so much at the body per se, but at the face of the woman and especially at her eyes. Since the process of gazing in a literal sense has to do with the establishment of a social relationship, the illusion of mutual eye contact plays a central role in fantasy as well.[53]

Second, the genre of the nude, like the genres of fashion, glamour and even portrait photography, involves the creation of a hierarchy of values such that some women are constructed as more desirable than others in terms that are presented as nearly absolute and universal. As a technique of dominance, this is the classic strategy of divide and rule, and it often proceeds along the lines of age, race and socio-economic position. The social function of the star system, its wedding to the fashion, cosmetics and perfume industries, its impact on patterns of female socialization and sexualization, have all been subject to feminist analysis and attacked by artists such as Anne Noggle, Jo Spence and Barbara Kruger (PLATE 38).[54] The ethnocentric and even racist aspects of the same system are also being scrutinized and repudiated in photographs by black women, who are nominally situated at the margin of this aesthetic hierarchy and therefore have special insights into its exclusivity.[55]

Finally, the work of lesbian image-makers actively repudiates the idea that there need be only one privileged male subject position from which to view the female nude or images of women in general. Laura Mulvey herself has acknowledged that any specific viewer's gender or sexual orientation is not "given" by a particular image being viewed.[56] However, lesbian-feminist critics especially have identified the particular problem of "beautiful" images of women within the lesbian context, its connection to pornography and its tendency to reinvent patriarchal standards of aesthetic judgement. Nevertheless, writers such as Jan Zita Grover, among others, have put the case for lesbian-feminist imagery as a sphere in which representations of Desire are less dialectic than dialogic.[57] Although this kind of work has emerged from highly restricted sites and venues, it clearly deserves far more recognition as a model form of praxis, one in which the gaze — *le regard* — is investigated for its exploratory, pleasurable, even caring associations, its ability to embody both the liberating and traumatizing aspects of sexuality of which we may be ignorant but never unconscious.

1. Kate Linker, "Representation and Sexuality," in *Art After Modernism: Rethinking Representation*, ed. Brian Wallis (New York: The New Museum of Contemporary Art, 1984), p. 393.
2. For an overview of this literature see Jane Gaines, "Women and Representation," *Jump Cut*, 29 (February 1984): 25-27.
3. Karen Slattery and Jim Fosdick, "Professionalism in Photojournalism: A Female/Male Comparison," *Journalism Quarterly*, 56 (Summer 1979): 245.
4. Beaumont Newhall, *The History of Photography from 1839 to the Present* (New York: The Museum of Modern Art, 1982); Helmut Gernsheim, *Creative Photography: Aesthetic Trends 1839 to Modern Times* (New York: Bonanza Books, 1962); Ian Jeffrey, *Photography: A Concise History* (New York and Toronto: Oxford University Press, 1981); Peter Pollack, *The Picture History of Photography* (New York: Harry N. Abrams, 1977).

5. These figures are based on the Society for Photographic Education's *1988 Membership Directory and Resource Guide* (Albuquerque: The Society for Photographic Education, 1988). Out of 1,482 members, 735 are men and 655 are women, leaving 92 unidentified or institutional memberships. The ratio of men listing institutional affiliations to those who do not is 141:594. That for women is 56:599.

6. See Juliet Mitchell, *Psychoanalysis and Feminism* (New York: Vintage Books, Random House, 1974).

7. See Russell Jacoby, *Social Amnesia: A Critique of Conformist Psychology from Adler to Laing* (Boston: Beacon Press, 1975), and his *The Repression of Psychoanalysis: Otto Fenichel and the Political Freudians* (New York: Basic Books, 1983).

8. See especially Erik H. Erikson, *Childhood and Society*, 2nd ed., rev. (New York: Norton, 1963).

9. The discussion here is based on Jacques Lacan, *Speech and Language in Psychoanalysis*, trans. Anthony Wilden (Baltimore: Johns Hopkins University Press, 1981); and Jacques Lacan, *Écrits: A Selection*, trans. Alan Sheridan (New York and London: Norton, 1977). For a brief introduction see Jacqueline Rose, *Sexuality in the Field of Vision* (London: Verso, 1986), pp. 167ff.

10. Laura Mulvey, "Visual Pleasure and Narrative Cinema," *Screen* 16,3 (Autumn 1975): 6-18. Reproduced in Laura Mulvey, *Visual and Other Pleasures* (Bloomington: Indiana University Press, 1989), pp. 14-26.

11. Ibid., pp. 6-7 (p. 14).

12. Ibid., p. 8 (p. 16).

13. Ibid., p. 10 (p. 18).

14. Ibid., p. 10 (p. 18).

15. Ibid., p. 11 (p. 19).

16. Ibid.

17. Ibid., p. 12 (p. 20).

18. Ibid., pp. 13-14 (p. 21).

19. In E. Ann Kaplan, *Women and Film: Both Sides of the Camera* (New York and London: Methuen, 1983), pp. 23-35.

20. Ibid., p. 31.

21. All quotations are taken from Abigail Solomon-Godeau's talk entitled "The Other Side of Venus: Erotic Photograph and Aesthetic Avatar," presented on 2 February 1988 as part of a conference on "The Photograph as Vulgar Document" sponsored by the Optica Gallery of Montréal. The author wishes to thank Anne-Marie Zeppetelli of the Musée des beaux-arts for making a tape of this lecture available.

22. For a parallel discussion see Christian Metz, "Photography and Fetish," *October,* 34 (Fall 1985): 81-90.

23. *Art After Modernism*, p. 406.

24. Sigmund Freud, *The Standard Edition of the Complete Psychological Works of Sigmund Freud*, trans. and ed. James Strachey (London: The Hogarth Press and The Institute of Psycho-Analysis, 24 volumes, 1953-1974), vol. 4, *The Interpretation of Dreams* (1953), pp. 310-338; vol. 10, *Two Case Histories ("Little Hans" and the "Rat Man")* (1955), pp. 488-508.

25. "Body Talk? A Dialogue between Ros Coward and Jo Spence," in *Photography/Politics: Two*, ed. Patricia Holland, Jo Spence and Simon Watney (London: Comedia Publishing Group, 1986), pp. 24-39.

26. Freud, vol. 14, *On the History of the Psycho-Analytic Movement* (1957), p. 55.

27. Freud, vol. 9, *Jensen's 'Gradiva' and Other Works* (1959), pp. 212, 215.

28. Ibid., pp. 217, 219-220.

29. Binarism has been an important part of those contemporary intellectual movements modeled on the information sciences, from Lévi-Strauss's structuralist anthropology to the artificial intelligence movement. As a model of perception and conception, it has been refuted by Hubert L. Dreyfus in *What Computers Can't Do: A Critique of Artificial Reason* (New York: Harper & Row, 1972), pp. 159-167.

30. See Victor Burgin, *Between* (London: Basil Blackwell, 1986), pp. 61ff. Similar criticisms have been made of the work of Mary Kelly (1983), which is explicitly based on a reading of Lacan.

31. "The Negro is the genital." See Frantz Fanon, *Black Skin, White Masks*, trans. Charles Lam Markmann (New York: Grove Press, 1967), p. 180 and throughout.

32. See Sander L. Gilman, "The Struggle of Psychiatry with Psychoanalysis: Who Won?" *Critical Inquiry*, 13,2 (Winter 1987): 303-304.

33. Freud, vol. 19, *The Ego and the Id and Other Works* (1961), p. 222.

34. See William J. McGrath, *Freud's Discovery of Psychoanalysis: The Politics of Hysteria* (Ithaca: Cornell University Press, 1986), and Marianne Krüll, *Freud and His Father*, trans. Arnold J. Pomerans (New York: Norton, 1986).

35. Quoted in Carl E. Schorske, *Fin-de-Siècle Vienna: Politics and Culture* (New York: Knopf, 1979), p. 160.

36. Freud, vol. 10, p. 6.

37. Ibid., p. 6.

38. Ibid., p. 143.

39. Ibid., pp. 71-72.

40. Ibid., p. 81.

41. Ibid., pp. 7-8.

42. Jeffrey Moussaieff Masson, *The Assault on Truth: Freud's Suppression of the Seduction Theory* (New York: Farrar, Straus and Giroux, 1984).

43. Freud, vol. 7, *A Case of Hysteria, Three Essays on Sexuality, and Other Works* (1953), p. 148.

44. *Selected Papers of Karl Abraham M.D.*, trans. Douglas Bryan and Alix Strachey (New York: Basic Books, 1927) p. 136.

45. Phyllis Greenacre, "Certain Relationships Between Fetishism and the Faulty Development of the Body Image," *The Psychoanalytic Study of the Child*, vol. 8, (New York: International Universities Press, 1953), pp. 79-98.

46. Juliet Hopkins, "The Probable Role of Trauma in a Case of Foot and Shoe Fetishism: Aspects of the Psychotherapy of a 6-Year-Old Girl," *International Review of Psychoanalysis*, 11,1 (1984): 79-91; I.K. Bond and D.R. Evans, "Avoidance Therapy: Its Use in Two Cases of Underwear Fetishism," *Canadian Medical Association Journal*, 96,16 (1967): 1160-1162; Arthur W. Epstein, "Fetishism: A Study of Its Psychopathology with Particular Reference to a Proposed Disorder

in Brain Mechanisms as an Etiological Factor," *Journal of Nervous and Mental Disease*, 130 (February 1960): 107-119; J.D.A. Whitelaw, "A Case of Fetishism Treated with Lysergic Acid Diethylamide," *Journal of Nervous and Mental Disease*, 129 (December 1959): 573-577.

47. Mulvey, pp. 14-17 and pp. 22-24.

48. See Hans Furth, *Knowledge as Desire: An Essay on Freud and Piaget* (New York: Columbia University Press, 1987); Michael G. Thompson, *The Death of Desire: A Study in Psychopathology* (New York and London: New York University Press, 1986); Joel Kovel, *The Age of Desire: Reflections of a Radical Psychoanalyst* (New York: Pantheon Books, 1981); Naïm Kattan, *Le désir et le pouvoir: Essai* (Montréal: Éditions Hurtubise HMH, 1983); Julia Kristeva, *Desire in Language: A Semiotic Approach to Literature and Art* (New York: Columbia University Press, 1980); Fred G. See, *Desire and the Sign: Nineteenth-Century American Fiction* (Baton Rouge: Louisiana State University Press, 1987); Peggy Kamuf, *Fictions of Feminine Desire: Disclosures of Heloise* (Lincoln: University of Nebraska Press, 1987); Judith P. Butler, *Subjects of Desire: Hegelian Reflections in Twentieth-Century France* (New York: Columbia University Press, 1987); Adrian Forty, *Objects of Desire* (New York: Pantheon Books, 1986); Rosalind Coward, *Female Desire* (London: Paladin, 1984); and Lisa Appignanesi, ed., *Desire* (London: Institute of Contemporary Arts, 1984).

49. See Michael Ignatieff, *The Needs of Strangers* (London: Chatto and Windus, 1984); James M. McGlathery, *Mysticism and Sexuality: E.T.A. Hoffmann, part 2, Interpretations of the Tales* (New York, Berne and Frankfurt: Peter Lang, 1985); Garrett Thomson, *Needs* (London and New York: Routledge & Kegan Paul, 1987); and Jean-François Lyotard, *Driftworks*, ed. Roger McKeon (New York: Semiotext(e), 1984).

50. Jean-Paul Sartre, *Being and Nothingness*, trans. Hazel E. Barnes (New York: Simon & Schuster, Washington Square Press Pocket Books, 1956), pp. 494-517. Sartre's chapter on "The Look" (pp. 340-400) is indispensable for understanding Lacan's "mirror stage."

51. G.W.F. Hegel, *Phenomenology of Spirit*, trans. A.V. Miller (Oxford: Oxford University Press, Clarendon Press, 1977), pp. 104-111.

52. Ibid., pp. 111-119.

53. This literature is reviewed in Mark L. Knapp and Gerald R. Miller, eds., *Handbook of Interpersonal Communication* (Beverly Hills, London and New Delhi: Sage Publications, 1985), pp. 407-408.

54. See Clara Gutsche, "Anne Noggle: The Tragedy of Fallen Flesh," *Photo Communique*, 5,3 (Fall 1983): 9-17; Jo Spence, *Putting Myself in the Picture: A Political Personal and Photographic Autobiography* (London: Camden Press, 1986); and Craig Owens, "The Discourse of Others: Feminists and Postmodernism," in *The Anti-Aesthetic: Essays on Postmodern Culture*, ed. Hal Foster (Port Townsend, Washington: Bay Press, 1983), pp. 57-82.

55. For examples of photography by black feminists see *Polareyes* magazine, published by Turnaround Distribution in London. A statement of purpose by Maxine Walker entitled "Polareyes: We Do Not Wish to Do It Quietly" appeared in *Ten-8*, 27: 42-45.

56. "Afterthoughts on 'Visual Pleasure and Narrative Cinema' Inspired by King Vidor's *Duel in the Sun (1946),*" *Framework*, Nos. 15-17 (Summer 1981): 12-15. Reproduced in Mulvey, *Visual and Other Pleasures*, pp. 29-38.

57. Jan Zita Grover, "Dykes in Context," in *Alternative Histories of Photography,* ed. Richard Bolton (Cambridge: MIT Press, 1989). A shorter version of this article was published in *Ten-8*, 30: 38-47.

12 Columbus Re-sighted

AN ANALYSIS OF PHOTOGRAPHIC PRACTICES IN A NEW WORLD OF POST-MODERNISM

DOT TUER

Everyone wanted to join in the quarrel about the objectivity of certainty;
no one dreamed of questioning the reality of certainty itself.

LOUIS ARAGON

On October 12, 1492, Christopher Columbus first "discovered" the New World and a conquest of the Americas began. Forged from the dreams of empire and etched in the blood of the vanquished, the New World became a vast colonial outpost of a mercantile economy, the distant land of a European imagination. Five hundred years later the New World is now the centre of a global technological economy, the heart of a new infrastructure of representation. The photographic medium, as a documentary reflection of this shift in empires, is critical to an understanding of the technological economy and its global influence. An object of popular culture, the photograph has both structured and mediated the visual projection of the American dream. A subject of fine art, photography has been the centrepiece of a modernist debate on a continent that lacks a tradition of painting. Integral to the production and dissemination of meaning in the New World, the photographic image is a repository of history, a cipher for reality. And as the mass media and telecommunications that bind the empire increasingly construct a representational infrastructure of domination at the centre and dependency at the periphery, the photograph has also become an object of theoretical controversy, a cipher for the contemporary uncertainty of artists in the United States, Latin America and Canada who confront the implications of this closed-circuit technology.

In what is referred to as the post-modern condition, or late capitalism, of North America, theories of representation concede only one point of consensus: photography no longer documents reality but shapes it. Cast into the shadows of a representational crisis that finds at every turn the imaginary of mediation consuming lived differences, the photograph is scrutinized for what it reveals of the clash of cultures, of the disintegration of an ethnocentric ego. The act of "seeing is believing" is interrogated for its dependence on a universalizing humanism. The old adage that "a picture is worth a thousand words" is critically examined and found lacking. From Edward Steichen's *The Family of Man* exhibition, launched in 1955, to *Life* magazine's postwar chronicle of Middle America, the photograph is analysed as an implicit reflection of a manifest destiny, a cul-de-sac of perception and reception that mirrors a dominant ideology.[1] Photographers who wish to register their opposition to this representational infrastructure no longer assume that the image "speaks for itself"; they incorporate in some way the context for the reception of an image into the process of its making.

Of the photographic practices that have emerged in response to the post-modern condition, the Sexual Difference school leads the way theoretically. While its origins lie in a number of British media artists who achieved critical prominence in the late 1970s through *Screen* magazine, its influence in North America as a political vanguard has become widespread.[2] Taking cues from the psychoanalytical investigations of Freud and Lacan, the Marxism of Althusser and the post-structuralism of French philosophy, artists such as Victor Burgin and Mary Kelly use photo-texts (in which words are intended to disrupt assumed readings of photographs) and photo-sequences (in which figures and objects are deliberately staged to fragment narrative and to rupture the pleasure of looking) to expose the "act of seeing" as an act of narcissistic overdetermination.[3] Reworking the formalist project of modernism and the surrealist bid for the unconscious, photographers of the Sexual Difference school propose to demonstrate that viewing a photograph has little to do with the image presented and everything to do with an analysis of the conceptual framework that underlies the construction of looking itself.

Sympathetic to the theoretical propositions of the Sexual Difference school, but taking cues from mass media by borrowing the images and codes of popular culture, the photographic practice of "appropriation" in the United States has also gained critical recognition. From Sarah Charlesworth's cool Cibachrome photographs of *National Geographic* "exotica" to Barbara Kruger's double-edged entrapments of the viewer in her black-and-white reworkings of advertising strategies, appropriation artists use popular imagery to reveal the ideological and social manipulation that underlies America's dominant culture.[4] Cindy Sherman, in an ongoing series of self-portraits, becomes a conduit of the technological order, donning wigs and costumes to catalogue the gestures and poses of women caught in the melodramatic codes of the Hollywood film industry, replaying sexual desire as a transvestite of a popular culture in which she is at once the exhibitionist and the voyeur (PLATE 42).[5] Chameleons of mediation, the appropriation artists do not deflect an investment in the image but insist upon its allure, creating perfect pin-up illustrations of a society bombarded by its own narcissistic reflections.

[182]

In 1985, when The New Museum in New York held an exhibition named *Difference: On Representation and Sexuality* and published an accompanying catalogue, the preeminence of the Sexual Difference school and appropriation was not only assured, but their respective origins fused into a *Who's Who* list of critically heralded artist/photographers. With essays by Craig Owens, Jacqueline Rose, Peter Wollen, Lisa Tickner and Jane Weinstock, and work by twenty media artists, this exhibition marked the establishment of a new Family of Wo/man that brought theories of Marxism, deconstruction, semiotics and psychoanalysis under one roof.[6] Treading gingerly between the ruins of a modernist debate and the obscurity of mediation, this post-modernist canon insists upon the active participation of the viewer in the "reading" of a photograph. The image becomes a screen that masks a murky territory of unconscious desires and conscious identifications. Reality becomes a simulacrum: raw material to be refined and recirculated like computer graphics on a video monitor. Guiding the viewer through the intricacies of a media-saturated environment that blurs the boundaries between documentation and simulation, the artists in *Difference: On Sexuality and Representation* question the legitimacy of the documentary image and point toward a contemporary collapse of representational values.

From the perspective of the Family of Wo/man, the reception of the photograph as a transparent copy of reality has not only constructed a sexual oppression of "looking" but created an imperialism of "seeing." As a medium that promised to capture a vast tabula rasa lying in wait to be documented as the United States began its expansionary move south at the turn of the century, photography becomes complicit with a history of domination.[7] Far from the neutral depiction of an external world the photograph is supposed to reproduce, images of reality are frozen out of time and context. That which cannot be assimilated by the value system of the new empire becomes foreign, exotic, the "other" in an otherwise comprehensible homogeneity of representation. Africans become the biblical victims of famine. Indigenous peoples become anthropological curiosities. Mugshots create a science of pathology. The stiff poses of the hysteric define the limits of madness. Death becomes a sensationalist instant. Sex becomes pornography. Locating documentary "truth" within a dialectic of context and culture, where the technological fiction of the simulacrum blends imperceptibly with the ideological fiction of a humanist vision, post-modernism sounds a death knell for a practice of photographic realism in North America.

In so doing, however, post-modernism has also created a hermetically sealed system of reading images in which all roads lead back to Rome, back to the representational infrastructure of the First World. For to imagine that reality is a simulacrum is to take McLuhan's "the medium is the message" to an absolute and pessimistic conclusion, where satellites feed images as commodities to passive viewers. To appropriate from mass media and Hollywood cinema or to deconstruct identification as sexual difference is to assume that all viewers are both formed and trapped by the structures of Western narratives. Choosing to read the photograph as the fiction of a mediated reality, the post-modernists presuppose that there can be no outside position of opposition to a closed-circuit technology. They accord to a technological economy the power to penetrate to the fringes of the developing world and simultaneously mirror back images of this world as part of dominant representation.

While the strategies embraced by the Family of Wo/man allude to a dialectic of the centre and the margin, the theoretical premises that frame their reading of a photograph limit the conceptualization of this dialectic to a movement within the field of language. By framing representation within the discourses of semiotics and psychoanalysis, a structural model is established wherein the relationship between the signifier/signified, the subject/object, the feminine/masculine becomes a relationship between a dominant and a dependent term. Boundaries for a photographic practice are created within which the centre frames the referent of the margin; presence frames absence. The evocation of "difference" evades the specificity of contexts in which economic, social and political differences are lived out. The societies and peoples actually marginalized by dominant culture are not given representational space to articulate their perspectives. As strategies that seek to challenge a dominant infrastructure of representation, the photographic practices of post-modernism veer dangerously close to replaying the very ethnocentricity they seek to dismantle, to creating from a surplus of images a circularity of references and a scarcity of narratives.

In an article examining the issue of reading dominant cultures, Caren Kaplan frames her argument by citing Ulf Hannerz's proposition that "marginal societies (here one can insert the terms 'third world' or 'underdeveloped') are not the passive recipients of ready-made images and consumer goods. Rather, these are complex, sophisticated cultures which filter and mediate first world imports, recreating local meanings, producing hybrid cultural artifacts and subjects."[8] For Kaplan, the threat of a new imperialism produces the destabilization of an old one, in which there exists the ability to simultaneously deconstruct *and* construct the conditions of reception. Through a process of deterritorialization, which accounts for both the centre and the margins as equal terms, Kaplan suggests that the spectre of a simulacrum evaporates into the complexity of lived differences. In this sense, the representational crisis of post-modernism not only encompasses the system of dependencies and domination analysed by the Family of Wo/man but, paradoxically, has created the potential for multiple locations of resistance and the potential for a dialetic of culture and context in which local meanings can challenge the homogeneity of a closed-circuit technology.

Moving geographically from the centre to the margins, crossing the Rio Grande into another America, Kaplan's theory of deterritorialization is realized in a photographic practice that is less concerned with deconstructing a representational infrastructure than with constructing a documentation of identity and self-determination. As artists and as photographers, Latin Americans do not confront a dominant ideology but an ideology of domination.[9] Economically debilitated by the external debt and politically destabilized by extremes of wealth and poverty and external intervention, Latin Americans have no need to interrogate what is self-evident. Lived realities contrast sharply with the chimera of development offered by mass media, satellite TV, and Hollywood cinema. Framed by a cultural tradition that owes more to the ideological narratives of Cuba's revolution and Chile's defeated socialism, photography is privileged as a medium which can reveal a popular opposition to late capitalism. It is not that Latin American photographers would disagree with a consensus that photography no longer simply records reality but shapes it; but from the perspective of the "other" America, the simulated world of images is a technology of alienation rather than a technology of deception.

[185]

In a series of conferences held in Mexico City in the late 1970s and early 1980s, photographers from across Latin American met to formally articulate a theory and practice defined by the conditions of production and reception specific to a Latin American context. The catalogues produced from these encounters and discussions provide an example of a photographic tradition and practice which challenges the prevailing attitudes toward images and reception espoused by the post-modernist canon of North America. Raquel Tibol, in the introduction to *Primera muestra de la fotografía latinoamericana contemporanea*, suggests that

deeply affective similarities, surprising contrast and historical differences emerge from this first concrete action that permits us to detect some of the features common to Latin American photographers: the rejection of an alienating and unjust society; the denunciation of exploitation, marginalization, and colonization; a rupture with conventional aesthetic models; an impulse towards a reaffirmation that recognizes in concrete things an inexhaustible quarry of creativity; a conscious reading of the geographic and ethnic peculiarities in order to place them, within the image, in their levels of signification; the beginnings of new interrelations, new orders to conquer greater scope and complexity; a contempt for superficial description that does not tend to reveal man's relations to his social and natural space; a neatness of execution that demonstrates a capacity to see and feel; the rejection of the technical subterfuges placed before the photographer by a consumer industry; a denial of sophisticated techniques that make perfection an end in itself to the detriment of creativity and imagination; a will to transmit those facts from daily reality which many choose to ignore and others deform and conceal, considering them bothersome or offensive; a will to interpret deeper into meanings for all they have to say; a repugnance to appropriate, through insipidly taken plates, a reality that oscillates between violence and hope; an acceptance of the fact that it is not the camera but the photographer who lies when making use of his right to explore symbolism; the avoidance of all manipulation and a strict respect for the subject; and finally, a will to serve the viewer without seducing him.[10]

While Tibol's observations appear to echo the *Family of Man*'s claim to a humanist vision, her support of a photographic practice that can "transmit those facts from daily reality" is not a call for a new universalism but the manifesto of an ideological position unaccounted for by the U.S. version of truth and its deconstruction. From the perspective of Raquel Tibol, to argue for a "conscious reading of the geographic and ethnic peculiarities in order to place them, within the image, in their levels of signification" is to argue for a dialectic of culture and context that is created from a North/South dichotomy, predicated upon a critical understanding of local meanings and lived experiences "deformed and concealed" by the representational infrastructure of the First World. For while the modernist paradigm of consciousness, shaped by European philosophies and mutated by American technologies, is under siege in North America, the consciousness of Latin America is still in the process of becoming. And it is this process, Paulo Freire's *conscientizaçao* of "learning to perceive social, political, and economic contradictions, and to take action against the oppressive elements of reality,"[11] that frames an oppositional practice in Latin America as a practice of photographic realism.

Ronald Kay, writing in Chile in the late 1970s, suggested that the modernist debate that pitted painting against photography was a red herring in the colonized space of Latin America. Rather, the absence of a painting tradition created a situation in which photography first visualized a landscape unknown to itself and in which "we collectively recognize the Latin American space only by a random number of photographs."[12] In the context of Latin America, photography's claim to reality becomes a link, not to the ambitions of the colonizers to make the world over in their own image but to the failure of modernism to ever totally penetrate the social and political landscape. Photography becomes a medium that makes less random the history of economic and political intervention, revealing the dialectic of culture and context as a dialectic of oppression and liberation. The decolonized body does not surrender to a postmodernist mystification but confronts the camera to denounce a representational infrastructure of oppression. For as Harry Gamboa, a Chicano artist, states, "Chicanos are viewed and related to as a phantom culture. As Chicanos refer to their own personal lives, we refute and combat falsifications. In the '80s, we self-define our

[186]

imagery and enter the global consciousness as a valid entity with experiences/messages/dreams to share."[13]

There is a search, then, within Latin American photography to appeal to the viewer not as a reader of theory but as a participant in a reality which is refused documentation. Economically, socially and culturally penetrated by North American images, Latin American photographers embrace a strategy of autonomous representation. Alberto Korda's 1959 photograph *Entrada de Fidel a La Habana* or Mario García Joya's *Somos Cubanos* (PLATE 43) do not appropriate or deconstruct the images of history but simply desire to record and communicate the imagination of a revolution deformed and despised by the media in the United States.[14] From the ironic capsule of the Mexican ruling-class arrogance in Pedro Meyer's portraits to the defiant stares of the *mujeres bolivianos* in Sara Facio's work, the images seek to juxtapose alienation and vision, to create from a photographic realism a localized context for the understanding of exploitation and *conscientizaçao*.[15] As such, the crisis of representation that threatens the legitimacy of documentary image at the centre of the empire creates the conditions for its validity at the margins. In an odd twist of culture and context, it is the erosion of the "real" in North America that creates the potential to express the other reality of Latin America.

While the photographic practices of North and South America confront each other across a border of ideological, social and political differences, producing diametrically opposed readings of the image within a closed-circuit infrastructure of representation, the conditions of reception that shape Canada's dialectic of culture and context reveal a paradoxical location for mediation, breeding a territory of contradiction for the reading of the photograph. As a First World country ideologically and economically aligned with the United States, Canada at first glance would appear to share with her "friendly" neighbour a post-modern condition of representation. Yet Canada's cultural imperative, articulated as a restless and often anxiety-riddled search for a "national identity," also suggests an affinity with a Latin American history of colonial domination. Simultaneously at the heart and the periphery of the empire, technologically assimilated but culturally marginalized, Canada's dialectic of culture and context is constructed from a conflation of the margins and the centre, framed by a location of "exile in the technological world."[16]

[187]

[188]

Phillip Monk, a Canadian critic, argues in his book *Struggles with the Image*, as Ronald Kay did for Latin America, that Canadian contemporary art has "passed from pre-modernism to so-called post-modernism without a history of modernism."[17] But with a militarized DEW Line to the north and the "longest undefended one-way mirror in the world"[18] to the south, Canada's response to photography shares little allegiance with a Latin American position. While visual artists use photography extensively as a conceptual medium, they take care to distance themselves from a documentary tradition, instead aligning themselves with a post-modern condition. The results of this collaboration, constructed within a representational landscape of a borderless simulacrum, reveal less about the intricacies of ideological structures and constructed identifications than the profound insecurities which shape the Canadian conditions of reception. For to look for the political and social landscape of Canada through the photographic practices of its art world is to discover a country where the contradictions between the imaginary of the simulacrum and the lived differences of reality have created an absence of references.

Michael Snow, in *Authorization* (1969), taped onto a mirror Polaroids of himself looking into a mirror, doubling and fracturing a reflection of an artist whose access to the technology of representation produces a paradigm of self-referentiality.[19] Mediated space in this work creates from a phenomenological model of perception a claustrophobia of reception. The viewer becomes both a consumer of and consumed by a mirror image of the producer, creating what Phillip Monk describes as a "rich social history of a *Canadian* artist" in which the "social referent itself is missing from his work."[20] Ten years later, Jeff Wall's *Double Self-Portrait* (PLATE 44) constructs an autobiographical subject who confronts the camera rather than being swallowed whole by its apparatus. Two Jeff Walls, one with hands folded and the other with one hand placed tentatively upon an empty chair, stare at the viewer from a room bare of other images. The chair, resembling a satellite dish, holds empty promises and catches a mediated reality which is devoid of content. A double exposure of the social referent's absence, Jeff Wall's piece reworks Snow's process of authorization, constructing from a paradigm of self-referentiality a claustrophobia of perception.[21]

Doubling again the stakes of technology and domination, feminist and/or feminine readings of photographs produced by Canadian women through the veil of sexual difference reveal a relentless search for identity in a colony of the simulacrum, mirroring the wounded and appropriated gestures of a mediated lack. From the trapped figure of Geneviève Cadieux's *La blessure d'une cicatrice ou Les Anges* to the scratched and mutilated reproductions in Janice Gurney's *Portrait of Me as My Grandmother's Faults*, from the dreamy dissections of Shelagh Alexander's cinematic psyche to Sorel Cohen's multiplication of a narcissistic self-imaging in *Tablet*, the images point to an erosion of the "real" in Canada where the absence of external referents becomes a desperate subjectivity. [22] In the face of an imaginary mediation that has exiled both lived realities and women's bodies from an infrastructure of representation, a self-referentiality in these photographs no longer constructs an authorization but documents the disintegration of self as fragments of a technological society that has peripheralized everyone.

While a contemporary obsession with a mediated self-referentiality can be read as a symptom of Canada's paradoxical exile inside a closed-circuit technology of representation, the absence of a social referent within a Canadian photographic practice also reflects the deception of an officially sanctioned past. For, in an effort to unify a vast territory fractured by regional, linguistic and racial conflicts, Canada's history is constructed from a selective chronology of facts and figures, framed within an ideology of a model landscape that has exiled narratives of opposition. The search for a national identity in Canada smooths over the rebellions of 1837-39 in Upper and Lower Canada, the armed insurrection of Louis Riel, the Winnipeg General Strike of 1919, and the FLQ Crisis as momentary disturbances in an otherwise tranquil progression from colonialization to federalism. The struggles of self-determination by native peoples are erased by the cultural mythology of a northern "wilderness." The urban realities of the majority of Canadians, who live clinging to the 49th parallel, are absorbed by a literary imperative of survival. [23] Policies of bilingualism and multiculturalism conceal the scars of political, economic and cultural difference. Official history becomes a history of official amnesia, constructing from an imaginary Canada a representational landscape that has been emptied of people, conflict, context. [24]

Framed by this double-edged paradox of exile within technology and exile from history, a photographic practice in Canada that seeks to challenge the closed-circuit technology of the empire has neither a popular culture to deconstruct nor a narrative of resistance to privilege. There are no Marilyn Monroes or John Kennedys to appropriate. There are no popular armies of liberation to document. There is no oppositional vision of a New Latin American cinema to embrace nor the cinematic codes of a Hollywood industry to appropriate; images of Canada as Mounties and mountaintops were traded in the 1940s in exchange for a full-scale invasion by and vertical integration into the American movie industry. [25] In Canada, the failure of modernism to totally penetrate a social and political landscape has not lead to the recognition of a colonized space through a "random number of photographs" but to the historical prominence afforded the Group of Seven as the painters of a foreign and hostile nature. To propose a "conscious reading of the geographical and ethnic peculiarities" in Canada is to confront a dialectic of culture and context, where the conflation of an imaginary wilderness and an American mediation has simultaneously seduced and alienated the viewer.

In *Geography Lesson, Canadian Notes*, American photographer Allan Sekula travels from Ottawa to Sudbury to discover how the image of Canada, engraved on its money as a "productive industrialized Nature ... [is] repeated in an official architecture of Canadian finance, and within the productive (and not so productive) 'landscape' itself." [26] Images of the garden court of the Bank of Canada's interior and of experimental vegetable farming in a non-producing mine offer parallel locations for an artificial independence from a hostile environment. The settings for the Group of Seven paintings that hang in the National Gallery of Canada, in the Eldorado reception room and in the office of the president of the Mine, Mill and Smelter Workers Union, Local 598, all suggest the extent to which a mythological wilderness has overwhelmed representations of lived differences. Juxtapositions of the Bank of Canada and replicas of giant nickels on the blighted Sudbury landscape (PLATE 45); the embossed series of Canadian paper money and the encased sculpture of The Last Indian (1901); and a model tour-guide posing inside a museum built by Inco and the president of Local 598 posing inside the union office construct a narrative of visual clichés that disentangle the conflation of the centre and the margin, of ideology and landscape, of industry and labour in Canada.

By accompanying his images with a text that traces the development of the miner's union and of Inco's global aquisitions, Sekula supplements a strategy of juxtaposition with the exposition of history that lies concealed below the surface representations of Canada's rich dependency. Excavating an oppositional narrative of militant labour organization and multinational exploitation, Sekula, as an American who crosses the 49th parallel in search of a dialectic of culture and context specific to Canada, suggests that "more is at stake than the keys to the Bank of Canada."[27] For as the third term of the Americas, Canada offers not only a paradigm of "exile in the technological world" but also a location for resistance, where reclaiming a social referent offers a "promise of geopolitical decentring."[28] The process of deterritorialization initiated by the confrontation of mediated representations and "lived realities" between North and South becomes in the context of Canada a process of simultaneously deconstructing and reconstructing an infrastructure of representation. Recreating local meanings from a paradoxical location of integration and alienation within the simulacrum, a hybrid photographic practice does not simply challenge a closed-circuit technology; it also takes an active role in the shaping of an oppositional culture.

In *Spadina Avenue*, exhibited at A-Space in 1984, Rosemary Donegan's juxtaposition of historical photographs with the contemporary architecture of a city street in Toronto constructed a documentary context for a social referent in which the viewer him/herself became integrated into the process of recreating local meanings. A linear grid of photographs by Peter McCallum documented the façade of each building on Spadina Avenue, situating the viewer as a pedestrian walking the length of the street from the waterfront to Bloor Street. Above and below this grid were images culled from archives, private collections, newspapers, amateur photographers and the past and present inhabitants of the buildings themselves. Reaching from the floor to the ceiling, the photographs of communist party demonstrations, trade union marches, industrial interiors, poetry readings, hippie havens, Black church groups, ethnic communities, rich landlords and tenement housing were only some of the diverse representations that revealed a complex social fabric and a

tradition of political activism that lay hidden behind the buildings'
exteriors. Involving the past and present residents of Spadina Avenue
in the process of reconstructing personal memory as documented
history, Donegan reclaimed both a social referent exiled from official
history and a context for the photograph as a document of a lived
history erased by a dominant ideology. [29]

Through the construction of an oppositional culture, Sekula and
Donegan provide models of representation that confront not only the
paradox of exile facing Canada but also, by extension, a global
dilemma. They create a condition of reception in which the image, as
a document of lived reality, can be read inside the already mediated
space of a technological present. In a New World of rapid
technological evolution and rampant disinformation, the potential to
declare a strategy of cultural autonomy away from the glare of the
empire's simulacrum of images is fading. And while the realism of
Latin American photography stands in ideological opposition to the
late capitalism of North America, the empire's infrastructure of
representation is steadily absorbing the periphery's imperative of
self-determination. A retreat into an obsessive self-referentiality, or
the active participation in the construction of an oppositional
narrative, foreshadows the dilemma facing all of the Americas as a
bid by multinational conglomerates to realign technology and
ideology on a global scale, transforming the parameters of image
reception and blurring the borders between countries. As a paradigm
of a colonial location within post-modernism, Canada offers a
location from which to consider the implications of this technological
determinism, to construct a photographic practice that does not
capitulate to the screen of the simulacrum, a practice that instead
reflects the complexity of realities lived inside an infrastructure of
mediation.

1. For an elaboration of this debate see Allan Sekula's "The Traffic in Photographs"
and audience responses in *Modernism & Modernity*, eds. Benjamin H.D. Buchloh,
Serge Guilbaut and David Solkia (Halifax: Nova Scotia College of Art and Design,
1983).
2. *Screen* magazine, published by The Society for Education in Film and Television,
was instrumental in bringing psychoanalytical discourse to photography and film
in an English-speaking context. Among the theorists and practitioners who
contributed to the development of a theory of sexual difference through *Screen*
magazine were Mary Kelly ("Re-Viewing Modernist Criticism," *Screen*, 22,3

[Autumn 1981]), Victor Burgin ("Photography, Phantasy, Function," *Screen*, 21,1 [Spring 1980]), Stephen Heath ("Difference," *Screen*, 19,3 [Autumn 1978] and "Narrative Space," *Screen*, 17,3 [Autumn 1976]) and Laura Mulvey ("Visual Pleasure and Narrative Cinema," *Screen*, 16,3 [Autumn 1975]).

3. For examples and a discussion of the work of Victor Burgin and Mary Kelly, see the catalogue for the exhibition *Difference: On Representation and Sexuality* (New York: The New Museum of Contemporary Art, 1984).

4. For examples and a discussion of Barbara Kruger's work, see the catalogue for *Difference*. For a discussion of Sarah Charlesworth, see Dot Tuer, "Sarah Charlesworth," *Vanguard*, 16,1 (February/March 1987): 32.

5. Cindy Sherman's on-going series of film stills are featured in the catalogue *Cindy Sherman* (New York: Pantheon Books, 1984).

6. The twenty artists featured in the exhibition *Difference: On Representation and Sexuality* were Max Almy, Ray Barrie, Judith Barry, Raymond Bellour, Dara Birnbaum, Victor Burgin, Theresa Cha, Cecilia Condit, Jean-Luc Godard, Hans Haacke, Mary Kelly, Silvia Kolbowski, Barbara Kruger, Sherrie Levine, Yve Lomax, Stuart Marshall, Martha Rosler, Philippe Venault, Jeff Wall and Marie Yates. The exhibition was curated by Kate Linker, with Jane Weinstock curating film and video.

7. The United States of America occupied Cuba and Puerto Rico in 1889, Panama in 1903, the Dominican Republic in 1905 and Nicaragua in 1909. A detailed analysis of America's southward expansion can be found in Noam Chomsky's *Turning the Tide: U.S. Intervention in Central America and the Struggle for Peace* (Boston: South End Press, 1985).

8. See Caren Kaplan, "Deterritorializations: The Rewriting of Home and Exile in Western Feminist Discourse," *Cultural Critique*, 7 (Fall 1987): 188.

9. See Chomsky, *Turning the Tide*. In Chapter two, Chomsky describes in detail a history of American policies regarding Latin America as a sphere of influence. Woodrow Wilson's secretary of state, Robert Lansing, is quoted as saying that "in its advocacy of the Monroe Doctrine the United States considers its own interests. The integrity of other American nations is an incident..." (p. 59); while Dexter Perkins is quoted describing the Monroe Doctrine, announced in 1823, as a policy that "was intended for the protection of Latin-American states by the United States [and evolved] into one that justified and even sanctified American interference in and control of the affairs of the independent republics of this continent" (p. 60).

10. Raquel Tibol, in *Primera muestra de la fotografía latinoamericana contemporanea* (Mexico City: Consejo Mexicano de Fotografía, 1978), p. 28.

11. This definition of *conscientizaçao* is given by translator Myra Bergman Ramos in a footnote to the Preface of *Pedagogy of the Oppressed*. See Paulo Freire, *Pedagogy of the Oppressed*, trans. Myra Bergman Ramos (New York: Herder and Herder, 1971), p. 19.

12. Ronald Kay, quoted by Nelly Richard in "Margins and Institutions: Art in Chile Since 1973," *Art & Text*, 21 (1986): 42.

13. Harry Gamboa, quoted in *Segundo coloquio latinoamericano de fotografía* (Mexico City: Consejo Mexicano de Fotografía, 1981), p. 229.

14. Mario García Joya and Alberto Korda are featured along with Raúl Corrales, Ernesto Fernández and Osvaldo Salas in *Cuba: La fotografía de los años 60* (Havana: Colección Calibán, Fototeca de Cuba, 1988).

15. Sarah Facio's photography is featured on pages 142-148 of *Segundo coloquio latinoamericano de fotografía*. Pedro Meyer's work is featured in *Primera muestra de la fotografía latinoamericana contemporanea* (unpaginated).

16. Arthur Kroker, *Technology and the Canadian Mind: Innis/McLuhan/Grant* (Montréal: New World Perspectives, 1984), p. 19.

17. Philip Monk, *Struggles with the Image: Essays in Art Criticism* (Toronto: YYZ Books, 1988), p. 93.

18. Quoted by Allan Sekula in "Geography Lesson, Canadian Notes," *Ten-8*, 29 (1988): 4.

19. *Authorization* is reproduced in Phillip Monk, *Struggles with the Image*.

20. Ibid.

21. *Double Self-Portrait* is reproduced in the catalogue for *Difference*, p. 13.

22. For a discussion and examples of Geneviève Cadieux's work, see Nell Tenhaaf's review in *C*, 18 (June 1988): 44-45. For a discussion and examples of the work of Janice Gurney and Shelagh Alexander, see the catalogue *Subjects in Pictures: An Exhibition Curated by Philip Monk* (Toronto: YYZ, 1984). For a discussion and examples of Sorel Cohen's work see Reesa Greenberg's review in *C*, 12 (1987): 44-45.

23. In my reference to the imperative of survival, I am thinking of Margaret Atwood's analysis in *Survival: A Thematic Guide to Canadian Literature* (Toronto: House of Anansi Press, 1972).

24. The thesis of an imaginary Canada was first argued by Tony Wilden in *The Imaginary Canadian* (Vancouver: Pulp Press, 1980).

25. Ibid., p. 82.

26. Allan Sekula, "Geography Lesson," p. 4.

27. Ibid., p. 25.

28. Ibid.

29. Rosemary Donegan's *Spadina Avenue* was exhibited at A-Space in Toronto in the spring of 1984 and subsequently published as a book entitled *Spadina Avenue* (Vancouver and Toronto: Douglas & McIntyre, 1985).

A Fly in Paradise

RAYMONDE APRIL

His shadow lay over the rocks as he bent, ending. Why not endless till the farthest star? Darkly they are there behind this light, darkness shining in the brightness, delta of Cassiopeia, worlds. Me sits there with his augur's rod of ash, in borrowed sandals, by day beside a livid sea, unbeheld, in violet night walking beneath a reign of uncouth stars. I throw this ended shadow from me, manshape ineluctable, call it back. Endless, would it be mine, form of my form? Who watches me here? Who ever anywhere will read these written words? Signs on a white field.

JAMES JOYCE
Ulysses

SUMMER

I am here for the summer.

I often think of my work in terms of the seasons, because it follows such a definite rhythm. I trust this rhythm, which I know from experience never changes. Each time I head into a new creative period, I feel the need to step back and look at my life from a distance. My creative cycle is not unlike that of a school year. Summer is an important season.

During the spring and summer I make a lot of photographs. My contact sheets are filled with outdoor scenes, with landscapes and, most of all, with people in landscapes. In the summertime I step outside my everyday existence. I plunge into another life, timeless and fundamental, though less familiar; a life that I observe even as I live it.

Then, before fall sets in, I go back home. I pore over my contact sheets, establishing relationships between the images gathered so spontaneously. I arrange them into series, give them titles, decide on formats. I begin to really see their content and the elements at play. I plan what shape to give them. The more I look at them, the more they seem like illusions or like visions whose origins will be remembered for a while longer. They are like white pebbles hidden in the hollow of my being. One day, almost without my noticing, they start to shift and become disorganized again.

In the deep of winter I settle down in the darkroom and begin transforming these images into works of art that I will later exhibit somewhere. I look them over affectionately, then renounce my claims on them forever. After that they belong to those who will view them. Some people read them as biographies, as though they were personal histories recorded in literary form, like a diary or memoirs. But I prefer to think of them as expressing a photographic present, a never-ending now that lives on in my favourite images, within a space that is theirs alone.

THE OBSERVATORY

I said that I was here for the summer.

I am living with Gérald in a house overlooking the St. Lawrence River like an observatory. It is an imposing structure that could easily have been a hotel. It has a name because the people who used to live here made wood, leather and metal crafts, and they ran a shop here to sell their work. The house is called La Chimère, and it lives up to its name.

Perched on a cliff, it has what is curiously known as a "view." We soon realized that it did not offer that sensual connection with nature that is the charm of summer cottages; no direct contact with the dry, rustling branches of the trees, no rising tides to flood the castles in the sand. Its windows open only to the wind and the scent of freshly mown hay wafting through its rooms on the breeze. We live on the third floor, and I work in the attic. Our feet never touch the ground. A pathway leads through the woods and over the fields to the river. We go there on expeditions, equipped with all sorts of paraphernalia. The surrounding area we explore by car.

We spend a lot of time on the roof. We look through binoculars at the vast perspective. We enter into it through the tiny details — the changing shape of the clouds, the flight of the sea birds. We sweep the horizon in a pattern that would drive a sea captain crazy. The landscape is so immense.

Faced with a panorama like this, the camera is powerless. All it can do is clip out a few scraps of horizon with no depth — as if we needed a visual reminder of our own insignificance. So I take no photographs. I love being here like this, buoyed up on the wind from the sea, looking across at mountains as unreachable as the stars, sitting on the sidelines like an attentive spectator. I am profoundly moved by the differences of scale, by the boundless perspectives, and I feel that I am living in a romantic painting, with an ocean of mist at my feet.

But then one day there are cracks in the roof.

In a fortress built to withstand the elements, childhood memories flood my mind with tales of legendary storms. We have so much water below us, but it is water from above that finally filters down on us. Grey and yellow drops seep in around the joists of the ceiling, dripping onto the curtains, the table, the musical instruments and the boxes full of negatives.

We are caught in a trap, like mice.

ROOM OF LIGHTS

We lie in bed in the master bedroom. Eyes open, I watch the walls where the headlamps of passing cars cast squares of light. Following the twists and turns of the road, the beams appear from a distance, pale at first, then flood the entire room for a brief second at the curve. After that, nothing. The night grows even darker than before. Then the cycle resumes, in a sequence repeated over and over again. Hurrying home, the drivers know nothing of the effect they create.

I get up and go to the window to watch for the next car. My eye is caught by the shadows of the trees against the house, dancing a stately saraband. Inside, the windows project geometric patterns. I start to plot the trajectory of the beams and shadows, as though I had to choreograph the whole performance for some future ballet.

Now we are both watching, holding hands. We are silent and still, small and gentle, together and alone, like in a movie theatre. I am reminded of a friend's mother who used to say it was always better to be two, if only to look at something beautiful together.

We are spectators. If we were actors in a film, there would be a script. We are merely present. The only action is the creation of a marvelous setting with no characters. It is like a film of which the critic writes, "The real star is the rugged landscape of such-and-such a place."

A few years ago I made photos out of thin air, with effects created entirely through lighting and perspective. I transformed everyday objects and studio walls, and gave substance to the space between the objects. Under neon light or flash, these airy nothings became fleeting structures in the afternoon sun. I turned light bulbs into comets. I made grandiose compositions from simple images. Often the back or the silhouette of a spectator would enter the realm of my special effects, adding a human dimension, caught up in my game of worlds in miniature.

My summer home reminds me of the studio in Montréal where I created *Cabanes dans le ciel*. Located on the fourth floor of an apartment building, it too was perched high above. Faint sounds of the street drifted up to its windows. The sun poured in and all the floors were creaky. I would go there to think, to read, to make photographs. My friends had set up tables there, and the materials they left lying around — brushes, pieces of wood, cardboard, found objects — were my treasures.

For a few seconds more, my eyes follow the path traced by the light as it rises and falls. Then I go back to bed. I fall asleep in a giant camera.

THE LANTERN

In the evening, the house is a lantern instead of a giant camera. No one can see me, sitting on the roof of my giant lantern. But I see all the lights shining below me: the yellow rectangles and diamonds of windows lined along the fields, and the sign of a diner gleaming in the distance. Hidden from view, I can watch my friend when he comes to the kitchen window to stare at the moths fluttering there, pensive, a cigarette in hand, in the listless attitude of someone looking out with no inclination to actually go outside. Like the shadow of the trees, his shadow is the merest whisper of his presence.

In the country, people take an interest in the performance put on quite unintentionally by their neighbours. There is always useful information to be gleaned, rudimentary but reliable: "Someone is home, because there's a light on," or "They must be home, the car is in the yard." It is tempting to circumvent a logic so naive. Lovers having an affair will park at a distance, but even on the back roads someone is sure to discover them.

RHUBARB AND SMALL TOMATOES

I am still photographing myself with a tripod-mounted camera. Despite all my experience with the field of the camera lens and the space in which I persist in posing, I never get used to it. I still have trouble focussing, because I cannot see myself. I have given up all hope of technical perfection; now I just take my chances. I do not always have my tripod within reach, nor is there always a large piece of furniture or flat rock on which to place my camera. Sometimes I ask someone to help me. Occasionally people volunteer spontaneously, and so the photo they take of me becomes one of my photographs.

There is something very touching about couples on vacation. They are victims of the camera's cruel limitations. They cannot simultaneously kiss, see themselves kissing and click the shutter. They are forced to ask for help from the first passer-by with a camera around his neck, and they have to settle for just any kind of kiss.

One day in September 1985, I went out into the street to photograph. I was looking for lost and lonely objects. The night before I had set up my tripod to photograph myself in my apartment, and got nowhere. I photographed trees near Jeanne Mance park; they were side by side in front of the hospital wall, their shadows reaching out for each other without connecting. I was alone and feeling sad that day. The empty park benches echoed my mood. But not the people. There were old men playing cards and young people riding their bicycles. I would have liked to be invisible. In the shadows, trying to avoid attention, I held my camera at arm's length and began to aim it at my face. A passer-by saw me, and came up and offered to help, but I refused. I kept on going, photographing myself outside store windows filled with drab mannequins, in front of houses and inside a crowded café. That day I got four uneasy images that are now part of the series entitled *De l'autre côté des baisers*. Apart from these images, the series includes portraits of friends looking right at the lens, offering their faces to the camera, and pictures of myself in various situations, taken by friends.

Two years later, again in September, I went out into the yard to photograph myself in front of the tool shed. With its doll-house appearance and its tiny, climbing tomatoes, it looked like something from a fairy tale that day. I had never seen it in this light before, although I passed it every night when I came home.

Trying to be inconspicuous as always, I first concealed my tripod between the two doors. This was because of my landlord, who lived downstairs. A retired man, he spent much of his time looking out the window and chasing away strangers who tried to park in the yard. But the screen door made it very difficult to move. Cautiously, I set up the tripod on the landing. No sooner had I finished than my landlord stepped out to chat about the weather.

I was trapped. I was very fond of my landlord. There was no way I could go back inside, much less ask him to leave me alone. I valiantly kept on with what I was doing: adjusting the camera, setting the timer, moving in front of the lens to pose — a procedure I repeated over and over again. My landlord did not seem to notice anything unusual. If I moved, he moved with me, talking about complicated matters even as the shutter clicked. Yet not once did he enter the camera's field of view. I watched the neighbours coming and going in the street as if nothing was wrong, all the while staring into the distance or at the sky. Then we had an aperitif, and I went back upstairs with a gift of small tomatoes.

I like to think that the words spoken when a photograph is made remain hidden somewhere in the printed image, and I often try to remember the words associated with a favourite photo. I know it does not really matter. But that day's photographs are true to their origins.

Yesterday I photographed myself for the first time since coming here. I was alone, the way I used to be. I was on the roof, badly dressed, my hair straight. I was holding a large bunch of rhubarb and looking off into the distance. Gérald was on the shore down below. Standing on a rock at the edge of the underwater world, holding his telescope, he was shouting insults at the gulls. He was too far away for anyone to make him out in the photos. He did not respond when I waved at him. I was alone, and for once no one would come to help me.

MONA LISA OF THE PARKING LOT

There was a time when I made small, very dark prints of my photographs. Some were no larger than a postage stamp, mounted on a large sheet of white paper. This size intrigued me because of the intimate dialogue it set up with the viewer, the factual details that could be tucked away and the intellectual rather than visual impact it created.

Later I made large prints that became lighter and lighter as I incorporated documentary accuracy into the composition and began to appreciate the beauty of facts experienced through fiction. Hand-developed in large fibreglass window boxes, these images had a strong presence both physically and visually. Held at arm's length, their grainy texture commanded attention and slowly led the eye to discover networks of lines, spots and details unnoticed at first glance. On the wall, they left the viewer free to draw closer or move back, and to accept their figurative and abstract content like a painting.

The largest photo I ever made was installed in the Algoma Steel parking lot in Sault Ste. Marie, Ontario, in the very centre of a multicoloured field of cars and trucks. It was a black-and-white print depicting a tiny figure of a woman sitting in an imitation leather chair, under a television set, between an air conditioner and a telephone, in what was obviously a motel room. It was a photo of me, which I composed and which was taken by a friend in Portland, Oregon.

I had been invited to create a large-scale work for a public area in Sault Ste. Marie. I thought it over a long time before accepting the invitation.

The only image I brought with me was this one, entitled *Femme au motel*, printed the size of a billboard, three metres by four metres. I looked around for a place to install it. There were some lovely natural settings. Then, in my car, I drove to one of the parking lots on the edge of the Algoma Steel Company industrial complex. I circled the lot several times under a sky grey with clouds that seemed to pour out of the factory's countless chimneys. I had found my second image. I did not go to look round the factory, preferring to keep a safe distance from this infernal city that belched red.

After installing *Femme au motel* in the parking lot, I often went back to see the two of them together, the woman and the factory, the woman's back to the factory, a Mona Lisa smile on her face, the steel mill looming over the horizon with its ash and its black smoke. Sometimes, through a trick of perspective, the factory looked like a toddler playing at the woman's knees. Most often, however, the woman seemed to disappear among the chimneys and the metal roofs. *Femme au motel* was like a postcard lost among hundreds of cars. Yet the woman's face alone measured thirty centimetres across, and there was enough room to park two trucks underneath the photo. But it was only an image, and a small gesture: a woman greeting the workers.

Leaving the factory in small groups, the men would stop, their curiosity aroused. I would try to tell from their faces what kind of work they did. They would ask me jokingly if I were a boozer, or if I often went to motels. I would reply that the photograph was a story. They often compared the installation to a motionless drive-in theatre or suggested their own interpretation: their wives were at home and their mistresses waiting for them at the motel.

I did not want to say too much, or admit that sometimes I waited for the telephone to ring. They were in a hurry to get home after work. I left an image there that would greet them day after day for months.

HEROES OF THE IMAGINATION

I choose to photograph everyday life. I want to work where the distinction between life and art is as narrow as possible. My images must be ordinary, concrete and easy to recognize, but they have to be strong and meaningful as works of art. Photographing myself among the rhubarb leaves, I know that I will simultaneously look like someone else and myself. If I succeed, the same will be true of my clothes and the rhubarb. I seek transformations and levels of meaning. I want to create a poetic journey that is inviting and open to the most ordinary interpretation.

There are people who look for omens at every step they take, creating a system of mysterious associations. Others are terrified by thunder and will gladly tell you why. Still others give nicknames to everyone they meet but forget their real names. There are some people who never throw away photographs, even when the people in them are strangers. Others have no concept of the meaning of fiction; they believe sad stories and cry at the movies. There are also people who clown around and adopt exaggerated or ridiculous poses when they are photographed, but whose faces remain expressionless the rest of the time. Finally, there are people who imagine they can make the sun come out again by keeping their Bermuda shorts on, even in the rain.

I am attracted by people who mould reality to fit a secret and highly personal anarchistic vision. They do not necessarily produce works of art. But that is not their goal. They relate to the world in a magical way that transforms and fictionalizes. People who describe their dream lives are not trying to leave their mark on the world. They create something they do not finish — perhaps because they love it too much, or they keep wanting to change it or they have nothing with which to replace it.

I like this fable-making form that fragments reality, changes facts into symbols, speaks in solemn tones and mixes its tenses, periods and characters. It helps me to compose my images, to see them and most of all to put them together. I am also fond of images suggested to me by storytellers, fetishists and superstitious people.

THE GUITAR

Gérald found the white guitar that was stolen from him years ago. A subway musician sold it back to him. Gérald paid cash, without even bargaining. He is happy to have it in his hands again. But it is in terrible condition. Tonight when we came home, he set it down under the coffee table, speaking to it tenderly. Time to rest now. Tomorrow he will take it apart completely so he can repair and repaint it before putting it back together again.

The next day, sitting at the kitchen table, equipped with tiny screwdrivers, he dismantles it piece by piece, placing the parts in small, numbered slide trays. Once the sorting is complete he puts the trays in a shoe box, which he tucks away on the top shelf of the cupboard. The only parts he keeps out are the neck and the body, two carefully shaped pieces of wood as sensuous as sculptures. After covering the table with newspaper, he turns his energy to the marks left by rough handling. He sands by hand with finer and finer grades of sandpaper. He enjoys this kind of work, it calms his nerves. Suddenly he realizes that it is dark outside, he is still in his housecoat and he has not eaten all day.

A day later he begins to spray on the paint, coat after coat, sanding between applications. He uses the paint left in the case by the subway musician, but there is not enough. He gets dressed and goes to the hardware store. He tries to find the same colour and brand. After making the rounds of all the hardware stores in the area, he has to settle for a similar colour in another brand. Inevitably there will be small differences in colour, but the old colour, antique white, was too yellowish for his taste anyway.

He works in the summer kitchen which serves as a storage space in winter. It is cold there in December. The room is poorly ventilated. Black specks of dust keep landing on the freshly painted surface. Still another coat is needed, and it is never quite perfect. One evening Gérald announces that the painting is finished, and he begins applying the varnish. The odour of the varnish is strong. He has to open the window. The cold is bad for the wood — especially for the neck, which might warp. Feeling dizzy from the fumes, Gérald decides to get some fresh air. A few days and several coats later, he notices dark lines under the varnish, probably caused by the sandpaper. Frustration sets in, and he considers turning his attention to some other project.

The completed neck is smooth and shiny. He wants to decorate it with some ornament, a sort of good-luck charm. He tries several before choosing a bright red little bird and a sparkling blue stone. Eventually he decides he does not like either one. He takes them off, sands and varnishes again, and sets to work on some sketches. After three afternoons of painstaking work, the masterpiece is complete. It is a magnificent red and black fire-breathing dragon, worked entirely in nail polish.

But that is not the end of the story. Now the body of the guitar looks dirty because of the black streaks. This tarnished look is simply unacceptable. Gérald thinks it over, then decides to change the colour. He always dreamed of having a fiery red guitar. He likes red clothes. That settles the matter. This time the dust will not show so much. He will be able to finish the work in less time.

After a few coats of bright red, he is satisfied and begins to apply the varnish. He is anxious to finish and get on to something else. He uses varnish of the same brand as the paint; you never know. But for some inexplicable reason, the varnish does not harden. It feels tacky, even after several hours. Exasperated, Gérald scratches it, at first by accident and then on purpose, with perverse delight. His fingers are stained with red. Close to tears, he throws the ruined part into a corner of the workshop. Three days later, he realizes that the varnish has dried as hard as nails, leaving the scratches plainly visible.

Rather than getting upset, he goes out to buy new pegs to replace the old ones. The ones he finds do not fit the small holes in the neck. No matter, he will simply make new holes with a drill, being very careful. But the red body of the guitar seems to be scolding him; Gérald decides to resand the whole thing and go back to the original colour.

After a vigorous sanding that leaves his fingers skinned, Gérald starts over with antique white. He accepts the dust specks calmly. He feels relieved to see his white guitar again. The red set him on edge.

He buys a new plastic varnish that is supposed to dry to a hard finish. At the first drop, another catastrophe: the varnish dissolves the paint and it starts to blister. On the verge of depression he decides he has better things to do. He would sooner play music. He sets the guitar aside in a corner. He will wait till summer to strip it down to bare wood, and then he will stain it. Cherry red. Yes. The other colour was not the right red.

A few months later, sitting at a proper workbench, Gérald makes a first attempt to strip the guitar using a solvent. It does not work. So he goes to the shopping centre at the corner to buy a stronger paint remover. It works well except on the undercoat, which is probably a plastic; he has to sand again. A friend lends him her small electric sander. After a whole day's work, Gérald concludes that he will have to do something with the neck of the guitar. But he likes the dragon. That night he dreams that the wood is of poor quality and not worth the trouble to restore. He gets up to check, then falls asleep again, still worried.

The moment of truth is at hand. Without making a single test, Gérald applies the stain directly to one face. The effect is like a fake mahogany finish on cheap cupboard doors. It is botched, the way a bad haircut is botched. Gérald gives up. Obviously, the guitar is the stronger of the two and wants to be white. Luckily, the neck is not ruined. Pretending to laugh, Gérald pantomimes throwing the guitar out the window.

He is becoming a familiar face at the corner hardware store. Today he bought two cans of antique white spray paint and two cans of the same brand of varnish. He does not have much time left. It is late August. He has to work on some new music for a production. He remembers the quality of the sound of his little white guitar. "To hell with it," he says to himself. "I'll just get the job done without worrying about it too much. Or maybe I'll start over next year when I have more time."

THE OTHER SIDE

When we sit on the roof at night with all the lights out, we gaze at the stars. We look across to the other side of the river where tiny lights glimmer in the distance, though we cannot tell exactly what they come from: a beacon, a house, a fire, a plane, a telephone pole, a car? Their constant flickering has an uneven rhythm. Probably because the light has to pass through several layers of air before reaching us.

Gérald asks me suddenly, "When you were little, watching the lights in the distance, did you ever wish you were over there? Over there instead of here, I mean?"

I rummage around in my memory. I think not. I liked to watch the lights and repeat to myself the words "over there." But I knew that the lights over there were the same as here and came from a beacon, a house, a fire, an airplane, a pole, or a car. I loved them from afar. He confesses he has never looked at the lights in the distance without feeling in himself a deep longing to go over there.

"Even now?"

"Even now."

PARADISE

Fall is coming. The air feels crisp already. In the evening the sun sets in a different place. At night we have to wrap up in plaid blankets to watch the shooting stars. The birds are already congregating in flocks along the river's edge. They no longer sing the same songs as they did in summer, at the height of July, when the sun drenched our hair. Maybe they are not the same birds. The fields are alive with giant grasshoppers. We talk of all these changes to make ourselves realize how time is passing, as though we have neither watch nor calendar to count the days we have left to spend here.

Back when the sun drenched our hair, we spoke of paradise, of a magical state that would go on forever, fresh and new every day. We were bathed in a golden light that cradled us in the air and calmed our bodies. We told ourselves we could live here for the rest of our lives, that we had never known anything like this before. Night after night we were present as the setting sun turned the sky to flame, and we felt honoured and blessed. The tiny lights on the other side of the river sparkled, and we talked about this strange, numbing, frightening happiness. We spoke of our irrational fears. The fear of being pulled under and drowning in the current of the falls where we used to swim. The fear of having a car accident. The fear of a witch hiding in some cranny of the house. The fear that the other might suddenly stop loving and leave. Montréal seemed far away to us. We were in a little corner of paradise. When I thought about it, I realized I had been striving for a state like this in my photographs, especially the latest ones, the ones of figures with their eyes closed, standing in the light, formal and unreal like statues of saints in churches. These figures surrounded by surrealistic visions, substantial and shadowy at the same time, I called *Les cœurs en bois de rêve*. They were like trees in the forest that one takes for living creatures.

At night we dreamed dreams in which objects and animals could speak. In the morning we awoke younger, as though we had somehow returned to childhood and, like children, were eager to greet the day. We set up studios in holy places, like the attic or the old workshop, and we would go there to dream again by the windows. We were not disappointed that we had produced no masterpieces. All the photographs I took seemed dull and empty, grey, faded and small compared to the life I was living.

Although I had always worked in black and white, I began to long for colour. I started taking photographs like an amateur, trying to store up memories like supplies for winter. Of course the colour in the pictures disappointed me. Then, out of curiosity, I printed them on black and white paper, and I liked them best of all.

The composition was different, crude, sensual, happy. I saw the original colours more clearly when they were hidden under the black and white. And I wanted to keep these photographs to myself, like secrets.

Our friends who were spending the summer near us were the first to go. Gathered together one last time around a fire on the beach, we talked about how quickly time passes and how difficult it is to have no regrets. I questioned my friends about paradise. Some spoke of their fears. We talked about time, about the tenses of verbs in language and the expression of time in photographs. There are past-tense photographs so full of death they hurt the eyes. Others are in the imperfect, as improbable and as inviting as the intoxication of some evenings. There is the present in its multitude of forms. I wanted my photographs to be in the present, because the present is immense. They told me that some are in the present and some in the present perfect, and that only the past is infinite. And that summer is the best time for reading Proust.

As the fall approaches I once again see my images gain power. They become almost phantasmal. A brooding sky underlines their strangeness. They will take over the darkroom. Already their only reality is their separate existence, their life as photographs.

August 1988
Saint-Roch-des-Aulnaies
Quebec

RAYMONDE APRIL

WORKS CITED

Cabanes dans le ciel 1984-85
Twenty-five photographs, each 50.8 x 76.2 cm. See *Voyage dans le monde des choses*, Musée d'art contemporain, Montréal, 1986 (catalogue). Also April / Davey / Grauerholz, Agnes Etherington Art Centre, Kingston, Ontario, 1985 (catalogue).

De l'autre côté des baisers 1985-86
Fourteen photographs, of various sizes, approximately 40.7 x 50.8 cm each. See *Voyage dans le monde des choses*. Also "Raymonde April autour du portrait," by Serge Bérard, *Parachute*, 43 (1986).

Femme au motel 1987
Extract from the series *Les chansons formidables*. Black-and-white photo approximately 3 x 4 m mounted on plywood, installed in the Algoma Steel Company parking lot at Sault Ste. Marie, Ontario. Invitational exhibition jointly organized by Visual Arts Ontario and the Art Gallery of Algoma. See *Sans démarcation*, Visual Arts Ontario, Toronto, 1987 (catalogue).

Les chansons formidables 1986-87
Eleven photographs: eight images, each 88 x 121 cm, and three texts, each 62 x 88 cm, originally exhibited at the Galerie René Blouin, Montréal. See *The Impossible Self*, Winnipeg Art Gallery, Winnipeg, 1988 (catalogue). Also "Telling Stories: Raymonde April's *Chansons formidables*," by Cheryl Simon, *Photo Communique*, Summer 1987.

Les cœurs en bois de rêve 1987-88
Five unrelated triptychs, approximately 82 x 400 cm each. See *Les Temps Chauds*, Musée d'art contemporain, Montréal, 1988 (catalogue).
(Translated from French)

Biographical Notes

RAYMONDE APRIL

Born in Moncton, New Brunswick, Raymonde April now lives in Montréal. Her works are featured in the collections of a number of major institutions in Canada, including the National Gallery, the Musée du Québec, the Musée d'art contemporain de Montréal, the Canada Council Art Bank, the Department of External Affairs, the Canadian Museum of Contemporary Photography, and in other countries, notably the Bibliothèque nationale in Paris. Raymonde April's approach, work and art have been extensively discussed in articles and critical essays appearing in magazines and periodicals (such as *Canadian Art*, *Spirale*, *Parachute*, *Art Press*, *Le Figaro*, *Vanguard* and *Photo Communique*), in catalogues and in other publications. She has had many solo exhibitions throughout her remarkable career, including *Voyage dans le monde des choses*, *Les montagnes d'aimant*, *Jour de verre*, and *Chroniques noires*. April has also participated in the following group exhibitions: *Tenir l'image à distance* (Montréal, 1989); *Photographie québécoise* (Nice, France, 1989); *Montréal 89: aspects de la photographie québécoise contemporaine* (Ivry-sur-Seine, France, 1989); *The Impossible Self* (Winnipeg and Vancouver, 1988); *Image/Double/Shadow – Raymonde April/Lise Bégin* (Halifax, 1986); *Montréal Art Contemporain* (Lyons, France, 1985); *Visual Facts* (Glasgow, Sheffield and London, 1985); *Esthétiques actuelles de la photographie au Québec* (Arles, Paris, Brussels and Rome, 1983).

KEITH BELL

Combining university studies in history and art history at Hull and Cambridge, England, Keith Bell's special expertise lies in early 20th century British art and photographic history. A professor of art history in the Department of Art and Art History, University of

Saskatchewan, Saskatoon, since 1974, Bell's other art-associated activities are recognized nationally and internationally. In 1980, he curated and wrote the catalogue for the London Royal Academy of Arts exhibition, *Stanley Spencer R.A.*, consisting of two hundred and eighty-two paintings and drawings. He also curated the first Canadian exhibition of the *Photographs of David Octavius Hill and Robert Adamson*, that originated in 1987 at the Mendel Art Gallery in Saskatoon, travelled across Canada and had its finale in 1989 at the Hunterian Art Gallery, University of Glasgow, Scotland. Among his many accomplishments, Bell has organized numerous other exhibitions, including one of Picasso prints, and others on aspects of Canadian art. He also contributes art criticism for various journals on contemporary Canadian art. He is currently writing a *Catalogue Raisonné* of the paintings of Stanley Spencer R.A.

Georges Bogardi

An eminent member of the teaching staff at the School of Visual Arts of Laval University in Québec City, Georges Bogardi became full professor in 1988. For the last twenty-five years, he has been passionately interested in photography as a practitioner as well as a critic. His works have been shown in European as well as Canadian art galleries, and as part of such exhibitions as *Véhicule* at the fair in Basel, Switzerland, in 1974; and *Canadian Photographers* in Budapest, Hungary, in 1989. In addition to contributing to some of the most prestigious Canadian art magazines (*Parachute*, *Vie des Arts*, *Chimo*, *Vanguard*, *Canadian Art*), Bogardi was an art critic for the *Montreal Star*, to which he contributed over 400 columns. He has also been a guest curator at the Banyaszati Muzeum in Budapest, the Musée d'art contemporain in Montréal and the Canadian Cultural Centre in Paris, a Canadian correspondent at the 10e Biennale in Paris, and a much sought-after speaker. He is the author of an article on Pierre Boogaerts published in *Contemporary Photographers* (New York), as well as an essay on Donigan Cumming for an exhibition at the 49th Parallel Centre for Contemporary Canadian Art in New York. He has also participated in a number of symposia in Canada, the United States and Poland, and has sat on juries of the Québec Ministry of Cultural Affairs, the Canada Council in Ottawa and various cultural bodies and universities.

GAIL FISHER-TAYLOR

Recognized in Canada and abroad as the founder, editor and publisher of *Photo Communique* (1978-1988), Gail Fisher-Taylor's extensive credentials have led her into print and electronic media. From 1979 to 1989, she wrote, edited and narrated five one-hour programs for CBC's *Ideas*, two about incest (*Family Secrets: Social Tales*) and three for a series called *Photography*. As executive director of the Holocene Foundation, Fisher-Taylor was responsible for "Talking Pictures, a Conference on Art and Photography," an international symposium at the Ontario College of Art in Toronto in 1987. Other notable experience includes being a correspondent for *print letter*, a journal published in Zurich, Switzerland, and *American Photographer*, published by CBS in New York. Early in her career, Fisher-Taylor worked as a photographer, writer and art director in New York City and Mexico City. From 1982 to 1984, she served on the Board of Directors of the Toronto Photographers Workshop, and since 1975 she has been involved as a juror on photography and a speaker at numerous workshops and conference panels across Canada and the United States. She lives in Toronto.

MONIKA GAGNON

Since 1985, Monika Gagnon has amassed to her credit a considerable number of publications on contemporary art. Among the best known are "Tony Brown, Geneviève Cadieux, David Tomas, Raymond Gervais" (in the exhibition catalogue *Elementa Naturae, 1987)*, "Work in Progress: Canadian Women in the Visual Arts, 1975-1987" in *Work in Progress: Building Feminist Culture* (Toronto: Women's Educational Press, 1987), "Al Fannanah 'l Rassamah, Jamelie Hassan" (*Vanguard, 1988*) and an exhibition catalogue *Beauté Convulsive* for Vancouver's Artspeak Gallery 1989). Her latest publication appeared in the book anthology, *AIDS and Feminism: Exploring Representations* (University of Toronto Press, 1990). Since 1985, she has also contributed many art reviews to *C*, *Parachute* and other magazines. Among other related activities, Monika Gagnon has been a member on the editorial collective of *border/lines* magazine and a contributing editor to *Public*. She also guest-lectured at the Ontario College of Art in Toronto and Concordia University in Montréal in 1989. A graduate of York University's Master's program in Social and Political Thought, Monika Gagnon currently lives in Toronto.

ROBERT GRAHAM

Since 1980, Robert Graham's literary skills and profound interest in art have enabled him to produce a succession of works for the leading Canadian art journals *Parachute*, *C* and *Vanguard*. As well as being well-versed in art, photography and architecture, he writes lucidly on the subject of cultural politics. In addition, Graham has written catalogue essays for exhibitions organized by the Canadian Museum of Contemporary Photography and the Musée d'art contemporain de Montréal. In 1986, Graham received a Canada Council "B" Grant for the Visual Arts (curators and critics category). After graduating with a B.A. from McGill University in 1973, Graham later returned to McGill where he completed an M.A. in Communications in 1989.

SERGE JONGUÉ

A freelance photographer and journalist since 1981, Serge Jongué lives in Montréal. His work on urban phenomena, immigration and work, including *Haïti, P.Q.*, *Entrevues citadines* and *Identités métropolitaines*, exemplifies his areas of concentration. He writes a regular column on the visual arts for *Vie des Arts*, as well as feature articles for *L'Actualité*, *Marie-Pier*, *Châtelaine*, the French daily *Libération*, *Les Annales de la recherche urbaine* (France), *Steelabor*, *Informatique et bureautique*, *Éducabec*, among others. Jongué has also written several monographs, including works on the cartoonists Schulz, Mordillo, Gabellini and Ungerer. He has exhibited in France and Canada. Group exhibitions include *Entrevues citadines*, organized in Marseilles, Barcelona, Algiers and Naples, and *Tout l'art du monde*, which travelled around Québec. Jongué has also taken part in conferences, radio and television interviews, and a variety of research activities. He is a member of the International Association of Art Critics.

DENIS LESSARD

With an M.A. in Art History, Denis Lessard has taught Contemporary Art at the University of Ottawa, Art History at Concordia University and the History of Architecture at the National Theatre School of Canada. A distinguished art critic, he has published many articles and essays in *Vanguard*, *Vie des Arts*, *Parachute* and *artscanada*, as well as a number of monographs (Raymonde April, Lise Bégin, Marie Fréchette). Conferences, radio shows, films and videos (*Petits tableaux*), performances (*Dix petites pièces classiques, Goethe*), solo and group exhibitions of photography, contributions to various catalogues (*En cinq temps, la photographie* and *Notes pour écrire une histoire*), and exhibition reference material (*Photographie actuelle au Québec, Dessin contemporain canadien, 1977-1982, Dessin ↔ installation*) bear witness to Lessard's active involvement in the visual arts. Born in Sherbrooke, Lessard lives in Montréal.

MICHAEL MITCHELL

Michael Mitchell's long list of academic achievements, teaching positions and exhibitions attests to his prowess as a freelance and fine art photographer. With two photographic arts degrees from Ryerson Polytechnical Institute and two degrees from the University of Toronto, he has been an instructor and lecturer at many prominent schools across Canada, including the Ontario College of Art in his home city of Toronto and the Banff School of Fine Arts in Alberta. Mitchell has been a juror, editorial board member, president, moderator and curator of various photography-related activities in Toronto, and was a board member of the Harbourfront Art Gallery and director of *Fine Art Photography Publications* during the 1970s and 1980s. His solo exhibitions include *Nightlife* (1978), *Staying Home* (1982), *Sonora* (1985), *Nicaragua: After the Triumph* (1985) and *Mask* (1988). His work has been shown at many group exhibitions, including *Farbwerke* (Zurich, Switzerland, 1980); *Seeing People/Seeing Places* (London, England, 1984); *Structured Paradise* (Banff, 1987); *Faire Image* (Québec, 1989) and *Baden/Mitchell/Rosten: Three Contemporary Photographers Celebrate the 150th Anniversary of Photography* (1989). As well as writing articles for prestigious Canadian art journals, Mitchell is the author of *Monsters of the Gilded Age: The Photography of Charles Eisenmann* (1979) and *Singing Songs to the Spirit: The Culture History of the Inuit* (1980). He was also the photographer for *Fighting Back* (1972) and *Parade* (1984).

CAROL COREY PHILLIPS

Lecturer, teacher, writer, Carol Corey Phillips earned an Ottawa Teachers' College diploma in 1962 and an Honours B.A. in Photography at the University of Ottawa in 1983. Later, she continued studying at Carleton University in Ottawa, where she graduated with an M.A. in Canadian Studies/Women's Studies in

1987. An Ottawa resident, Phillips is emerging as a commentator on photographic activity in the area. In 1983, she published "Michael Schreier, Recent Photographs" and "Lynne Cohen, Vincent Sharp, Geoffrey James, Yarlow Saltzman Gallery, Toronto" in the University of Ottawa publication *Objekt*. Phillips is also the author of *Ten Ottawa Photographers*, a brochure for Ottawa's SAW Gallery exhibit, and worked as an educational guide for the National Film Board exhibit *Contemporary Canadian Photography*. She taught a History of Photography course at the University of Ottawa in 1989.

DOT TUER

Dot Tuer is a versatile writer, journalist and filmmaker. Fluent in English, French and Spanish, she has accumulated an impressive list of projects since her post-graduate studies at York University in Toronto in 1983-1984. Several major articles have appeared in *Fuse Magazine* ("Radioactivating Nicaragua: A Report on the AMARC 3 Radio-Conference," 1989; "The Good, The Bad, and The Ugly: Resistance in the New Age of Everyday Life," 1988) and she regularly reviews for *Parachute* and *C* ("Gestures in the Looking Glass: Performance Art and the Body"). Other publications include "The Embattled Body: AIDS and the current crisis in representation" (*Canadian Art*, 1989), "Stolen Doubles" (*Site Specific*, 1988), "Evocations of the Heroic/Mediations Upon a Site" (*Heroics: A Critical View*, 1988) and "Mary, Mary, Is Quite Contrary" (*Impulse*, 1986). Among her films are *My Disgusting Flower* (1984); *It's Confidential* (1985), *Boarding House* (1985) and *In the Shadow of the Body* (1988). Tuer has also appeared as a panelist and lecturer at numerous conferences and art institutions across Canada and in the United States.

IAN WALLACE

An instructor in Art History at the Emily Carr College of Art and Design in Vancouver since 1972, Ian Wallace earlier lectured in Art History at the University of British Columbia, from 1967 to 1970. Wallace has also lectured frequently at various prominent institutions across Canada. Wallace was a reviewer and regular contributor to *Vanguard* from the early 1980s ("Dan Graham at David Bellman Gallery, Toronto," 1983; "Ken Lum: Image and Alter-Image," 1986-1987; "Roy Arden, Image and Alter-Image," 1987). *Vanguard* and *artscanada* have featured many articles and many reviews on

Wallace's own work. Wallace is the author of two catalogues for exhibitions of Jeff Wall's work, the first in Chicago in 1982 and the second at the Institute of Contemporary Arts, London, in 1984. As both a solo and a group exhibitor of paintings and photographic murals since 1965, Wallace has been involved in more than sixty exhibitions in Canada, the United States and Europe. In 1988, the Vancouver Art Gallery produced a major exhibition and catalogue, *Ian Wallace: Selected Works 1970-1987.* His works are found in several public collections, including the Canada Council Art Bank and the National Gallery of Canada in Ottawa.

PETER WOLLHEIM

Freelance photographer and writer Peter Wollheim holds an M.A. in Communications from Simon Fraser University in British Columbia (1978) and is a doctoral student in Communications at McGill University in Montréal. As well as thirteen academic awards, he has received five non-academic awards, including a Canada Council Travel Grant (1986) and two Canada Council "B" Grants for Photography (1981, 1984). A well-published critic since mid-1970s, Wollheim's articles have appeared in *Vanguard*, *Canadian Forum*, *Photographer*, *C* and *Doctor's Review*, to name a few. Photographer for the book *The Birth Report* (1983), and editor and contributor to *New: West Coast Photographers* (1981), he also has many cover photographs to his credit (*Rights of the Pregnant Parent*, 1985; *Victoria's Monday Magazine*, 1982; *Mountain's Dream*, 1980; *Second Harvest*, 1980). Wollheim's photographs have been exhibited across Canada including the exhibition *Nuclear Winter* which toured in 1988-89. He has produced or been actively involved in several film productions, such as the 30-minute "Greater Vancouver Mental Health Service." Since the early 1970s, he has been sought after as a lecturer or conference/ workshop speaker at such leading institutions as the National Gallery of Canada in Ottawa (1985), the Canadian Centre for Photography in Toronto (1983), Simon Fraser University (1974, 1977, 1979), and the Emily Carr College of Art and Design in Vancouver (1974, 1977, 1980).

PLATE I
C. P. CURRAN
James Joyce in 1902 in
the Curran family's garden

PLATE 2
WEEGEE
(Arthur Fellig)
Life Saving Attempt
1940

PLATE 3
ANDREW DANSON
The Right Honourable
John N. Turner, P.C.
Leader of the Opposition in
the House of Commons
Ottawa, March 4, 1987

PLATE 4
RON GALELLA
Sean Penn leaving his apartment
New York, November 20, 1985

PLATE 5
UNKNOWN
Lachlan McKinnon family,
Dalemead, Alberta.
L-R: Maggie, Isobel, Edwin, Annie,
Jessie and Don (on horseback),
May, Angus, Charlie
1910

PLATE 6
W. J. Oliver
Harvesting grain crops, Arrowwood
1927

in bushels per acre, of the Western Provinces as compared with some of the principal North Central States in 1905:—

	Wheat.	Oats.	Barley.
SASKATCHEWAN	**23.09**	**42.70**	**27.11**
Alberta	21.46	39.18	27.36
Manitoba	21.07	42.60	34.20
Wisconsin	15.80	39.00	29.90
Kansas	14.10	27.10	22.00
Nebraska	14.00	31.00	27.50
The Dakotas	13.90	39.00	29.00
Iowa	13.80	35.00	26.00
Minnesota	13.30	37.50	27.00

The crop reports for Western Canada for 1906 show:—

90,000,000 bushels Wheat
70,000,000 bushels Oats
17,000,000 bushels Barley

which means that the value of the grain crop for 1906 is upwards of $100,000,000.

Horses, cattle, sheep and hogs thrive on the rich and nutritious pastures of wild hay and prairie grass. These grasses mostly form in tufts, and make good fodder during both the winter and summer.

THE FAMOUS SASKATCHEWAN WHEAT BELT.

A few years ago the lands around Regina were practically unsaleable. Today they are changing hands at prices ranging from $20 to $50 per acre. Development of the surrounding country has brought about this change. This same

10

SHOULDER DEEP IN WHEAT   FIFTY BUSHELS TO THE ACRE

PLATE 8
UNKNOWN
Pages of booklet on farming in
Saskatchewan (The Heart of the
Famous Saskatchewan Wheat Belt),
published by the Saskatoon and
Western Land Company of Montreal

PLATE 9
GABOR SZILASI
Shawinigan
1988

FÊTE RELIGIEUSE PORTUGAISE, MONTRÉAL, 1980.

PLATE 10
MICHEL CAMPEAU
Fête Religieuse Portugaise, Montréal,
extrait de la série
« Week-end au 'Paradis terrestre'! »
*[Portuguese religious celebration,
Montréal, from the series "Weekend in an
'earthly paradise'!"]*
1980

PLATE 11
NORMAND RAJOTTE
Sans titre
[Untitled]

PLATE 12
ALAIN CHAGNON
Extrait de la série «Calepin de voyage
provenant du sud — Le Sénégal»
*[From the series "Travel notes from
the South — Senegal"]*
December 1987

PLATE 13
PETER PITSEOLAK
The Nascopie, Sinking
1947

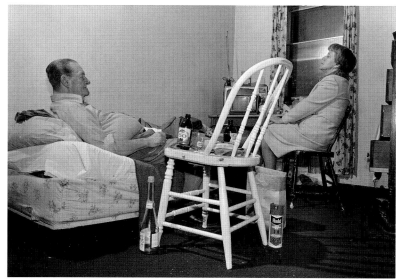

PLATE 15
DONIGAN CUMMING
Untitled
March 27, 1983

Untitled
June 9, 1982

PLATE 16
DONIGAN CUMMING
Untitled
July 19, 1985

PLATE 17
DONIGAN CUMMING
Installation view:
*Reality and Motive
in Documentary Photography*
Centre national de la photographie
Palais de Tokyo, Paris, France
Dec. 17, 1986 – March 2, 1987

PLATE 18
LISE BÉGIN
Turbulence, *detail*
Photograph, mixed media

PLATE 19
LUCIE LEFEBVRE
Pont d'or et nappe d'eau
[Bridge of gold and sheet of water]
1986

PLATE 20
SUZY LAKE
Installation view:
Confrontation with Shadow
Gelatin silver print, foamcore
and charcoal on wall
Galerie John A. Schweitzer
1985-1986

PLATE 21
MARIE-JEANNE MUSIOL
Le trou noir de l'histoire,
Fragment (Tulum)
*[The black hole of history,
Fragment (Tulum)]*
Photographic installation,
altered colour photograph
1987

PLATE 22
IAIN BAXTER
(N.E. Thing Co.)
A Portfolio of Piles
Illustrated publication
1968

Once these photographs are processed, there are several uses to which I might put them. For example, someone might be invited or constrained to hold the 36 small photographs on his lap in a moving car, flip through them as the car moves along, and attempt to "relate" them to a particular journey. I might bury them alongside the roadway or try to have them published in an automobile magazine. The car, just by its very nature & seemingly unconsciously, has created here a vast defeatured region in which all information is ren-

PHOTO 33   TIME 4:35 P.M.
SUN BREAKING

dered useless through the continuous and apparently imperceptible (at least to those not speaking this particular language) input of "energy" in the form of simultaneously continuous and apparently fragmented imagery.

In any case, whatever the process to which these small casebook photographs are subjected, they will comprise a basic and central factor in the structure of this ongoing analogue for real experience. As the project continues, however, it is becoming more and more apparent that this "ongoing analogue for real experience" is a great deal more "real" than much "other" experience---which is considered ceaselessly to be insistently "real". The high degree of self-consciousness in this analogical situation never detracts from its immediacy, but instead distinctly intensified that immediacy, meanwhile adding a functional precision. For art-making, this condition reduces one's needs----on all levels---to the near-zero point. (see photos attached)

attached photo — (extension) precise draithing — away intersections — interjected (multiple) possibilities etc.

A — possible (future) LOCATION

attached photo (reflection-extension) Note — divisions (further projected movement within A & B

TWO CAR RIDES

The two car-rides are---in another way of speaking, two aspects of the same car ride. That is, one of the car rides is a "reconstruction" of the other car ride, using photographs, maps possibly, written accounts, film-strips, tape recordings, even verbal accounts by some of the people involved in the car rides.

2

The truly important factor in these car rides is the consciousness of the participants of their own ability to make real-time abstractions or to form real-time image-systems concerning their activities in the widest possible context.

pleasant tree-lined road

CAR RIDE A: a bright, cool, sunny autumn day; I am riding at a considerable speed (50 miles an hour) on a tree lined road. The road itself has uneven patches and when the car rides over them I am subjected to fairly violent vibrations---enough to make photography difficult if the goal of this photography is the attainment of a clear, unblurred image. The car comes to a halt at a red stop sign, and, after a short pause, turns right, accelerating rapidly. 35 seconds brings us---up a very slight incline---to the end of one stretch of road moving in one direction and the beginning of another stretch moving in another direction--- a 90-degree left turn. We proceed along fairly level ground for 2 minutes or so, begin to ... the crest of a low hill, begin to ... and after 3½ minutes of running time, ... her red stop sign. After another short pause, we continue along the same straight route, descending another long incline; when it flattens out again, we continue for 1 minute 49 seconds on level ground, then stop at at third red stop sign, then turn right onto another wide flat area which after somewhat

more than one minute running time, begins to slope upward. As the pitch of the incline suddenly increases, we reach a fourth red stop sign, pause on the hill, and make another right turn, and continue to climb. We run on a wide relatively smooth surface for more than 3½ minutes, then slow down and make a U-turn to the left and proceed back in the direction from which we came, this time on the opposite side of a grassy median. We proceed at a steady 33 or 34 miles per hour, running between lawns, houses and sidewalks. The car is cool---the windows in each

up a very slight incline---

Notes camera locations
1. - i'm CAR
2. - i'm HOUSE (back to windows etc.)
3. - i'm YARD (looking through concrete-block fenced)

(future---(unspecified---unorganized??) activities etc.---cameras running simultaneously---& so including each other)

of the front doors is rolled down, and the air vents under the dashboard are wide open. The riding compartment is filled with noise---the sound of the tires on the road, the engine, the wind pouring in and out of the car, the noise of other cars passing in an erratic stream. On the back seat is a coloured service-station street-

3

PLATE 23
JEFF WALL
Landscape Manual
Illustrated publication
1969

PLATE 24
RODNEY GRAHAM
Installation view:
75 Polaroids
Vancouver Art Gallery
1975

PLATE 25
KEN LUM
Anonymous
Offset reproductions
1977

PLATE 26
CLARA GUTSCHE
Bain de Soleil, C. Vakis Pharmacy
5001 Park Avenue, Montreal
1978

PLATE 27
CLARA GUTSCHE
Kimon Caragianis, Architecte
4113 St. Lawrence Blvd., Montreal
1978

PLATE 28
LYNNE COHEN
Observation Room

PLATE 29
LYNNE COHEN
Emergency Measures Auditorium

PLATE 30
GENEVIÈVE CADIEUX
Nature morte aux arbres et au ballon
[Still life with trees and ball]
1987

ONE SISTER WAS NORMAL, THE OTHER WAS NOT—

Strange Sisters

ROBERT TURNER

They were both indescribably lovely—
yet one wanted a man's love...while
the other craved a woman.

THE SAVAGE NOVEL OF A LESBIAN ON THE LOOSE!

B526F 50¢ K

BEACON
SIGNAL

PLATE 31
NINA LEVITT
From the series
Conspiracy of Silence
1987

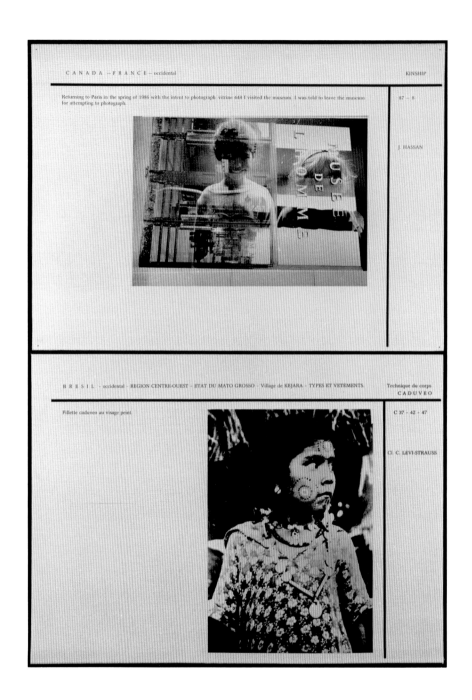

Returning to Paris in the spring of 1986 with the intent to photograph vitrine 448 I visited the museum. I was told to leave the museum for attempting to photograph.

87 — 8

J. HASSAN

B R E S I L - occidental - REGION CENTRE-OUEST – ETAT DU MATO GROSSO - Village de KEJARA - TYPES ET VÊTEMENTS.

Technique du corps
CADUVEO

Fillette caduveo au visage peint.

C 37 - 42 - 47

Cl. C. LEVI-STRAUSS

PLATE 32
JAMELIE HASSAN
vitrine 448
1987-1988

PLATE 33
ROY ARDEN
Abjection, *detail (one of ten panels)*
Black-and-white silver prints
and black silver prints
1985

PLATE 35
SUZY LAKE
Authority is an attribute of a critic
1986

"The ideology of the domestic sphere and the love of a good woman allowed people to treat their homes as if the economic world did not exist and as if individuals were not implicated in the injustices of the world."

Rosalind Coward

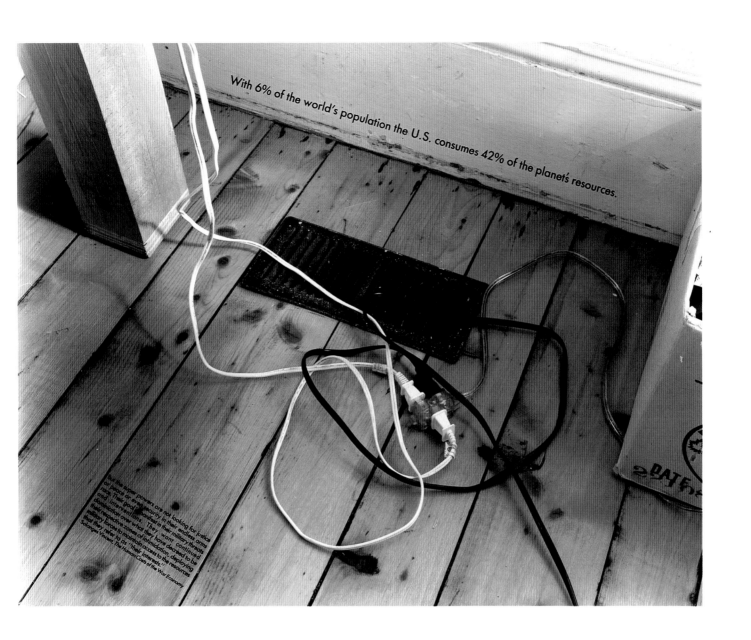

With 6% of the world's population the U.S. consumes 42% of the planet's resources.

PLATE 37
SUSAN McEACHERN
On Living at Home
Part Four: The Outside World (detail)
1987

PLATE 38
BARBARA KRUGER
Untitled
1981

PLATE 39
JO SPENCE
From "Mother and Daughter"
work circa 1948. In a photo therapy
session Jo re-enacts the relationship
between herself and her mother
(the working class daughter who is
'never at home', always 'hanging
around' the streets hoping to
bump into boys); the factory worker
mother who feels she is used
like a "hotel keeper."
1988

PLATE 40
VICTOR BURGIN
Sigmund Freud Haus,
Bergasse 19, Vienna
1981

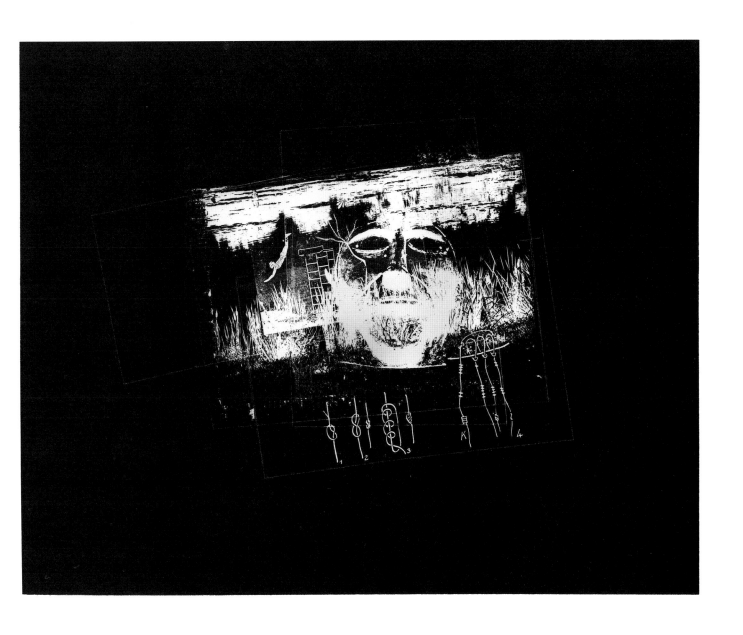

PLATE 41
CHERYL SOURKES
Relegative Relation
1989

PLATE 42
CINDY SHERMAN
Untitled Film Still #56
1980

PLATE 43
MARIO GARCÍA JOYA
Somos Cubanos
1959

PLATE 44
JEFF WALL
Double Self-Exposure
1979

NICKEL IS A CURIOUS METAL, A PROMISCUOUS ALLOY, BUT THE NICKEL IS A MODEST
COIN, MORE MODEST THAN ONE OF JOHN D. ROCKEFELLER'S DIMES. IN OTTAWA,
GOLD IS HIDDEN. IN SUDBURY, NICKEL IS ON DISPLAY, ALTHOUGH ITS MANY USES
ARE ECLIPSED BY ITS EXAGGERATED PRESENCE AS A TOKEN OF EXCHANGE.

PLATE 45
ALLAN SEKULA
Big Nickel Mine, Sudbury
Cibachrome print
1986

PLATE 46
RAYMONDE APRIL
Une mouche au paradis nº 1
[A Fly in Paradise #1]
1988

PLATE 47
RAYMONDE APRIL
Une mouche au paradis nº 2
[A Fly in Paradise #2]
1988

PLATE 48
RAYMONDE APRIL
Une mouche au paradis n° 3
[A Fly in Paradise #3]
1988

PLATE 49
RAYMONDE APRIL
Une mouche au paradis nº 4
[A Fly in Paradise #4]
1988

Photograph Sources

PLATE 41:   Cheryl Sourkes
PLATE 42:   Metro Pictures, New York
PLATE 43:   Mario García Joya
PLATE 44:   Schirmer / Mosel Verlag GMBH
PLATE 45:   Allan Sekula. Photograph and text excerpted from *Geography Lesson:*
              Canadian Notes, photographic installation, 1986.
              Courtesy Vancouver Art Gallery
PLATE 46:   Raymonde April
PLATE 47:   Raymonde April
PLATE 48:   Raymonde April
PLATE 49:   Raymonde April

THIS EDITION WAS PRINTED IN 1750 COPIES.
TYPE COMPOSED BY ZIBRA, MONTRÉAL. THE PLATES ARE
175 LINE, PRINTED OFFSET BY HERZIG SOMERVILLE, TORONTO.
THE BINDING IS BY JOHN DEYELL COMPANY, TORONTO.
TEXT PAPER IS 160M MOHAWK ANTIQUE VELLUM AND 200M
WARREN CAMEO DULL. TEXT TYPE IS LINOTYPE JANSON,
ATTRIBUTED SIMULTANEOUSLY TO ANTON JANSON (1620-1687)
AND MIKLÓS KIS (1650-1702). DISPLAY TYPE IS LINOTYPE
FUTURA, DESIGNED BY PAUL RENNER, 1930.
BOOK DESIGN BY ROBERT TOMBS.